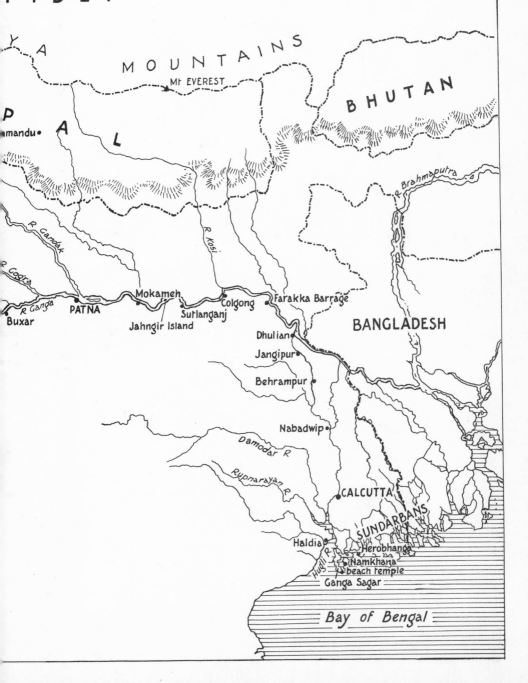

T I B E T

M O U N T A I N S

Mt EVEREST

B H U T A N

Y A

P A L

amandu

R Brahmaputra

R Gandak

R Kosi

R Cogra

R Ganga

Buxar

PATNA

Mokameh

Jahngir Island

Sutlanganj

Colgong

Farakka Barrage

Dhulian

BANGLADESH

Jangipur

Behrampur

Nabadwip

Damodar R

Rupnarayan R

CALCUTTA

SUNDARBANS

Haldia

Herobhanga

Namkhana

beach temple

Ganga Sagar

Bay of Bengal

From the Ocean to the Sky

By the same author

HIGH ADVENTURE

NO LATITUDE FOR ERROR

SCHOOL HOUSE IN THE CLOUDS

NOTHING VENTURE, NOTHING WIN

EAST OF EVEREST (with George Lowe)

THE CROSSING OF ANTARCTICA (with Sir Vivian Fuchs)

HIGH IN THE THIN COLD AIR (with Desmond Doig)

FROM THE OCEAN
TO THE SKY

by

Sir EDMUND HILLARY

THE VIKING PRESS   NEW YORK

Published in 1979 by The Viking Press
625 Madison Avenue, New York, N.Y. 10022

LIBRARY OF CONGRESS CATALOGING IN PUBLICATION DATA
Hillary, Edmund, Sir.
From the ocean to the sky.
Includes index.
1. Ganges River—Description and travel. 2. Ganges
Valley—Description and travel. 3. Hillary, Edmund, Sir.
I. Title.
DS485.G25H54   915.4'1'044   78-23668
ISBN 0-670-33172-4

Printed in the United States of America
Set in Monotype Bembo

Contents

		page
1	From the Ocean to the Sky	13
2	Organisation	23
3	The Team	33
4	Tiger Country	50
5	Calcutta	63
6	Up the River	77
7	Rural India	92
8	Varanasi — the Holy City	105
9	To the Gate of God	122
10	White Water	142
11	"You can go no further"	169
12	Advance on Foot	185
13	Hillary in Devlok	200
14	Rescue and Success	217
	Appendix One Expedition Diary by Mike Gill	239
	Appendix Two Ganga and Hinduism by Jim Wilson	242
	Appendix Three Distance and Elevation of the Ganga	260
	Appendix Four Jet Boats by Jon Hamilton	261
	Appendix Five Glossary of Indian Terms by Jim Wilson	268
	Index	271

Colour Illustrations

between pages 112 and 113

Circling Jahngir island[1]
Ganga sailing dhows[2]
Varanasi, holiest city of Ganga[3]
A *puja* at Varanasi[4]
Young men at Chait Singh Palace[1]
A peaceful temple near Garhmuktesar[2]
The jet boats approach Deoprayag[3]
Crowds lined the water at every *ghat*[3]
End of the jet-boat route[3]
Above Nandaprayag[3]
A mountain village above Govindghat[3]
The Alaknanda at Badrinath[2]
High Camp, with Akash Parbat beyond[5]

CREDITS

[1] Peter Hillary   [3] Graeme Dingle
[2] Mike Hamilton   [4] Mike Gill
              [5] Jim Wilson

Black and White Illustrations

	facing page
A *puja* for the boats[1]	16
Ed Hillary[2]	17
Mike Gill[3]	17
Harish Sarin	17
Jon Hamilton[2]	17
Jim Wilson[2]	17
Bridhiv Bhatia ('BB')[2]	17
Mike Hamilton[2]	32
Max Pearl[2]	32
Prem Vaidya[4]	32
BG Dewari[4]	32
Mike Dillon and Waka Attewell[5]	32
Murray Jones[1]	33

ILLUSTRATIONS

	facing page
Joginder Singh and Mohan Kohli[2]	33
Graeme Dingle[2]	33
Peter Hillary[2]	33
Mingma Tsering[1]	33
Pemma[2]	33
Ding paints on *Kiwi*'s name[1]	48
Floating haystack in the Sundarbans[3]	48
Under Calcutta's Howrah Bridge[1]	49
Pedal power near Farakka[4]	49
Prayer and peace in a busy city[1]	64
The island temple, Jahngir[1]	65
Deserted palace of a thousand doors[6]	80
Ancient carving on Jahngir island[3]	81
An enthusiastic welcome[7]	96
Jet crew forging ahead[2]	96
The author takes to *lungi* and beads[4]	97
Bathers at Varanasi[1]	128
View from the Maharajah's palace[2]	128
Everywhere people wanting to shake hands[2] [4]	129
Away from the crowds, contemplation[3]	144
A *yogi* at Mirzapur[2]	145
Waiting crowds at Rudraprayag[2]	145
Facing the rapids above Rishikesh[1]	160
Going up The Chute[2]	161
The rapids above The Chute[2]	176
Turban ceremony at Nandaprayag[5]	176
Mohan tied his on with string[2]	176
Paying off the porters at Base Camp[1]	177
The author contemplates mountain alternatives[2]	208
Pouring Ganga *pani* onto the snow plateau[3]	208
The unmistakable symmetry of Nilkanta[2]	209
Behind the cairn, Akash Parbat[1]	224
Crossing the plateau to Nar Parbat[2]	224
Climbing to the summit ridge of Akash Parbat	225

CREDITS

[1] Peter Hillary   [4] Mike Gill

[2] Graeme Dingle   [5] Max Pearl

[3] Jim Wilson   [6] Jon Hamilton

[7] Murray Jones

Maps and Drawings

	page
The Hardwar Barrage	144
Rishikesh Rapid	152
Moonlight Rapid	159
Viyasi Rapid	160
Rudraprayag Rapid	170
Deer's Leap and The Chute	174
Nandaprayag Falls	183
Badrinath and the Mountains	202
Distance and Elevation of the Ganga	260

Author's Note

Many people helped with this book and I deeply appreciate their assistance. Our expedition was a combination of the skills and enthusiasm of its members and so the story of the journey reflects their feelings and experiences. Mike Gill and Jim Wilson made a considerable contribution to the manuscript and I also had the use of the diaries of Graeme Dingle, Murray Jones and Peter Hillary. The Appendices written by Mike Gill, Jon Hamilton and Jim Wilson demanded a considerable effort, which is also greatly appreciated.

Above all I must thank those many Indian friends whose kindness and generosity made our adventure one that I will always remember.

Ed Hillary

From the Ocean to the Sky

I

From the Ocean to the Sky

FOR MORE THAN FIVE YEARS I HAD DREAMED OF A NEW ADVENTURE —
to travel with a group of friends from the mouth of the Ganges River
upstream against the current as far as we could go. We would use jet
boats, those lively and speedy craft, and penetrate for 1,500 miles
through the centre of the country, seeing a new view of India from the
holiest of its rivers. And, when the waters became so violent that even
a jet boat couldn't handle them, then we'd travel on foot and climb up
into the mountains where the river had its beginnings ... and so
ultimately we'd reach up to the sky itself.

I could think of many good reasons for such a journey. In 1968 we
had taken two jet boats to the Sun Kosi River in Nepal, with the aim of
making our way upriver for 250 miles to the outskirts of Kathmandu.
It had proved a remarkable adventure. Early on in the trip we struck
disaster when exploring a tributary river, the Arun, which was in full
flood. One of the boats dipped into a huge vortex and sank. The four
members of the crew managed to get safely to the bank. That left only
one boat, and the major journey still ahead of us. Should we risk it or
abandon the venture? We decided to go on, but to reduce our party to
six men — Jon Hamilton, our chief driver; Jim Wilson; Doctor Michael
Gill; Mingmatsering Sherpa; Siku Sherpa; and myself.

For two weeks we forced our way upstream, overcoming great
rapids, relaying our fuel, manhandling our supplies around difficult
sections so that the boat could go through, light. We camped each
night in beautiful locations on the banks of the river and enjoyed the
friendship of the local people who lived many days' walk away from
the nearest road. Finally we battled our way up the last big rapid and
drove on to our destination. It had been a tremendous adventure — one
of the best I'd ever undertaken. The ambition to do another similar
journey had simmered in the back of my mind ever since.

And so I thought of Ganga — as the Ganges is universally called in
India. In its upper reaches there would be all the action we could
desire or handle. And in the long journey from the ocean we would

see and experience the heart of India—for to hundreds of millions of Indians Mother Ganga *is* the heart of India. Our journey would not only be an adventure but a cultural pilgrimage as well—we would learn much of the history and religion of this great country. We would have the chance, too, to meet and experience the rural India away from the bursting millions in the cities with their extremes of poverty and riches.

And at the end I would meet my old love, the Himalayas. We would climb up into their airy heights and complete our journey amongst the icefields from which Ganga draws its first drops of water. The journey would be full of excitement and variety, and have its share of danger, too—what more could one ask than that?

*   *   *

Ganga is not nearly the longest river in the world nor does it contain the greatest volume of water. But it is surely the most sacred and the most loved. It has been revered at least since the invading Aryans reached it before 1000 B.C.; it was already old in history by the time of the Buddha in the sixth century B.C.; to the present day it is continuously holy to millions of Indians.

The *Imperial Gazetteer of India*, written in 1886 by the Department of Statistics for the Government of India, breaks away from its dry recital of facts and figures to become eloquent when it considers the Ganges:

> Of all the great rivers of India, none can compare in sanctity with the Ganges, or Mother Ganga as she is affectionately called by devout Hindus. From her source in the Himalayas to her mouth in the Bay of Bengal, every foot of her course is holy ground; and many of the other sacred rivers of India borrow their sanctity from a supposed underground connection with her waters. To bathe in the Ganges, especially at the great state festivals, will wash away the stain of sin; and those who have thus purified themselves carry back bottles of the sacred water to their less fortunate relations. To die and be buried on the river bank is a passport to eternal bliss. Even to exclaim "Ganga Ganga" at the distance of a hundred leagues will atone for the sins committed during three previous lives.

Ganga herself is described as the daughter of the Himalayas, who is persuaded, after infinite solicitation, to shed her purifying stream upon the sinful earth.

Some of the most moving words were written by Jawaharlal Nehru, that great Indian statesman who, when I spoke to him in 1953, impressed me more than any other man I have met before or since. In his *Last Will and Testament* he wrote:

> The Ganga, especially, is the river of India, beloved of her people, round which are intertwined her racial memories, her hopes and fears, her songs of triumph, her victories and her defeats. She has been a symbol of India's age-long culture and civilisation, ever changing, ever flowing and yet ever the same Ganga. She reminds me of the snow-covered peaks and the deep valleys of the Himalayas, which I have loved so much, and of the rich and vast plains below, where my life and work have been cast.

India is, of course, a country of many religions besides Hinduism. Sixty million Indians are followers of Islam, and Islamic art and architecture and politics have immeasurably enriched the country. India was also the birthplace of Buddhism and, though this proved basically an export, yet marks of her Buddhist age abound. Sikhs and Jains, while often regarded as under the umbrella of Hinduism, can well be considered members of separate religions. About 2 per cent of the population are Christian and there are important communities of Zoroastrians (Parsis) and Jews. To Indian adherents of all these religions Ganga is very special. But it is to Hinduism above all that she is the sacred river, a goddess and a pre-eminent place of pilgrimage. So while our motive for going from the ocean mouth to the mountain source of the Ganga was initially more adventurous than religious, yet we could expect the overwhelming religious association of the river for all Hindus to be impressed on us at every stage of the way.

Every Indian knows the myth of Ganga, of how her waters were brought down from heaven to earth. This is how Bridhiv Bhatia, liaison officer for our expedition, told it to us as we camped one evening in a mango grove on the banks of the river:

> At the beginning of each cycle, as Vishnu re-forms the universe, he makes Ganga flow from his toe as a celestial river. There she flowed serenely across the skies in the white torrent known to Westerners as the Milky Way. And though she was an object of great beauty and sanctity, she was of little use to the parched earth below.
>
> So matters might have remained but for the death of one thousand sons of a king. In ancient days in India, kings of substance used to perform a rite known as Aswamedh — the "horse sacrifice". A fine young stallion was let loose, and chosen warriors would follow it

while it wandered where it willed for a year. Whatever territory the horse crossed without challenge, the king of that territory had to acknowledge the other's superiority and pay levy to him. Wherever the horse's movement was challenged or hindered, the king would challenge and fight the ruler of that territory and, if victorious, would make that king his vassal also.

Maharajah Sagar was a king of great substance, and also of great virility and fertility. He had one thousand sons, and when they had grown into strong young warriors he decided the time had come to perform Aswamedh. A horse was set loose and the sons set off to follow. For a while all went well, for rival kings knew of the wealth and strength of Maharajah Sagar and wisely chose to pay tribute rather than challenge and meet defeat. But at length the horse in his wanderings came to an island in the Bay of Bengal where lived the great Kapil *muni*, one of the greatest of all sages. Ancient Hindu sages were notoriously unimpressed by kingly reputation and power, and when Kapil's meditation was disturbed by the arrogant stallion prancing over his island, he ordered some of his disciples to tie it up. The thousand sons of the Maharajah came sweeping up, found the horse hobbled, and demanded of Kapil *muni*, "Who are you, and why have you tied up our father's horse?" Foolhardy words to direct to a sage of Kapil's powers and irascibility! Looking up in annoyance from his meditation, he seared them to ashes with his glance.

When Maharajah Sagar heard what had happened, he hastened to Kapil *muni* and pleaded with him to restore his sons to life. "It is impossible to undo what I have done," the sage replied, "but if you can persuade Ganga to come to this island and touch the ashes, then only will your sons be restored to life."

The Maharajah went to Bhagirathi, another great sage, and persuaded him to intercede with Ganga. "How can I come down to earth?" Ganga replied. "I am so mighty a torrent I would shatter the earth's foundations." So Bhagirathi, after doing penance for a thousand years, went to the god Shiva, the greatest of all ascetics, and persuaded him to stand high above the earth amidst the rock and ice of the Himalayas. Shiva had matted hair piled on his head, and he allowed Ganga to thunder down from the skies into his locks, which absorbed gently the earth-threatening shock. Ganga then trickled softly out on to the earth and flowed down from the mountains and across the plains, bringing water and therefore life to the dry earth. In the huge flat area at the head of the Bay of Bengal she divided into many streams, one of which, the

A *puja* for the boats at Ganga Sagar.

Ed Hillary, *top*, and Mike Gill, deputy leader and chief cameraman; *centre*, Harish Sarin, past president of the Indian Mountaineering Federation and Government adviser, and Jon Hamilton, jet boat expert; *bottom*, Jim Wilson, specialist on culture and religion, and liaison officer, Bridhiv Bhatia (B.B.).

Hugli, at length reached Kapil's island—Ganga Sagar Island as it is now called. Gently she touched the ashes lying there, and the thousand sons of Maharajah Sagar were restored to life. And so the earthly Ganga was born.

★   ★   ★

The spot where Shiva stood to receive this great gift is in the Garhwal Himalaya, a region teeming with the gods of the myths of Hinduism. In Garhwal are the headwaters of Ganga, for it properly takes this name at Deoprayag where two rivers come together, the Bhagirathi and the Alaknanda. We would have to choose one of these two rivers for our jet boats as our route into the mountains.

The shorter and smaller tributary is the Bhagirathi. It flows from a cave of ice in the snout of a glacier, and the cave is known as Gomukh, "the cow's mouth". A day's walk below Gomukh is the temple of Gangotri, one of the most sacred shrines of Hinduism and a famous site of pilgrimage. Equally famous is the temple of Badrinath at the head of the other and larger tributary of Ganga, the Alaknanda. From their respective headwaters the two tributaries flow in deep gorges to Deoprayag, where a temple and a cluster of houses cling to the steep slopes of a prow of rock narrowing to a point where the waters of the two rivers mingle. Prayag is the Sanskrit word for any point of union of two great tributaries, and above Deoprayag are four others before Badrinath is reached.

Still in deep gorges, Ganga flows down to Rishikesh, breaking out then on to a broad sloping plain. Across the plain in shingle bed she flows, then narrows to squeeze through a gap in the last outliers of the hills—Hardwar, the Gate of God. Then she is set fair on her long run across the plains, the Indo-Gangetic basin, over 1,200 miles to the Bay of Bengal.

On the way across the plains she receives many great tributaries. Most sacred is the Jamuna, and the Prayag, at Allahabad, is one of the chief holy spots on the river. Lower down, beyond ancient Varanasi, the Son and the Gandaki and the Kosi enter, and what started as a tiny mountain torrent has become a great tawny flood in the monsoon, and a mighty river even in the dry season, bringing water and hence life to the land as she promised, and giving transport to people and goods. Then at length she nears the sea, and on the final flat coastal run spreads out into a host of tributaries in her great delta. Most of these channels flow through Bangladesh, but the westernmost one, the Hugli, remains in India, flowing past Calcutta and on to Ganga Sagar Island, the ashes of the Maharajah's sons, and the sea.

From sky and mountain, to the ocean . . . 1,500 miles of constantly changing river. Our plan was to do Ganga's journey in reverse: from ocean to sky. From Ganga Sagar Island, up the Hugli past Calcutta into the main Ganga, and on up past Varanasi and Allahabad, Hardwar and Rishikesh, to the mountain gorges and the holy confluence at Deoprayag. From there on we would push as far as possible up the Alaknanda tributary towards Badrinath. The choice of Alaknanda over Bhagirathi was later to get us into an argument with a religious poet anxious that we go to the true (religious) source at Gangotri. But to us, all the sources of Ganga were exciting, and the larger Alaknanda should allow us to penetrate further into the mountains. And besides, Gomukh, Gangotri and the upper Bhagirathi are forbidden territory to foreigners. We didn't have any option.

For me there was another reason for going to Badrinath. It was from there, in 1951, that I set out on my first Himalayan expedition, and it was there, in Badrinath, that I received the telegram inviting me to join Eric Shipton on the Everest Reconnaissance of that year, an expedition which in the end was to change my life so completely.

When I planned the expedition it was as an adventure as much as anything else, but as the weeks went by my attitude to it slowly changed. I was told that Hindus believe there are four stages in their lives. The first is that of the child and student learning about life; the second is devoted to acquiring a home, family and material goods; but in the third and fourth stages a man should leave these behind him, to seek to draw closer to the creator of the universe. Many seek this in a pilgrimage to the holy places of Hinduism, nearly all of them on the banks of the Ganga: Badrinath and Hardwar, the Prayag at Allahabad, Benares, Ganga Sagar — we would visit them all. I learned, too, of the concept of *darshan*, which means that a person can acquire merit simply by standing in the presence of someone making a great pilgrimage or by touching him. Often I had people touch me or kneel down briefly to touch my feet and thus share in my *darshan*. For me, too, it became a pilgrimage and one that I was sharing with an immensely warm and hospitable people.

*   *   *

On the morning of August 24th we drove out into the Bay of Bengal on the first day of our journey. It was a Wednesday, an auspicious day on which to set forth, we were told. To the south-west the sky was an inky black where a storm of monsoon rain was sweeping towards the Ganga delta, but in our quarter the sun shone brilliantly. A strong offshore wind was throwing up steep choppy seas in which our three jet boats pranced and thumped. In the rough areas we had a series of spine-shattering crashes as we surged over the waves—our shallow planing hulls were much more suited to rivers than to the open sea. We drove down a long, shelving, sandy shore, mile after mile of it crowded with thin black Bengalis sitting in groups on the foreshore, or wading with their nets in the warm brown water, catching the fish that teem here where the Ganga meets the Indian Ocean. Behind, the land stretched flat and featureless, hardly more than a few feet above sea level. So many people. So little land.

Thirty miles south we turned east around a flat promontory bearing a solitary building crouching low to the ground, with a weather-beaten palm tree standing guard over it, its trunk bent inland, its leaves blown to tatters by the prevailing winds. I recalled those devastating cyclones that sweep inland here off the ocean: great tidal waves of devastation carrying all before them, except a few who cling to the tops of trees or enjoy some miraculous escape.

Somewhere along this coast was our destination, the temple of Ganga Sagar, and we planned to do *puja* there, a Hindu religious ceremony to bless the boats and our journey. To the people of India, for the past 3,000 years Ganga Sagar has been the place where Ganga meets Sagar, the ocean, the place from which any great pilgrimage must start. If you wish to gain infinite merit by walking, hopping, crawling, or measuring your length for the full 1,500 miles of the Ganga up to its source (and back again if you have survived the journey up) then this is where you begin. For a long time we saw nothing but the surf rolling in, but suddenly we saw the spires of a small temple hidden behind the sand dunes. Beside it was a small, partly sheltered inlet. Jon Hamilton turned inland, settled his jet boat into an advancing line of calm water with a big breaker following behind and another in front. In a few minutes, troubled only by the thought of how we were going to get out again against the run of the surf, we were ashore. Jim Wilson, following with a flourish, was brought to an abrupt halt by a hidden sandbank, and a corner of the boat's sun-awning collapsed as one of our camera-men arrested his forward flight by hanging on to an aluminium upright.

Jim and I, with Prem Vaidya and Mike Gill, walked up an almost empty stretch of beach and over the white sand dunes. The temple, a recent construction draped with power lines, was no architectural masterpiece. Perhaps they thought the sea and sky provided setting enough. Perhaps the temple was so susceptible to cyclones that it was not worth building for posterity. It was used, none the less, for a few villagers were sprinkling water and crimson flower petals on the image of the goddess—simple acts of devotion that we were to see countless times at innumerable temples on our journey up the river.

We were met by a frail little priest, so thin that it seemed a fresh southerly wind would have carried him inland most of the way to Calcutta. He had a wispy beard and bright eyes. He looked like Merlin the magician. Prem translated for us. Like their temples, Hindu priests can vary, and Jim Wilson, as our cultural and religious adviser, had been afraid we would not find a priest worthy of so important an occasion. He need not have worried. I could see that he was delighted with this quick little man.

The importance of this *puja* had grown in our minds over the last few days. We had three new boats. We were setting out on a long and perhaps dangerous journey to reach the source of the Ganga. No Hindu would contemplate setting forth on such a venture without the blessing of the gods. Although I have no formal religious beliefs, I am not a complete disbeliever, either. It is always worth having the blessing of a good and holy man. The priest showed not a trace of surprise at our request. Of course he would do *puja* for us. It was as if jet boats drove in through the surf from the ocean every other day. Hastily he brought together a few small boys to carry for him the offerings of coconut, flowers, apples and crimson powder for the *puja*.

With bells ringing and the priest chanting, our procession trudged over the dunes, across the shelving beach to where the three boats stood, stranded in six inches of water against a backdrop of thundering surf. We steadied the rocking boats. As he broke coconuts over the bow of each boat, with the milk running down their shining chrome and clean fibre-glass, the priest blessed our pilgrimage and invoked for us the blessing of the Hindu gods. On each of our foreheads he placed a spot of pigment, the *tilak*, which was part of any traditional welcome or religious ceremony we attended. The priest looked at the boats for a few moments, uncertain as to which part of a jet boat was its forehead, the bow or the windscreen. He chose the bow, imprinted a *tilak* on it with his thumb, and added for good measure a garland of flowers. Finally he filled a small copper vessel with Ganga *pani*, the water of Ganga, and we stowed this carefully, for it would travel with us to the end of our journey. Ganga *pani* is renowned for its miraculous properties. It keeps fresh and unspoiled indefinitely in its container whereas water from any other Indian river becomes tainted and unpleasant. Old sailing ships used to take on water in the Ganga delta because of its legendary purity. Today, Ganga water is known to kill disease-carrying bacteria, and its sacred origin brings good luck to the bearer.

The *puja* took a long time, but at length we were ready to drive out to sea again. We had one last look at the beach of Ganga Sagar, which was still surprisingly deserted apart from a group of women in saris, up to their waists in warm water, picking tiny silver fish out of a net. Although we didn't realise it at the time, it would be close on 1,500 miles before we found a place with so few people.

By now the surf had grown in size and, even beyond the breaking waves, the going looked decidedly rough. The Calcutta pilot, Commander Minocha, who was accompanying us and now perhaps regretting it, had warned us of the danger of driving small boats in the Bay of Bengal at this time of year. "We know you are all heroes," he had said, "but we do not want dead heroes." It was a sentiment we all agreed with. Driving in through surf is easy, even if the waves are thirty feet high, for the boat simply drives forward in the patch of flat water between waves. Going out is a different game altogether. If the boat meets a big wave just after it has broken and the nose goes under, water pours over the front into the cockpit and within seconds the boat is settling on the sea-bed. As with all jet-boat driving, the secret is in the timing, which comes partly from some inbuilt sixth sense, partly from experience. Jon Hamilton has both, and with consummate skill he drove out through the big breaking waves, racing along parallel to each until he saw the right moment to turn seaward and climb over the moving wall of white water.

Jim Wilson is generously endowed with natural ability, but his range of experience was minute compared with Jon's and he was uncomfortably aware of the fact that the only jet boat ever sunk by Jon had been in the surf. This was Jim's first encounter with surf of any sort. That day I was with Jon in the front boat, but all through that crazy drive seaward I was watching Jim behind us. Once I saw his boat rear in the air until it seemed almost vertical and, as the hull slammed back down on to the water, sheets of spray flew outwards. The already shaken awnings half-crumpled as a couple of poles fell out, but the boat kept going. Further back still, Mike Hamilton, too, was having a rough passage, but at length all boats were free of the shoreline and driving across deeper water. The wind was rising and an ominous black cloud filled the horizon; the afternoon was well on and I was keen to turn into the estuary as soon as possible.

At this point a fearful sound came from under the engine-housing of Jim's boat, and the motor cut. Mike Hamilton was our engineer, and it took him only a few moments to establish that the engine had ridden off its mountings. Apparently a few vital nuts had not been tightened properly. For half an hour we worked desperately, while the boats tossed up and down in the steepening seas rolling in from the ocean. I had terrible visions of us having to abandon the crippled boat on the first day of the expedition, but with the sun low on the horizon, it was moving again. Minutes later the motor cut and we discovered that the alternator had been damaged beyond repair. Mike had a spare under the front seat and in half an hour that too was repaired. Two miles further on, with the dusk closing fast around us, Jim's boat was again spluttering and slowing until once more it came to a halt. This time it was a clogged fuel filter.

"I'm not sure that *puja* helped us a lot," I said.

It doesn't do to criticise Hindu customs to Jim. "Without that *puja* we'd never have got the motor going again," he flashed back. "In fact we'd have sunk in the surf without it."

There didn't seem any point in arguing. It was dark now; a few drops of rain rattled on the awnings and we could hear the hiss of a monsoon rainstorm approaching, thrashing the surface of the sea into a fine dancing spray. Then the motor roared into life and we turned inland up the estuary of the Ganga. This time the boats didn't fail us, and indeed that was the last trouble we ever had with any of them. Half an hour later, peering through the darkness with our eyes stung by the torrential rain, we saw lights ahead. It was Haldia, the first step on our journey upriver. We were launched at last on our journey from the ocean to the sky.

2

Organisation

AN EXPEDITION STARTS LONG BEFORE THE FIRST STAGE OF THE ACTUAL journey begins. An extensive period of planning and organisation is necessary to turn a dream into a reality.

In 1973 at a dinner in Delhi I mentioned my hopes to Mr M. A. Rahman of the Ministry of External Affairs, and to my great delight he expressed interest and confidence in the project, and went to the trouble of having a report compiled on possible river routes from the Hugli to the Himalayas. About this time I also had a long discussion with Mr Harish Sarin, President of the Indian Mountaineering Foundation, and he too showed great interest in the project, and offered his assistance and advice. These reactions were encouraging enough to make worthwhile a reconnaissance of the river and, at the beginning of 1975, Jim Wilson and Murray Jones carried out an extensive journey on the Ganga.

The reconnaissance had two aims. First we had to make sure that the journey by jet boat was possible. We had read a magnificent account by Eric Newby of a descent of Ganga from Hardwar in a variety of local craft. In the stretch below Hardwar, where a great deal of water is drawn off for irrigation by the Upper Ganga Canal, and again in Bhagirathi-Hugli on account of the silting of that channel's intake, Newby's problem had been insufficient water. Time and again he and his small party found themselves aground on boulders, or lost amidst a dry sea of sandbanks. It would be embarrassing, to say the least, if we went to a lot of trouble to get permission for our trip, shipped the boats over, and then couldn't even reach Hardwar or, worse, ran inextricably aground a few miles above Calcutta. And it was pretty important to know in advance which of the main tributaries of Ganga would give the best boating, and to have a rough idea of how far we could get up.

Secondly, it was a major part of the expedition to make a documentary film of the journey. While many of the detailed decisions about what to film and how to work it into a story would have to be made in the field, we needed some initial idea of what parts of the river were likely to prove most interesting, and what general shape the film might have. So the reconnaissance was to produce both a "river report" and some guidance for the film-makers.

Murray and Jim were expeditioners first and foremost, and as film men they came a distant second. So they went first to where they thought the action would be, the violent mountain headwaters. From Rishikesh, buses left daily for Badrinath, 300 km away at the head of the Alaknanda gorge. It was the height of the pilgrimage season, mid-May, and health regulations demanded that all pilgrims be vaccinated against cholera before being permitted to buy a bus ticket, let alone actually board a bus. Murray had left his international vaccination certificate back in Delhi. He is not keen on vaccinations at the best of times, and the crowded heat of the Rishikesh bus terminal didn't look terribly sanitary. Desperation lent honesty to his face, and just before the bus pulled out he managed to convince a kindly old official that he did have a valid vaccination certificate back in Delhi. A leap and two quick wriggles, and the two of them were on the moving bus.

The road followed the river fairly closely. But the bus was very crowded, a seat next to the low small windows difficult to acquire and defend, and the road often many hundreds of feet above the river. Jim and Murray had both done some jet boating and had a reasonable idea of what the boats could and could not handle, but under these jolting conditions it was not at all easy to assess the rapids they did see – and many rapids were not seen at all, hidden below in folds of the steep-sided gorges, or missed by their being on the wrong side of the bus. However, what they lacked in vision they made up for in optimism. Their report was later to become required and hilarious reading in the evening camps when at length we were in the boats amongst the waters it described.

"From Rishikesh to Deoprayag we had a good view of the river all the way, and though we saw this stretch only once, we are both sure there is no difficulty – a broad flow in confining but not sheer banks." (In fact, we had to contend with no fewer than five very lively rapids in this section.)

From Deoprayag to Rudraprayag they did not see any major difficulties either, but the report disarmingly admits that the river was "getting livelier, quite a few rapids, but not many right across. Interesting but not difficult." Above Rudraprayag, however, even from the moving bus it was clear that conditions were much more challenging:

Two miles above Rudraprayag there is a short, narrow, sheer

rock-sided gorge—$\frac{1}{2}$ m in length. The gorge itself is fine, although a very confined flow. At the lower end there is a rock "gate", where the total flow goes through a 20 ft. gap, with considerable boils. It would be no trouble at all at the level of flow when we were there; but in flood it could be very turbulent. At the upper end of the gorge, there is a chute which I think is fairly tricky, although Jon might sail up it. There is a very "boily" and turbulent take-off for a jump on to a really narrow boiling tongue. The gap through which the chute comes is again about 15–20 ft., I guess, but the river drops about 5 ft. in a 20 ft.-long tongue, and as the whole flow comes down this tongue the result is quite impressive.

On the final section to Vishnuprayag, the point below Joshimath where the Alaknanda from Badrinath joins the Dhauliganga from Nanda Devi, Jim craned despairingly from the wrong side of the crowded bus, the penalty for using an out-of-date map. Their Indian fellow pilgrims had never been able to understand at the best of times why these two had to see every inch of the river, and turned a deaf ear to Jim's pleas to change sides. So Murray alone gazed down nearly two thousand feet, for the road here ran high above a deep gorge, and he had to guess what the tiny bright ribbon of water might be like in a boat.

Another long bucketing bus ride on India's incredible mountain roads took them up to Uttarkashi on the Bhagirathi, and convinced them that this smaller tributary, no matter how sacred, was not nearly so suitable a boating prospect as the Alaknanda. Since, in addition, border restrictions would make it very difficult for us to get permission to climb at the head of this tributary, the choice of the Alaknanda and a climb above Badrinath seemed the logical one.

The Wilson/Jones report on this crucial upper section was encouraging, as was their enthusiasm for the excitement and beauty of the mountain gorges. Jon Hamilton, our chief jet-boat expert, had some reservations about the chute and the river beyond, when he saw the photographs, but remained enthusiastic about the prospect of pitting the boats against these difficulties. In general we were optimistic that we would have a good chance of getting the jet boats as far as Vishnuprayag, below Joshimath.

Confident now that there was exciting and worthwhile boating in the upper reaches, Murray and Jim travelled down-river by bus and train, checking on man-made obstacles and on possible filming locations:

At *Hardwar* there is a low dam right across the river, and this diverts a lot of water down a canal past the really beautiful waterfront. In my view it has the best waterfront of all—clean *ghats*, two nice islands with grass and trees and retired businessmen meditating, and bridges across to them. The name means Gate of Hari (God—usually a name for Vishnu), and that is where Ganga finally debouches on to the plains of India. When we were there the canal (the Rourkee irrigation canal) was taking considerably more than half the river. You will need to find out in Delhi where this canal comes back into Ganga, and what obstructions there are. At the head, when we were there, we could get the boats through the control gates and into Ganga above the dam—and it would be nice to have the boats in the canal where it passes the bathing *ghats* and temples. The main river used to flow close to the town, but diverted across its bed leaving the *ghats* dry, I gather. The dam and canal fulfil a holy as well as an agricultural purpose, sending Ganga-*pani* close past the city again.

On the long central portion of the river, across the plains, Jim, who had lived there for two years, was sure there would be no major problems. Temporary pontoon bridges were placed across during the period of low flow, but they were removed for the monsoon. Quite large sailing vessels plied their trade up and down the river, we knew, and where they could go a jet boat would have no difficulties. But we were concerned about the lower reaches of the river. The Bhagirathi-Hugli had been silting up badly for many years, and to divert more water down it from the main river a huge barrage had been constructed at Farakka. A quick visit to Farakka by Jim allayed these fears. The increased flow in the Bhagirathi would make the trip up that river easier for us, and there did not seem to be too great an effort involved in hauling the boats around the barrage. As it turned out, even this effort was not necessary as, with the kind co-operation of the project engineers, we were able to drive our boats through one of the barrage gates.

Still travelling in reverse, Murray and Jim finally tackled the problem of an ocean starting-place for the expedition. They looked at some rather distant ones—the famous pilgrimage centre of Puri, and the ancient "sun-temple" at Konarak. But the temples were well back from the sea, and the beaches were nothing out of the ordinary. A long sea crossing to the mouth of the Hugli would be involved if we started from there, and both places, though sacred and beautiful, were ruled out. Enquiries in Calcutta, however, led them to the island of Ganga Sagar, the generally accepted "mouth of Ganga".

The reconnaissance report left plenty of unanswered questions, but it did give a detailed basis for planning, both for the trip and for the film.

Jim and Murray also helped to clarify my ideas about the best time of year. The Indian cycle of seasons begins with the summer months of April and May, when the rivers are low and the temperatures building up to the terrible heat preceding the monsoon. July through to September are the monsoon months, with the rains inundating the continent and the rivers in flood, the peak levels being usually reached in September. By October the weather is clearing and the rivers are beginning to fall quickly to the low levels of winter. For the people of the plains, November to March are the best months, dry and clear, with warm days and cool nights.

There were two overriding considerations for us, the first being that mountaineering in the Himalayas is impossible in winter because of the cold. The second was that we needed as much water as we could find for the ascent of the upper gorges, and this meant either the rainy season or the period after it, when the rivers would be falling from their September peak. Looked at in that light we had little option. We would do our climbing in October, the greater part of our river travelling in September, and that brought us back to a starting date in late August.

In the event, our timing was proved right and I was gratified to find that no less a person than Jawaharlal Nehru himself, in a letter to a European film-maker in 1939, advised starting in the rainy season. "It is difficult to suggest a definite time . . . During winter the Ganga shrinks and is not much to look at in many places. The rainy season would be the proper time . . ." He added a note about the name of the river. "I hope you will not use the name Ganges. I dislike it. 'Ganga' sounds infinitely better. I wonder how your forebears managed to change this good name into Ganges."

By the middle of 1975 I had clear in my mind the broad outline of what looked to me an unusually good expedition. I called it "Ocean to Sky".

All this was irrelevant, however, without the time in which to do it. 1976 was a busy year and I thought no more of the expedition. But then came the beginning of 1977. The year ahead looked surprisingly empty. I brooded on it all through January, and slowly the conviction was borne in on me that it should be this year or never for "Ocean to Sky". I decided to make the first moves. I could still not make an absolute commitment, for that would depend on raising finance – about ninety thousand dollars, I estimated – and I gave myself until April 20th to find money from various sources to trim this figure down to a residue that I might be able to handle myself.

And so I began planning and organising, both in New Zealand and India. There was much to do. Official permission would need to be obtained from the Government of India; substantial finance would be required; suitable boats would have to be ordered, built and delivered in India on time; the membership of the party would need to be finalised, the filming problems resolved; and all the details of logistic support in India clearly set out.

At first I was concerned as to how quickly permission would come through from the Government of India, but I need not have worried. From the moment I began seriously to seek permission, right through to the conclusion of the expedition, the Indian Government in all its departments was magnificent. I received the warmest encouragement wherever I went, and soon I was receiving very substantial financial assistance as well. It was clear to me by now that this was not a New Zealand expedition: it was a shared venture and its official name became the Indo-New Zealand Ganga Expedition. In giving credit for this tremendous assistance, I remember three people in particular. One is Harish Sarin, President of the Indian Mountaineering Foundation who, until his recent retirement, had been a powerful and influential civil servant. He used his many contacts and great influence on our behalf and was responsible for smoothing our path in many directions, including Customs and permits. The second person was Miss Vatsala Pai, Deputy Director General of the Department of Tourism. It was always a pleasure to work with her, for she was a woman of great charm, and supremely efficient. The third person was Captain Mohan Kohli, Air India Manager for East Australasia, for it was through him that we made what was perhaps our greatest step forward, an offer from Air India to transport eleven expedition members plus 600 kg excess baggage from Sydney to India and back. This was a tremendous boost to our plans, for it immediately reduced the cost of the expedition by a quarter. Air India even contemplated freighting our three jet boats in a Boeing 747, but they wouldn't fit. This time the Indian Shipping Corporation offered their help, by giving us free space on the *Vishva Vikas* for our three boats – and that was another 4,000 dollars I could forget about.

This generous support from Air India encouraged me to make the fateful step of ordering our three jet boats from C. W. F. Hamilton & Company in Christchurch, New Zealand. Financially it was not an easy decision for me to take. I still needed a major additional source of finance, which could only come from book, magazine and film rights, and nothing could be finalised in that direction for at least a month. Yet unless I ordered the boats early in March, they would not be completed in time. By now, however, my blood was up. I decided to take the risk. I flew to Christchurch, where Jon Hamilton, Jim Wilson and I had a pleasant meeting at the boat factory, working out the specifications and size of the boats we felt would do the job. Meeting schedules would be a problem, but I was assured that every priority would be given. Hamiltons also generously agreed to a very substantial reduction in the price of the boats which, with spares and modifications, would have been around 10,000 dollars each. Our jet boats would be 16 ft long with strongly reinforced fibre-glass hulls. They'd have 250 h.p. V8 automobile engines, detuned for the 83-octane petrol available in India, but still very powerful. Instead of propellers and rudders like ordinary runabouts, they'd drive sophisticated three-stage jet units which sucked the water from a grating under the flatish hull and ejected it at the back with great force. Our boats would have a top speed in excess of 45 m.p.h. and immense manoeuvrability as they pivoted on their jet units. With nothing hanging down below the hull, they could operate in very shallow water and even slide over rocks with the minimum of harm. We made a number of modifications to the standard boats. As well as the ordinary bilge pump we incorporated an electric bilge pump operating off the battery, and a third hand-operated pump for extreme emergency. Realising that we should be experiencing warm temperatures, we had installed a blower in the bilge to remove any possible petrol fumes before starting the engine. To increase our range we built in extra fuel tanks. There were two 16-gallon tanks at the rear of the boat and one 24-gallon tank under the floor in front of the engine. This 56-gallon capacity, we hoped, would give us a 150-mile radius, but in practice we found we were lucky to get more than 130 miles with the heavy loads we were carrying and the high speed of the Ganga current.

To shelter us from both sun and rain (in the latter part of the monsoon we'd have plenty of both) I designed collapsible canvas awnings overhead on the boat, supported by aluminium poles. They were made by Sears Roebuck, the American firm with whom I have been associated over the past fifteen years as their adviser on camping equipment. I have always taken a fatherly interest in the latest design of tents (or awnings) while using them on expeditions, my general philosophy being that if they stood up to one of our expeditions, they'd probably stand up to anything. I hoped our boats with the awnings up would also serve as sleeping quarters if no suitable land site was available. Hanging down from the sides of the awnings were netting flaps, zipped together at the corners to keep out mosquitoes and outside these again were rain flaps, giving a completely enclosed space over the open deck. I wrote to Jim asking him to discuss with Jon how best to sleep five people aboard the boats and received the following reply:

Dear Ed,

Jon and I crawled round, in and over the boat looking for nooks in which a six-foot-three person like yourself could fit, along with four or five others. We decided that sleeping in the boats should only be resorted to in the most unfavourable situations, such as those occasions when tigers can actually be seen strolling along the banks. We can indeed use sheets of plywood to cover in the rear half of the boat behind the front seat, but of the three positions thus made available, only the central one will be comfortable. The outer berths will be sloping and we recommend that people using these should wear a life-jacket and smear themselves with crocodile repellent before falling asleep, as they have an excellent chance of going overboard.

The fourth person, sleeping on the front seat, will need to be less than five feet tall, and we suggest you bear this in mind when selecting expedition personnel.

The fifth person, God help him, will be bent across the curve of the windscreen up forard (as we say afloat) with a chrome bollard protruding into his back. We feel that he is likely to defect at a fairly early stage of the expedition.

I, as sixteenth man, would always prefer the Sacred Bank of the Sacred River, however muddy, to such cramped quarters as the boats will provide for all but the lucky man in the premium middle place.

The boats, though considerably bigger and more powerful than the Sun Kosi ones, will still be crowded when laden with our fifteen-man party, camping and cooking gear and above all film gear. I'm wondering if some advance warning should go out that personal gear must be kept to an absolute minimum. I would suggest one dirty *dhoti* each would be sufficient on the plains. And it seems to me essential that any climbing gear, and indeed even warmer personal gear for the upper reaches of the river, be sent to Hardwar or Rishikesh from Calcutta. In the upper reaches it becomes less important for all to be in the boats, as the road is always pretty close, but I have a feeling that in the delta area and in some other places we want to be able to move everyone in the boats in one lift.

On the reverse side of Jim's letter were some additional instructions headed

University of Canterbury – Religious Studies 1

With special reference to the Ringatu and/or Ratana movements, discuss Maori religious responses to Christianity.
Note: Maori essay due on or before May 2nd.
   Hinduism essay due on or before July 14th.

Jim had added a note to the bottom of this:

P.S. Since you've been busy organising the expedition I will grant you an extension on your Maori religion essay – but only until June 25th – if you haven't written it by then I'll give you an oral in Auckland – or mouth to mouth resuscitation or something!

For the next two months I was away and the organisation continued from Chicago, Toronto, London and New Delhi. In Chicago, Sears agreed to supply and ship all our camping equipment, another very useful contribution. And then in London, my literary agent, George Greenfield, gave me the glad tidings that he had been able to arrange some very satisfactory advances on book and magazine rights. I cabled the good news back to New Zealand. We were now past the point of no return.

And so to New Delhi where, on May 31st, I attended a most important meeting in the office of Mr Naik, Secretary in the Ministry of Tourism. My old friends Harish Sarin and Miss Pai were there and also representatives of the Army and of Indian Oil. Yet another load was lifted from my shoulders when Harish said that we had been granted free Customs entrance for the boats, provided they were either re-exported within three months or else donated to a suitable organisation within India. We would not have to lodge a financial guarantee, and if the Liaison Officer confirmed that a boat had been legitimately sunk or completely destroyed, then no duty would be payable – a mighty useful provision in an expedition which had a very good chance of a sunken boat.

There was more good news to come, for the Indian Army representatives went on to say that they could provide transport by road above Hardwar, with a jeep and a 3-ton truck keeping beside us on the road as we drove up the gorge, and staying with us at the road end during our climb into the mountains. We needed this support, for in the most difficult water it would be essential to keep the boats empty except for the driver. With all our camping gear, spare film and so on travelling by truck, our portaging would be confined to ourselves and the camera equipment actually in use.

From Delhi I went on to Calcutta to yet another round of meetings. I spoke with Mr Mitra, Chairman of the Calcutta Port Trust, who recommended that we unload our boats at the new port of Haldia, eighty miles downstream from Calcutta and close to the island of Ganga Sagar. The Secretary of Forests was insistent that we visit the tiger sanctuary administered by his department in the Sundarbans, the great mangrove swamp along the outer fringe of the Ganges delta, a most beautiful place, he assured us, full of wildlife; it was not unknown even for people to see tigers there. The local director of the Indian Oil Corporation discussed with me such questions as refuelling up the river, and the octane rating of the fuel obtainable in the smaller towns higher up the Ganga. Not only was petrol going to be one of our most expensive items while in India – about nine thousand dollars I estimated – but also I could see us spending many long hours carrying jerry-cans of fuel from the nearest petrol pump down to the riverbank. As a last gesture, Indian Oil offered us three free kerosene stoves. "They are very strong," said the Director and he called across someone who was, I suppose, some sort of junior executive. "Stand on it," he said, and the young man dutifully stood on it. The stove did not even begin to buckle. I left the meeting assuming that I would see little more of Indian Oil, an assumption in which I was fortunately wrong, for they later played a most important part in the expedition when they and the Bharat and Hindustan Oil Companies came to me with the exceedingly generous offer of free petrol along the whole length of the river.

I returned to New Zealand in June, enormously thankful for the assistance being given to me in India. It was hard to believe that it was only four months since I made the decision merely to investigate the possibility of going ahead with the expedition . . . and now we were fully committed to the task.

Top, Mike Hamilton, engineer, and Max Pearl, doctor; *above*, cameramen, Prem Vaidya and B. G. Dewari; *below*, cameramen, Mike Dillon and Waka Attewell.

limbers: Murray Jones, Joginder Singh and Mohan Kohli, *top*, with Graeme Dingle and Peter
Iillary, *centre*; *bottom*, Mingma Tsering, Sherpa Sirdar, and Pemma, Sherpa cook.

3

The Team

THE SELECTION OF EXPEDITION MEMBERS WAS NOT A DIFFICULT TASK
— on the whole they were people who had been with me on trips many
times before and had proved themselves hardy and successful characters.

To begin with, there was Jim Wilson. To have gone on a trip up
Ganga without Jim would have been inconceivable. My first expedition with him was to Nepal in 1963 when he was 25 years old, having just
completed an M.A. degree in philosophy. When the expedition was over,
he and his wife Ann settled for two years in Benares, the great holy city
on the banks of the Ganga. At the end of their stay, Jim returned to
New Zealand with a disturbed liver, a doctorate in philosophy — his
thesis was entitled "Grounds of religious belief in Hindu philosophy" —
and above all with a great love of India, its strangeness and diversity,
its myths and religions, its serenely beautiful landscape, the peoples and
their history. For their part, Indians immediately warmed to Jim, for
they quickly sensed his sympathy and understanding.

Jim's physical appearance is striking. When I first met him I noticed
particularly an aggressive and determined jaw, but of recent years he
has grown a massive beard, obscuring the jaw but retaining the same
general shape. One of the newspaper reporters described it as a long,
flowing beard but it was no such thing. It was a great thicket of a
beard, and when he strode through the streets of some village or town
on the banks of Ganga, wearing a few rags of old clothing, he looked
like a *sadhu* or holy man, and was widely accepted as such.

At 40 years of age he's still a forceful climber and canoeist, fit and
powerfully built, completely irrepressible when presented with any
crazy scheme. To his already considerable list of accomplishments he
added that of jet-boat driving. On the 1967 Sun Kosi expedition we
had set out with two boats, but only one experienced driver, Jon
Hamilton. Before leaving New Zealand, the other expedition members,
all mountaineers, had tried their hands at jet-boat driving. Jim turned
out to be a natural. He had better timing and co-ordination than the
rest of us and as a result he had the good fortune — or bad, according to

your point of view—to be appointed driver of the second boat. A few
days of sliding around shingle corners on a skinny little river outside his
home town of Christchurch completed Jim's driving. The next time
he was at the wheel was three months later when he was embarked on
the Sun Kosi, an immense river in high flood with breaking white
waves stretching from side to side—the sort of water he had never
driven in before. For two days Jim performed wonders, but on the
third, while trying to make the first ascent of the Arun Gorge behind
Jon, he dug the nose of the boat into a big wave. A wall of water
poured over the bow, over the windscreen, and in a moment filled the
boat, for there were no spray-covers then of the sort we had now with
us for Ganga. The boat sank instantly and was never seen again, except
as fragments being carried by cheerful Nepalis on their way back to
their houses. Since then Jim had put in a few more weeks' jet boating,
but so far as experience was concerned he was no match for Jon and
Mike Hamilton, our two other drivers.

Setting out without Jon Hamilton would have been equally inconceivable. We knew from previous experience on the Sun Kosi and on
many trips in New Zealand of his remarkable skill in difficult water,
his forceful approach to dangerous problems. By profession Jon is an
engineer and a director of the substantial engineering company established by his father. He had been the dominant force in many world-
wide jet-boat expeditions—the Colorado River in the U.S.A.; the
Zaïre River in the Congo; rivers in New Guinea and many others.
Having him as jet-boat leader also meant that I could delegate the
preparation of the jet boats totally to him—the size and shape of hull,
the power and make of the engine, the tool kits and spares, and the
mechanical maintenance on the river. It was a big load of work to have
lifted from my shoulders. Jon tended to be taciturn, but he had a wide
range of exact knowledge on many subjects, all spiced with a fine dry
sense of humour. Although 52 years old, when he gets behind the
wheel of a jet boat he still seems to possess the fire of youth plus the
wisdom of long experience. He was indeed a formidable lead man.

He was accompanied by his 26-year-old son Michael, who for three
years had been driving jet boats as a fulltime job on a wide variety of
New Zealand rivers—meeting changing water problems from day to
day, overcoming rapids when the rivers were high and white, or when
they were low and bony. Although this was his first major expedition,
we expected him to be an effective and forceful driver in all types of
conditions. He was also our mechanic—he had assembled the engines
and jet units in our three boats and had been responsible for the selection
and sorting of tools and spare parts for the journey . . . and in the field

he solved our mechanical problems quickly, without fuss and in such a way that they never recurred.

Mike Gill was the expedition's deputy leader. His wide experience as a mountaineer in New Zealand, the Himalayas and the Antarctic, and his considerable intelligence and drive made him a dominant influence in any party. Mike's medical career, like Jim's as an academic, had been shaped largely by his inability to refuse my invitations to go on expeditions over the past eighteen years. Like Jim he was 40 years old. I don't think anyone took the title of deputy leader very seriously, least of all Mike. Nevertheless, it served a useful purpose for him when writing expedition letters for, during those hectic months before we departed, he was more closely involved with the organisation than anybody apart from myself. With Jim and Jon 1,000 miles away in the South Island, Mike, who lived only a mile away, was the natural person with whom to share planning, and our meetings each evening between five-thirty and six-thirty p.m. over a glass of scotch became an important part of the daily ritual. Mike was also in charge of the film, which in itself involved a lot of organisation. When we found ourselves unable to raise any sort of financial advance on our proposed film, Mike offered to share the costs of production with me and for that alone I thought he deserved the title of deputy leader. It would certainly act as a powerful incentive to make the film a success.

In the later stages of the expedition we would be in the Himalayas and would need climbers of considerable skill. Murray Jones, at the age of 32, was a brilliant climber who had made his mark all over the world — in the European Alps where, with Graeme Dingle, he had made the first New Zealand ascent of the north face of the Eiger and the five other great north faces; in the Himalayas; in Yosemite, and in half a dozen other places. A successful climber must always have a combination of skill and determination, for the one quality without the other is never enough. Murray had plenty of both and in the climbing expeditions I had organised of recent years, he had been the one who led the hard bits. Over the same period of time he had helped me to do volunteer work with the Sherpas of Nepal and had built up a close relationship with them.

My son Peter was 22 years old and, quite independently of his father, had shown himself to be a climber of considerable promise, as well as being a ski instructor and pilot. In his recent climbing he had teamed up with Murray and I expected the pair of them to be our strongest climbing rope. I knew we would be short of time on our projected climb on this expedition, and Murray and Peter would probably be going ahead of the main group as we approached the head waters of the river, to carry out a high-speed reconnaissance of the mountain allotted to us, Narayan Parbat. In India one must obtain written Government permission to climb specific mountains, in the general interest of Border control. When I had put in our original request, I had had no particular mountain in mind, but in view of our circumstances and time schedule had asked for a peak of only moderate height and difficulty, attractive to film and easily climbed without a lot of gear. The Indian Mountaineering Foundation recommended Narayan Parbat. Although we had been assured that the mountain was easy — at 19,600 feet it was low by Himalayan standards — there is something ominous about the fact that it had never been climbed, or even attempted, so far as we knew. In our one photograph of the mountain, it looked anything but easy, and we had to assume that the easy route was on the side not visible in the photograph. Peter had travelled in the Himalayas before, but never on a climbing expedition, and he was desperately keen to launch himself against something difficult.

Murray and Peter had one other role to play. In the adventure films with which I had recently been involved, the two of them had emerged as the closest we had to star material. Murray, with his sinewy limbs and strong face scarred by an old motor-cycle accident, always caught the imagination of viewers and, compared with the rest of us, Peter had youth on his side. I had a few doubts about the patience of the two of them, that they might find the long flat stretches of the Ganga a little slow for their energetic tastes. I wrote a bluntly worded letter to the both of them, pointing out to them that they'd better be sure they were going to enjoy the long trip across the plains and that it wasn't just a free airfare for them to do a bit of climbing in Nepal. Murray wrote back: "Hi, Ed — I'm a very subdued chastened lad these days, not at all my usual obnoxious self though I'm sure I will be by the time the first campfire is ablaze in the Sundarbans. You're right though. I have taken the trip for granted but that doesn't mean I'm not really looking forward to being afloat on the old Ganga. It's going to be a great trip."

The third of our gun climbers was Graeme Dingle, commonly known as Ding, also 32 years old. Of the climbs that made him famous in New Zealand, many have been done with Murray. He had a natural flair for all types of outdoor sporting activities and over the past five years had established and directed a New Zealand Outdoor Pursuits Centre for introducing teenagers to the world of tramping, canoeing and climbing. Despite a total lack of money when he started, by imagination and hard work he built up a very successful centre — no small achievement. He'd written two books on mountaineering ventures, and I was relying on him, with others, to keep a diary of his view of our expedition up Ganga. His style had a tendency to be idiosyncratic, with a pungent turn of phrase that would not always get past the publisher's sub-editor. He was also an excellent photographer and because of this I had designated him official still photographer, although again this was an area where everybody could contribute. More than a little crazy at times, he made an admirable foil for Jim Wilson when they were in an irresponsible mood.

The last member of our New Zealand contingent was our medical officer, Max Pearl, aged 52, who has been associated with me on expeditions and in the medical work of the Himalayan Trust over the past fourteen years. It was never easy for Max to break away from his general practice in Auckland, but Ganga, he felt, was worth the supreme sacrifice of three months away from home, with his practice steadily dwindling. I couldn't worry too much about it. Max had been making the same supreme sacrifice almost annually now for as far back as I could remember and he seemed none the worse for it. He was an essential member of the team, as it turned out that there was more medical work on this expedition than on half a dozen Himalayan trips. Most of the problems were minor, but they caused a substantial drain on his medical supplies which, for the first time in his experience, nearly ran out. As well as being a skilful medico, Max has always been invaluable because of his logistic know-how and experience in organisation.

I was often asked two questions about the expedition members. The first was, how did they find the time to break away from their jobs for so long a period as three months? I could only shrug my shoulders about this. That was their problem, not mine. On the many expeditions I have organised in my time, the problem has always been how to restrict the numbers, not how to find those who can spare the time – and never was the restriction of numbers more difficult than on this expedition.

The other question, asked equally often, was what do expedition wives (or girlfriends) think of their husbands disappearing off overseas on a prolonged, exciting, and possibly dangerous adventure? One thing I have slowly come to realise is that wives of the 1960s and 70s are not the same creatures as those of the 1940s and 50s when I began going off on expeditions. In those days one expected a wife to stay pluckily at home caring for small children and generally keeping the home fires burning. Times have changed, and I find increasingly that when wives are around I need to treat them with some circumspection if I happen to be proposing a new trip. "Ocean to Sky" was more difficult than most, for it was clear to all that the first fifteen hundred miles of the journey required no great physical strength. Why couldn't we invite a few women as well? It was not an idea I entertained even for a moment. The problems and dissensions of multi-national expeditions pale into insignificance compared with those that can be brought about by a single woman in a party, or so it has always seemed to me. As the date of departure of the expedition drew closer I was interested to note the increasing respect with which people like Mike Gill and Jim Wilson treated their wives; the deference, the readiness to take sole charge of riotous children for a whole week-end at a stretch; the stockpiling of enormous quantities of cut firewood, presumably to keep the home fires burning. On the expedition itself there was a good deal of industrious letter writing and purchasing of presents, and when all else failed there was the standby of a direct phone call back to New Zealand, a feat not easily achieved from the towns and cities of the Ganges.

By the end of June I had sorted out who the New Zealand members were going to be. On the Ganga itself we would be joined by six Indian members. Without doubt the most distinguished of them was Harish Sarin who, at the age of 62, was also the oldest member, four years ahead of my own 58 years. While a student at Cambridge (England, not Massachusetts) just before the Second World War, Harish had cycled 2,000 miles around Scandinavia, and he had always had a taste for adventure. But when he returned to India after the war, the times were not propitious for launching mountaineering expeditions, for at that time India was embarking on the exciting and demanding first year of independence. Nevertheless, he loved the mountains and for the past twenty years had been President of the Indian Mountaineering Foundation, in a period when the sport had grown from almost nothing through to the great year of 1965, when an Indian Everest Expedition placed nine men on the summit. Over the past fifteen years, Harish had been in the highest ranks of the Indian Civil Service—Secretary of Steel, Secretary of Defence, Special Adviser to the Government of Andhra Pradesh at a time when it was going through a period of civil strife. He had widespread contacts with people in important positions. He was urbane, articulate, and used to wielding power. It would be, I thought, a bit like travelling with a prime minister, and in my more sombre moments I wondered how he would mix with the riff-raff I was bringing with me from New Zealand, none of whom takes very easily to authority. Fortunately none of the problems I feared arose, and Harish was an invaluable expedition member, always ready to help in a difficult situation. At the larger civic and social gatherings in the big cities and towns, he was the Indian partner in our Indo-New Zealand venture, and he shared

with me both the responsibilities and the limelight of those occasions.
He left us as we approached Rishikesh, as he had always planned to do,
and from there he led his own small All-Indian Expedition, with his
wife and our two Indian camera crew, to Gangotri at the head of the
Bhagirathi River, considered by many to be more truly the source of
Ganga than the larger Alaknanda which we would be travelling.

At Rishikesh we would be joined by Captain Mohan Kohli, a famous
Indian mountaineer with more than a score of Himalayan expeditions
to his credit, including the great Indian Everest Expedition of 1965,
when he had been leader and had climbed to above the South Col. His
intense enthusiasm had been a most important factor in getting the
expedition launched right from the very beginning and, without the
support arranged by him from Air India, the expedition would not
have been possible. As a Sikh, no matter what the conditions, he wore
a turban, a maroon one tied on with a turquoise band, and the sight
of this amidst the tossing white water of the upper gorges was always
inspiring.

Also from Air India we had Commander Joginder Singh, stationed
in Delhi where he played a most valuable role in sustaining our
organisation. He had a strong mountaineering reputation and had
recently led an important expedition on the first ascent of the re-
doubtable 25,170-foot Karakoram peak, Saser Kangri.

The fourth Indian member was our liaison officer, Major Bridhiv
Bhatia (or B.B. as everyone called him), an officer in the Indian Army
Engineers. In my time I have been associated with a variety of liaison
officers on expeditions, and they can make life difficult in some situations. B.B. was the sort of liaison officer you dream about — totally
committed to the success of the expedition; efficient in organising the
details of our daily movements, particularly in the big cities where
crowds were often a problem; and when, at the end of the expedition,
we had to obtain a new mountaineering permit immediately, he simply
told us to go ahead on the new mountain and he would accept the
whole responsibility back in Delhi. He was a good teller of tales, both
the strange myths and the legends with which Hinduism abounds, and
as the days went by, B.B. became a close and warm friend of all of us.

Finally I had two of my oldest Sherpa friends from Nepal. Mingma
Tsering had been my *sirdar*, adviser and friend in all my Himalayan
journeys and aid projects over the past twenty years. He is a man of
considerable executive ability, with the sort of memory that allows him
to recall exactly the contents of each one of a hundred loads, who has
been carrying it, how much he has been paid, and when. As a *sirdar*
he had become used to authority; with his eyes narrowed in his

weather-beaten brown face, he was a formidable man to confront, and few did so; though just as quickly his face could dissolve into laughter if he or someone else cracked a joke. Like many Sherpas he is short in stature but of nuggety build, with great strength and endurance, particularly at high altitude. At 48 he was older than most, but in the mountains I knew he would be every bit as strong as those half his age. Without Mingma, the party would have been incomplete both to me and to the others, who knew him well.

Pemma, our cook, was a much gentler soul, not *sirdar* material at all, but he had the same qualities of loyalty and willingness to work hard. When we staggered into a mountain camp at dark, completely done in, we knew that Pemma would have a cup of tea in our hands within half an hour, and a three-course meal ready an hour after that. The indolent heat and humidity of the plains of Ganga were, if anything, more foreign to the Sherpas than to us, but we knew they would both serve us as well there as when we reached their own environment in the mountains.

With the film crew thrown in, we had nineteen members, though this would be down to ten in the mountains. Taken all in all, it was an unusual mixture of people, but then the whole expedition was an unusual one. International expeditions have the reputation of being unmanageable, with a tendency to self-destruction half-way through. I remember reading a psychological analysis of a group of top climbers, describing them as intelligent, self-sufficient and resourceful, and also as withdrawn, detached, aggressive, self-centred and highly competitive. Not altogether the qualities one might look for in a group that would have to live close together for twelve weeks at a stretch! I wasn't too worried about this. We had a big span of ages, which I thought would help, and the New Zealand members at least have seen enough of each other to know their various weaknesses and strong points, and to make allowances as necessary. I felt I knew them all well enough to be sure there were no major incompatibilities.

I was then faced with the problem, which I shared with Mike Gill, of how to produce a film of the expedition. The easiest and cheapest way out would have been to have no film at all – I have rarely spent such large sums of money so quickly as I have when financing films, and the return, if any, comes back as a slow trickle – but on this occasion we had to have one. The Department of Tourism was justifying its support for the expedition in terms of the favourable publicity for the Indian tourist industry, and that required a film.

Until 1973 all the film shot on my expeditions had been amateur, low-budget affairs shot by a mountaineer with an interest in photography. Professionals had been derisive about this, but we had always returned with a film, and there had been no camera-man's fees. George Lowe had shown the way on Everest in 1953 when he shot all the footage above the Western Cwm. Without him there could hardly have been a film, and on later expeditions he developed his skills further. In 1963, by which time George was living in England running his own expeditions, the job had passed on to Mike Gill, and all through the 1960s, wherever we went, Mike was there with my small 100-ft-load Bell & Howell Combat camera. We always covered costs, including Mike's airfare and expedition expenses, and we always had a television film to show when we got back home.

In 1973 all that changed. For in that year began the saga of *The Adventure World of Sir Edmund Hillary*. The idea, which sprang from the fertile imagination of an Auckland businessman interested in film, sounded like a good one: to put together a series of films that would do for the mountains and rivers what Jacques Cousteau had done for the undersea world. I was not, fortunately, involved in any way in the production or financial aspects of the company—my part was to provide the ideas and lead the expeditions. Nevertheless, I observed the film-making process at close quarters, including its problems. Only one completed film emerged from *The Adventure World*. It was called *The Kaipo Wall*. Set in the primeval forests and mountains of the south-western corner of New Zealand, it was a journey in canoes and rubber dinghies down a wild river to the sea; down the coast on foot; and then inland up the Kaipo River to make the first ascent of a huge granite precipice forming a 4,000 foot cirque at the head of the valley. I had no difficulty persuading my mountaineering friends to take part, and I soon put together a basic group consisting of Mike Gill, Jim Wilson, Graeme Dingle, Murray Jones and my son Peter.

It was a magnificent adventure. The rivers came up in high flood; Ding and Jim paddled their way down seemingly impossible rapids that we had not even known were there; high in the mountains we were nearly blown off the face of the earth in the kind of devastating storm that makes the New Zealand alps one of the most rugged locations in the world. And we made the first ascent of the Kaipo Wall. It was also very expensive and I realised that we were in a much bigger league than in the old days of the clockwork Bell & Howell. We had a four-man film crew and a mountain of expensive camera equipment; the only way of moving from one camp to another was by helicopter. And when the company tried to sell *The Kaipo Wall*, it became clear that they would be lucky to recover costs, let alone make a profit.

All this should have warned me off the film business, but the strange thing was that I seemed to have been bitten by the film-making fever myself. It wasn't the belief that I could make money out of it. I wanted to make some good adventure films. Expeditions have been a way of life for me for thirty years; I have made my most lasting friendships in the hills; they have been a source of endless excitement and fun. Surely, somehow, we could capture this on film—perhaps even encourage a few people to get out into the hills and discover it for themselves. So I decided to attempt a couple of half-hour films on a much smaller scale. The first took us into the rough waters off the coast of New Zealand to a climb on a 200-foot pillar of rock rising from the depths of the Pacific Ocean. The scale of it was nothing like that of the Kaipo Wall, but it gave us a chance to get the old gang together again. We had lots of fun and excitement together, and we got ourselves a film. It had its faults, but within two months it was completed and I was eager to start into the next one.

For the second film I chose to use jet boats—on the Clutha, New Zealand's biggest river, which climbs up into some big white water in its upper reaches. Jon Hamilton agreed to come with us, bringing one of his own boats, but for Jim Wilson I would need to purchase a second boat myself. So I sent Jim a cheque for 2,000 dollars and told him to buy the best boat he could find for that price or less. As it turned out you can buy very little for that price or less, and we ended up with an ancient 14 ft jet boat which had spent the latter years of its life as a fishing boat on the west coast. Even on flat water it had a strange wavelike motion which it had no doubt acquired from many years at sea, and it handled very badly indeed in white water. Jim drove it with supreme courage, hurling it at big rapids that he should never have thought of attempting. It was bad for the boat, bad for Jim, but it did make superb film. There is one memorable shot of the boat impaled on a rock in the middle of a sheet of tossing white water, with Jim desperately trying to rock it afloat again. Ever since that he has regretted that he was not able to hang a sign over the side of the boat saying "For Sale—As is, Where is", and later on, when we had re-covered the boat from the situation, we shot another remarkable sequence of Jim driving the nose of the boat into a huge tongue of fast-moving water; a slow motion shot shows the boat dancing wildly sideways through sheets of spray, with a glimpse of Jim being hurled out of the driver's seat into the midst of a maelstrom of white water. It made a very good film.

When New Zealand's T.V.1 put *The Kaipo Wall* and our two smaller films together as a series in the winter of 1977, the reception ranged from the merely enthusiastic to the ecstatic.

Everything looked fine except that we were losing money. That was the situation when I sat down with Mike Gill to work out how we were going to put together a film of *Ocean to Sky*. The problem from a financial point of view was the length of the expedition, which could hardly be less than twelve weeks. The usual three-man film crew costs at least three hundred dollars a day in salary alone, and that was before buying the film stock or starting on the equally expensive second half of the film — editing, music, narration, and so on. Jon and Jim were sounding warnings about the load-carrying capacity, and it seemed certain that we could not afford the luxury of a three-man film crew. Somehow we would have to combine the roles of director, camera-man and sound-man into, at most, two people. Mike and I drew up a list describing the sort of person we were looking for. He would need to be compatible with the rest of the expedition; he would need to be compatible with India, for we knew from experience that not every-body falls in love with the country at first sight. He would need to be able to live under fairly primitive circumstances, whether in the swamps of Bengal or in the high névés of the Himalayas; he would need to be physically fit and agile. He should combine the roles of director and camera-man with a high degree of skill in both, and he would need to direct the film through its post-production phases of editing, script-writing, etc., for we had discovered by now that one thing that kills a film faster than any other is losing continuity between the shooting and post-production phases. He should have his own equipment and be able to maintain it through the heat and humidity of the lowlands and the cold of high altitude. Finally, we would expect him to do all this without pay — that, after all, was what everybody else was doing. He was going to be a very difficult person to find.

At this stage I received the following letter:

Dear Sir Edmund,

I am writing to express my great interest in being in some way involved in the Ganges Expedition Film Project.

Over the last four years I have participated in quite a number of film projects of this nature — in the Andes and the highlands of Timor; a film of an English Channel swim for A.B.C. Televison; and four films in the Himalayas. Some of these, including a documen-tary about a 200-mile trek in Nepal on which I acted as producer, director, sole camera-man and script-writer, have been sold to B.B.C. Television.

Although my mountaineering experience has been limited to a basic course at Mt Cook, I have done a lot of walking in remote parts of Australia and New Zealand, and over 400 miles of trekking in Nepal. Some of my Himalayan films have required me to carry and operate heavy camera equipment at heights above 17,000 feet and this has been done without much difficulty. Thus from past experience I feel I'm quite adaptable to most heights and climatic extremes and I certainly don't mind roughing it.

The most important thing I would like to mention is that I have a great love of India, having spent, in total, over a year there — often in very remote areas, filming, researching a travel book I am writing, or simply travelling. I was most recently there a few months ago, producing a documentary on Ladakh as guest of the Government of India.

I have a B.A. in Indian History from Sydney University and since graduating have read over two hundred books about India as background for my travel book and future film projects. In so doing I have accumulated a lot of interesting information about the Ganges. Having also travelled on various sections of it, I know what a beautiful and fascinating river it is and I have a tremendous enthusiasm for portraying this to the very best of my ability on film.

Yours sincerely
Michael Dillon

We met him a week later, quiet and diffident at first sight but with a surprisingly strong streak of determination showing through as one came to know him better. We saw his films and liked them. We made a few enquiries as to how he'd fitted in on the Himalayan expeditions. Mike scored well on all points. More than this, he had his own camera, an Eclair N.P.R., one of the expensive varieties that can be used while recording sound. And so to the final point: how much pay did he expect? Mike seemed almost surprised. "I wouldn't expect any pay on the expedition. This is going to be a very successful film and we'll have no trouble selling it all over the world. All I'd want is a share of the returns." All this and confidence too. The job was his. From that moment on, he worked in the interests of the film with monastic devotion. He could be distracted by an offering of Indian sweets but by little else. During our stops in cities he would disappear into his hotel room to repair and clean the mountain of equipment he had with him, but for the rest of the time, on riverbank or village, he could be seen wandering around with a camera in one hand and a tripod in the other, or sitting outside his tent, writing and rearranging details of the script written on minute pieces of paper. His knowledge of India was extensive, and included a fund of bizarre details such as how exactly a pilgrim measures his length up the whole course of the Ganges (he lies full length, scratching a mark in the dust with his out-stretched fingers for his next move – for extra merit he makes every fourth move in a backward direction). Even though Mike had never climbed a peak in his life, he kept up with the rest in the mountains. Peter and Ding still speak in hushed tones of watching Mike swaying down a steep ice-wall, carrying a hundred pounds of camera equipment during the descent from the High Camp, and wearing front claw crampons for the first time.

We still needed a sound recordist, and here again we were lucky, for we found Warrick Attewell (commonly known as Waka), a 22-year-old mountaineer who had been with Ding on Jannu in the Himalayas, and a camera-man who could also record sound if required. He was as agile as a cat and always good company. Like Mike Dillon he was unmarried, which made it less likely that he would be dependent on a steady income though, as later events proved, he was less unmarried than we had thought he was. He, too, agreed to come without pay, to record sound where required, and to act as second camera-man in the river gorges or in the mountains. With these two and Mike Gill I felt we had all the versatility we needed to shoot film under whatever circumstances we might encounter. Whilst we were finalising our selection of film crew, I received a letter from Harish Sarin reminding me that this film was to be a co-production with the Films Division of the Government of India. I had never been entirely enthusiastic about this. It sounded a bit like a committee trying to write a book, but as Mike and I talked about it we began to realise the very considerable advantages in having two Indians along with us. Their names were B. G. Dewari and Prem Vaidya, and we met them for the first time in Delhi, at a time when they knew absolutely nothing about what they were being seconded to. Would it be a luxury trip, moving gently from hotel to hotel, or were they being sent to almost certain death in the upper gorges of the Ganges and the mountain wastes of Garwhal? We were able to reassure them that neither was the case, and they soon became an integral part of the film team. B.G.'s father had been a famous still photographer in Bombay and through him B.G. had moved first into still photography and then to the Films Division, where he became a camera-man and later director. He had directed and shot films in the Himalayas and was completely at home wherever we went. Prem, as well as being a camera-man, soon settled into the important role of being the film crew's interpreter and, indeed, interpreter for the whole expedition when B.B. or Harish was not around. Despite being over 50, he still had the enthusiasm of youth where his filming was concerned, and at the end of each day would give us details of the day's filming. "A be-yoo-oo-tiful shot!" he would exclaim.

Sometimes Prem and B.G. travelled with us in the boats; sometimes they travelled by land, where they could get those additional angles that would be so valuable in the film. They certainly contributed much, and they became close friends in what was a truly Indo-New Zealand Expedition.

As the time approached for departure, the pace became increasingly hectic. Murray was assembling the ropes, pitons and other gear we needed for the climb, and writing to other expedition members to check that they had their personal equipment complete and ready to go. Mike Gill and Mike Dillon were involved in a frenzied exchange of letters between Auckland and Sydney, sorting out the complex details of what to take for the filming. Jim was our geographical expert as well as cultural and religious adviser, and I was often ringing him at his home in Christchurch. Once when I had an important matter to discuss I was answered by his 6-year-old son Mac.

"Hullo," I said. "Is Jim there, please?"

"Yes," said Mac who didn't waste words.

"Ahh. I wonder if I could please speak to him."

"No. He's chopping wood."

"Is that you, Mac? This is Ed speaking. Remember me?"

"Yes."

"Well, I'm a friend of Jim's. What I have to say is quite important. Do you think I could speak to him for just a few minutes?"

"No. He's chopping wood."

"I'm sure Jim would really like to speak to me, Mac. Couldn't you get him for me for a short time and then he can finish chopping the wood?"

"No," said Mac.

I tried bribes. I tried threats of violence. In the end I gave up. I suppose he'd inherited some of his old man's determination, or maybe he just wanted to be sure of big fires when Jim was away. After that I used to leave phone calls until late at night.

By the end of July our only worry was that the *Vishva Vikas*, containing our three jet boats, might become strike-bound in Singapore or sink in a cyclone in the Bay of Bengal. On August 5th we received a cable that our ship had reached Calcutta; and on August 16th we stepped out of the Maharajah luxury of an Air India first-class cabin into the sauna-bath atmosphere of Bombay airport. A small bus drew up at the foot of the steps, a crow perched on its roof protesting noisily at the movement of its perch. With a flourish the bus stopped a well-chosen few centimetres short of a large bus already waiting there. With a squawk the crow leaped indignantly to the roof of the large vehicle and complained to all within earshot of his displeasure at his human compatriots. We were in India.

Bombay was only a stopover for our main destination, Delhi, where a big Press conference awaited us and a round of meetings with government departments. From Delhi we flew to Calcutta; more Press conferences and another grand welcome. We visited the Calcutta Port Trust, who were endlessly helpful, producing piles of charts and all the details of tides and docking arrangements we wanted. That a meeting could be both efficient *and* relaxed and pleasant was welcome news to our anti-bureaucratic souls.

Thoroughly satisfied with our first meeting, we moved on to the next – the Department of Forests of the West Bengal Government. We wriggled up crowded steps and into a crowded foyer of a government building, and most of us squeezed inside an open-plan lift with its innards exposed for all to see and looking as though they should be wound by hand rather than suffer the indignity of motorised movement. We safely arrived and traversed a narrow corridor and entered a 15 by 15 ft concrete box, which a table and chairs attempted to disguise as an office.

Mr Battacherjee was the chairman, but he apologised that he had an important alternative meeting to drop in on and so he must leave us almost immediately for a few minutes – but he gracefully acceded to a Press request to be photographed with me. The rest of his staff of four seemed to have strongly differing opinions and powerful voices, and the sound reverberated in this enclosed space. It probably sounded as if murder and mayhem were being perpetrated, but all finally resolved into total harmony and the essential bits of information – dates, food, launch-size and fuelling – were agreed on.

As we rose to depart, Mr Battacherjee asked if we were taking any guns with us. We glanced uneasily at each other, feeling it unworthy of our well-organised expedition to answer "no", but honesty prevailed. Mr Battacherjee's kindly face creased in concern, and he turned hopefully to B.B. "Could the Army supply some, then? The Forest Department has guns, it is true, but they do not work very well." We left with visions crowding our imaginations – knee-deep in mud . . . gaping crocodile jaws inches away on one side, on the other

48 FROM THE OCEAN TO THE SKY

a ravenous Bengal tiger . . . and we armed with nothing but a Forest
Department rifle . . .

Haldia is a new dock eighty miles downstream from Calcutta, almost
at the point where the Hugli meets the sea. The countryside was
beautiful, with irregular areas of light green paddy fields, broken by
patches of trees and crumbling brick houses with sagging tile roofs.
There were people dotted over the paddy fields, working hard, ploughing
behind their white cows, planting out rice or netting fish. The Customs
clearance of the boats had been quick, the Customs man having confided that he had "orders from the top" in both Delhi and Calcutta to
make our operation go smoothly.

It was exciting to see the boats sitting in their crates on a big stretch
of new concrete. The dock was an ideal place for us, like a small lake
half a mile wide and two miles long, with a lock leading out to the
river. We set to work to uncrate the boats, and by midday the mobile
crane had lowered one of them into the water, with Jon Hamilton
standing in the sling and guiding the boat down. It was quickly fuelled.
I think we all wondered whether the engines would start, whether
something might have happened to them on the way across, whether
they might dislike the intensely hot and humid conditions, and whether
they might realise they were being fed on Indian petrol rather than
the brand they had been used to at home. Jon turned the key and the
big engine roared immediately into life. Next moment he was racing
up the harbour, the jet stream shooting gracefully behind, the boat
twisting and turning with remarkable ease. I had my first ride in these
particular boats and I was impressed beyond my expectations with
their power and manoeuvrability. We named the boats *Air India*, *Kiwi*,
and *Ganga* with Jon Hamilton driving *Air India*, Michael Hamilton in
Kiwi, and Jim Wilson the captain of *Ganga*. Ding, who had spent the
first year of his working life as a sign-writer, set to work to paint images
on the sides of the boats. On *Air India* went the bowing maharajah,
who, when travelling at speed, had his upturned shoes skimming the
surface of the water as if skiing. Mike Hamilton's boat carried a queer-
looking Kiwi bird with a pack on his back, ice-axe in one hand and a
glazed look in his eye, as he strode along the surface of the water. On
Ganga, Ding painted the traditional image of Shiva with his matted
locks into which, in those distant times, he had received the current of
Ganga in her descent from heaven.

For the first time since my arrival in India I began to relax. Despite
the heat, there was a strong breeze blowing in from the sea, bringing
in piled-up monsoon clouds. Sometimes the sky was clear, sometimes
mist would come across or, again, part of the sky would turn black

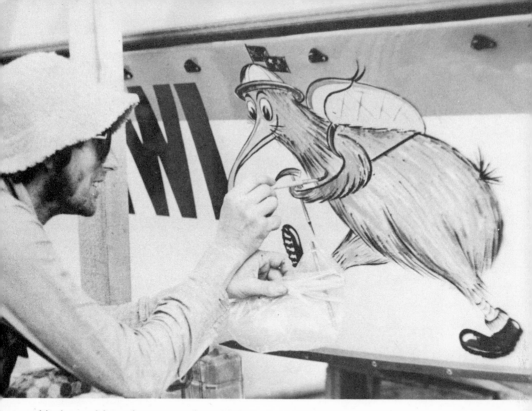

g puts his sign-writing talents to work on *Kiwi*.

oating haystack in the Sundarbans.

"No structural details!" Our boats skim under Calcutta's heavily protected Howrah Bridge.

Pedal power near Farakka.

and a shower of rain come across, very wet but so warm it didn't matter. The day turned to dusk and then there was the sudden closing in of the tropical night. We slept well.

The next morning, August 24th, we set off for Ganga Sagar on the first day of our great journey.

4

Tiger Country

THE DAY AT GANGA SAGAR HAD GIVEN US OUR FIRST TASTE OF THE river and had set the pattern of our journey. Ashore, we might be oppressed by the heat, inundated with hospitality, always aware, in the towns and cities, of the terrible press of humanity—yet back on the river all our lingering irritability was blown away by the first draught of warm breeze as our boats accelerated and skimmed out on to the broad waters of the river. At first we used the corrupt anglicised version of the river's name, Ganges, but as we came to love this great river we used the language of the people, and to us too she became Ganga, Mother Ganga. We were never happier than when travelling abroad on her sacred waters under a monsoon sky.

During the last 200 miles of her course, the Ganga spreads out into a delta built up by the mud and fine sand carried down from the head-waters. As the current slows in the delta, the river is no longer able to carry its burden of silt, and this is deposited, filling the beds of the watercourses or fertilising the fields over which it spreads. The whole of Lower Bengal, in which Calcutta lies, and which includes most of Bangladesh, is built up on this fertile bed of alluvial deposits.

Along the southern edge of the delta, where it meets the sea, is a vast region of mangrove-covered islands divided by small and large channels. It is called Sundarbans, meaning "beautiful forest". Before meeting the Forest Department of Bengal, I had never heard of the Sundarbans or of the tigers that still live there, and it was during an earlier visit that I was persuaded that we should explore these water-ways and mangroves before continuing upriver to the great city of Calcutta.

On August 25th we crossed the Hugli estuary, accompanied by our guide, Mr Minocha. Without him we should soon have been lost. There was the usual lumpy sea at first, and the boats crashed and banged a good deal, but we made good time. We passed a new silt island in the process of adding its expanse to the continent of India; at that stage it was only a foot or two above the high-watermark but in time, no doubt, mangroves would take root there, or the fine grass on which we had seen herds of buffalo grazing after being swum across the intervening channels. Pairs of big wooden fishing boats were scattered across the estuary with long lines of nets stretched between them. As we drove towards the bobbing floats of the nets, the fishermen danced and gesticulated, waving their hands to keep us away.

"Jet boats!" we shouted. "No propellers!" They're probably still wondering how we drove through without either cutting their nets to ribbons or getting ourselves hopelessly entangled.

We drove into a side channel. From here we thought we should be leaving behind us everybody except a few fishermen, but an hour later we swept around a corner to find a huge crowd thronging the banks. This, we were told, was the fishing village of Namkhana. An overwhelming smell of fish filled the air as we made some long, fast passes along the wooden wharf frontage, and amongst the crowd we caught glimpses of baskets of fresh fish, piles of crabs, prawns, squids and some strange-looking sea creatures none of us had seen before. Jim flicked the tail of *Ganga*, showering a crowd of children with the jet stream, and they shrieked and danced with delight.

The Forest Department of West Bengal were organising and supervising this part of our trip. They had expressed deep concern about the dangers of the tiger country and were strongly opposed to our camping aboard our boats, let alone ashore. Anchored in midstream at Namkhana were three large launches, and we were waved over to tie up behind. These launches would be travelling with us, and an even larger boat had gone ahead. We had arrived six hours behind schedule because of the work to be done on the boats that morning. We had had to refuel them, replace with bamboo poles the aluminium uprights that had been broken in the morning at Ganga Sagar. Jon and Michael had changed the oil in the boats and checked the motors and jet units to ensure that they were in perfect mechanical order, and we had been visited by Mr Mitra, Chairman of the Calcutta Port Trust, to take his party for a demonstration ride in the dock. Because of our late arrival, our guide suggested that we carry on through the night to reach our appointed objective, with the boats being towed. With some misgivings we tied our jet boats behind the launches and soon our fears were justified. The awning of *Ganga*, which seemed even at this early stage to be accident-prone, became jammed under a toilet cantilevered out over the back of one of the boats. Jim loped and scrambled across the deck of the launch and over the stern to cast *Ganga* free, before driving back and tying up in more satisfactory fashion. At ten p.m. we stopped for an excellent dinner, and then carried on into the moonlight.

We lay on the decks in the mild balmy air, watching the stars go past as the boat chugged on mile after mile deep into the Sundarbans. We really knew so little about the country we were moving into—most of the talk had been about the dangers of tigers and crocodiles. We were lucky to be there, for the sanctuary is closed to casual visitors.

Most of us drifted off to sleep. At two-forty a.m. we finally reached our accommodation vessel near Herobhanga. While some of the others slept out on deck, I thankfully fell into a comfortable bunk—it had been a marathon day.

We rose early, for we had a big day ahead of us, the plan being to visit a distant bird sanctuary. With a local expert to guide us, we roared off through a maze of channels—some calm, some choppy, for there was a brisk wind blowing. We kept to the main channels. Tigers can leap thirty feet, our guide told us, and he obviously wished to avoid having a tiger join us on the front seat of our jet boat. Although we passed the occasional small fishing vessel, there was no other trace of human beings in the area we were now entering. It was a monotonous landscape: the opaque water of the channel flanked by a thin line of mangroves on either side marked the edges of the swamp islands, and above that an empty sky.

After an hour's brisk driving, our guide pointed out a cloud of birds hovering over an area of mangroves to our right. We drove a short distance up a side channel to a spindly wooden landing with a raised walkway leading inland to a platform at treetop level, looking across an extensive nesting colony of white egrets and grey hornbills. There was a chatter of sound from the concourse of birds coming into land, making for their twig nests, or swaying amongst the foliage, digesting their last meal. A few pairs of egrets with outstretched wings were dancing gracefully in front of each other in what we presumed was some sort of mating ritual. Peter, the pilot amongst us, pointed out the aerodynamic skills of the arriving birds—the bringing forward of trailing legs to the outstretched forward position; wings flaring forwards towards the stall; and the loss of lift as they settled on to their perches.

When I returned to the landing, I noticed a narrow creek winding inland to the interior of the island. The tide was rushing out now, but I was curious as to what lay ahead. Jon, Murray and I set off on a wild exhilarating ride up the narrow channel with the planing boat side-slipping around tight bends, throwing waves of thick grey water on to the mudbanks on either side. The channel became smaller and shallower. Suddenly we came to the most gentle of halts. We were aground. A jet boat on the plane draws only three inches of water, but when settled back off the plane it needs fifteen inches to float free. I realised that the last stretch of the channel must be a few hundred yards back, and in a few minutes the tide had receded even further, leaving us high and dry. I cursed myself for an idiot—we were in the middle of jungle said to be infested with tigers and crocodiles, and it could easily be another eight or ten hours before the tide was high enough to float us off. Then, thirty feet to one side, across an intervening bank of mud and vegetation, I noticed a narrow stream of water still running briskly out—but how could three of us possibly move our 1,000 kg boat? In desperation we decided to try. We lowered ourselves overboard into knee-deep mud. With little faith in what we were doing, we heaved together, and to our absolute astonishment the boat moved—the mud was so slippery that the friction was almost nil. With much grunting and heaving we slid the boat over the muddy section and down into the fast-receding stream. The level was dropping quickly, so that we had to get going as soon as we could. The jet unit was clogged with mud; so while Jon cleaned it out, Murray and I paddled hard with the oars. Finally Jon had the jet going and we roared up on to the plane, swooping down the narrow stream and twisting crazily in water not much wider than our boat. A heavy overhanging branch wiped off one of the awning uprights, but we finally shot out into the open channel, and back to rejoin the other boats.

The two Mikes brightened when they heard of our grounding. Just what they needed to put some life into our film coverage of the Sundarbans; so *Air India* and *Ganga* headed back up the creek, taking care this time to go aground in deeper water, so that we could turn the boats and return the way we'd come. We wallowed around, sometimes up to our waists in mud and water, "like pigs in muck", as Ding put it. Two of our Forest Department guides, both wearing white shirts and neatly pressed trousers, had realised too late their mistake in accompanying us, and they too had reluctantly climbed overboard into the mud. They couldn't quite understand what we thought we were doing or why we didn't listen more carefully to their accounts of fifteen-foot crocodiles gliding through the slime. We nearly lost our first camera as B.G., one of our two Indian camera-men, slipped over and slithered gently down the mud slope on his back; fortunately he had the presence of mind to hand his ten thousand dollar camera to Ding as he slid past. We had little thought for the crocodiles and tigers that were meant to infest this area as we struggled our way up, roaring with laughter.

"You know," said Jon, "I've never seen such slippery mud. You could slide a long way on that."

I followed the drift of his thinking. "Let's try it," I said.

At the point where we rejoined the main channel, a long muddy corner stretched out. Jon turned sharply, gave a last burst of acceleration and cut the motor as we shot up the bank, slithering easily sixty or seventy feet overland, and popping back into the water again. "Just like the best powder snow," said Peter.

We repeated the exercise three times and, apart from further endangering our reputation with the Forestry Department and permanently jamming the speedometer at 34 m.p.h., there were no problems.

We had to move fast to make up time and catch up with the launches. Some of the route was protected from the wind, but in one long stretch we had a heavy sea dashing against the shore. Jon led an exhilarating run a few feet from the edge, where the backwash from the waves made the sea calmer. We saw a couple of deer on the way, and by the time we reached our rendezvous with the accommodation ship, at six p.m., I felt we had had a good day, with a feeling of shared excitement bringing the party together — something that always seemed to elude us in the cities.

That evening we went cruising in one of the smaller launches, equipped with a spotlight, to try to pick out a swimming tiger. Even though we had no success, it was a pleasant outing in the moonlight and we were told a number of tigerish tales. Once the jungles of India were infested with tigers, but now the species is in danger of becoming extinct. About 2,000 survivors are left and these languish in areas that man, for the moment at least, doesn't want. In the Sundarbans, one of these last retreats, tigers have had to learn to lead semi-aquatic lives in order to survive, eating crabs and fish as well as their more usual diet of deer and wild pigs when they can find them. They can swim very expertly from island to island, and they use this skill to creep up on sleeping fishermen and hook one of them out of their boats. One such incident had occurred just a few weeks before, we were told. The victim's brother fought the tiger and rescued the man, but he was still in hospital in Calcutta. The Forestry people estimated there were 170 tigers in their part of the Sundarbans, though probably many more in the large area in Bangladesh. Each year about seventy people are eaten by tigers, they said, the tigers having a higher preservation priority th the people. The villagers may get upset about this — the punishment for killing a tiger is six years "rigorous labour" in a Calcutta prison. I wasn't quite sure what was meant by "rigorous labour", but it didn't sound good. The official way to solve the problem is to keep people out of the tiger sanctuary; this makes life difficult for the locals, who rely on reclaiming new areas of the delta for their population growth.

When I asked about our chances of seeing a tiger during our final day in the Sundarbans, our companions were guarded in their replies. The picture became clearer as we enquired more closely how often they had seen tigers. We discovered, for instance, that our chief guide, who had been spending the greater part of each year around the sanctuary, had seen a tiger only twenty-five times in eight years. The head of the Forestry Department in Calcutta, also with us, had not seen one in thirty-two years, though admittedly he had not spent much time in the Sundarbans. Our guide had one photograph of a magnificent beast reclining on the mud under a mangrove tree, and this he said was the only one ever photographed in the sanctuary. It was clear by now that sighting a tiger was a very rare event indeed. I hadn't regretted our time spent in the Sundarbans, but from that time on I gave up hope of seeing a tiger.

We anchored that night alongside a tall watch-tower built beside a specially constructed tiger waterhole. Ding spent the night there, in a box covered in with heavy iron mesh, with his companion sweeping the banks of the pool below each hour with a strong light. It was, said Ding, a long night, full of the sounds of the jungle; in the small hours of the morning there was a torrential monsoon rainstorm; of tigers there was not a trace.

Next morning I was taken on a ceremonial visit through the area, with one man carrying a gun in front of me and one carrying a gun behind. They were obviously determined that *I* wasn't going to be eaten by a tiger. "The Sundarbans tiger is very ferocious, *sahib*," one of them confided to me. "If you are eaten by tiger, I will lose my job."

Over breakfast, back on the boat, we were told many more tales about the terrible activities of the local tigers but more than ever we were wondering if the creatures existed at all. We were tired of bumping around in wide and rough inlets, and instead wanted to get off to explore some narrow waterways. Our hosts were unhappy but, at length, with an armed officer in the second boat bearing a double-barrel shotgun, we went racing off up winding channels at full tide.

It was exciting, weaving in and out amongst the branches and tree trunks, and very beautiful. I saw a sea eagle, its rich bronze body and white head standing out amongst the olive green vegetation. Three brown monkeys swung rhythmically through the trees. With the motors cut there was no sound except the lapping of water; nothing to see except the thin bent trunks of the mangroves protruding from the water, an endless vista vanishing into the gloom of the great swamp surrounding us. We didn't envy the tigers the place they lived in. At high tide, four-fifths of the area is under water, and at this time the tigers are said to retreat to the remaining one-fifth of dry land. As the tide recedes, they move out on to the mud, searching for prey, or swimming across to a nearby island if they need new territory. We turned and fled back to the main channel as the tide began to recede.

We still hadn't filmed a sequence of the jet boats sliding overland, and as we still had two hours before lunch, Jon and I began hunting for a suitable location. We came to a small side-stream with a low, muddy peninsula protruding—better than the one of yesterday, for it was covered in grass three inches tall. To the immense consternation of our hosts, Mike Gill and Peter got out of their boat and went ashore, with the armed man following desperately behind them.

"You know what I'd like to see?" said Ding. "I'd like to see a crocodile bite that guy's foot and I reckon he'd give Gill both barrels."

Jon chose his line of approach at right angles to the small stream. He was getting ambitious by now. His aim was to put a fraction of turn on the boat before hitting the mud, slide gently through the grass, drifting through 90° as we went, leaving him in a position to take off upstream without pausing, once we landed in the creek on the far side. As we raced at the corner I could see Mike, Peter and the armed man directly in line with us, standing on the far bank of the small stream. We shot through the grass, plop into the stream at speed, with no chance of turning; in a fraction of a second we were across the channel and slithering up the mudbank on the far side. After missing Peter, Mike and the armed man by a couple of feet, the boat eased to a halt, hovered there for a second and then slid gently back into the creek.

"I thought I'd given up circus acts twenty years ago," Jon said with quiet delight.

"The old boy's still got a bit of dash in him," I said, and we turned round and did it again, this time perfectly, for we took off with a roar as soon as we emerged from the grass into the side channel.

We were back at the launches at one o'clock. *Air India* and *Kiwi* had tied up alongside, and we were all milling about on the high foredeck of the launch, awaiting lunch. Jim, with Mike Dillon, was still in *Ganga*, making it fast alongside the other two boats.

I don't know who saw the tiger first.

There was suddenly an air of electric excitement through the group, and one of our guides, eyes staring, seized me by the arm. "Tiger!" he said. "Tiger! Look, there, *sahib*! Big tiger!"

We were anchored in a channel a couple of hundred yards wide; the tide was low and a sloping bank of mud forty feet wide separated the mangrove forest from the sea. For a moment I saw nothing. Then my eye was caught by a movement, and there was a big cat just leaving the mangroves. Slowly it walked down the mud, tail aloft, slipped into the water and began swimming, intending to cross our channel some 200 yards upstream from us. Down in *Ganga*, Jim looked up at a scene of wild confusion: some people gesticulating and waving their arms, some pointing frantically upstream, while the rest of us had grabbed cameras and were piling over the side like a bunch of pirates. One thing was clear: something desperate was happening. The motor of *Ganga* roared into life, and Jim shot off like an arrow in the direction in which everybody was pointing. There was nothing to be seen except what looked like a small barrel bobbing about in the water. It was not until he was abreast of the small barrel that he realised that this was in fact the head of a tiger, at that stage swimming fast to shore.

Jon and I, in *Air India*, were following close on Jim's heels. Behind us someone was shouting, "Cut him off, Jon! Drive inshore and cut him off!"

That was easier said than done, for it was not at all clear as to who was going to get to where first. It seemed ludicrous to be in a position where we were in imminent danger of colliding with a Royal Bengal tiger. What happened if we did? If we killed the tiger, I supposed we'd get six years' "rigorous labour", if we hit the animal midships we might end up with a 400-pound tiger on our laps and there seemed every chance that at that stage the tiger would be thinking faster than we were. If we frightened him enough he might even turn and leap at us, and even Sears don't make their awning tiger-proof. In the end we took the easy way out and drove on the seaward side of the animal, who by now had his front paws ashore. In three immense loping bounds he was up the mud and into the mangroves.

An air of anticlimax came over the group. It seemed incredible that we had seen a tiger; incredible, too, that suddenly he was no longer there. With the boats rocking gently, we stood there gazing at the slope of soft mud, the row of pug-marks and the line of mangrove stems along the forest margin. And then, miraculously, we saw a movement in a thicket of mangroves; a big orange flank striped with black came into view for a few seconds and then vanished again.

"That's not the same tiger," someone said. "There's no mud on it."

We were tense with expectancy, certain now that the animal would reappear, and it did. A huge beast, eight feet long, not a trace of mud on him. He stalked slowly forwards into full view, the muscles of his powerful shoulders rippling under the sleek tawny skin, big head held aloft, staring straight at us, eye to eye. It was hard to guess what he was thinking. He certainly wasn't scared, nor angry either. In size and physical strength we were immeasurably inferior and he knew it. Turning, he walked slowly along the edge of the mangroves, glancing briefly over his shoulder. He gave a low growl, of contempt perhaps or disgust, and with not a sound glided inland into the gloom of the swamp. For a few moments we drifted in silence, spellbound by the aura of the great beast. We were aroused again by a deep-throated roar from less than fifty yards away, resonant with power and menace, like nothing I had ever heard before. The sound rolled upwards like distant thunder.

That was the last I saw of our tigers. Back on the launch, our Forestry guides were almost beside themselves in their attempts to wave us aboard, for they thought that, if we got into the boats, the tigers would return to the water and swim across, for they were obviously in search of new hunting territory. *Air India* and *Kiwi* tied astern, while *Ganga* drifted down the current with Jim and Mike Dillon watching the bank. They were in luck, for several times again they saw the tiger walking down the bank, and once he swam across a small side channel. Our guide told us that the animal which appeared first was a female, and the larger one, which we saw from close up, was a male. Seeing a tiger at all is a rare event, but to find two together was a new experience, even for the most experienced of our guides. The tiger will often have more than one mate, but they spend only short periods together. And yet by some miraculous coincidence we had found a pair of them. On one thing all were agreed: for the success of our expedition, such an event was auspicious beyond our wildest dreams. And we all felt with equal certainty that our *puja* at Ganga Sagar was directly responsible.

We motored on and passed through a narrow channel to a Forestry Compound where there was a thatched hut with an image of Banadevi, the goddess of the forest. The captain of the launch told a story about Banadevi and B.B. translated for us. Two or three thousand years ago, when all Bengal was one, the people of the Sundarbans used to live by collecting honey from the forests, in great danger from the many tigers then here. At one spot in what is now Bangladesh there lived a man who was told by a spirit that, if he brought a young boy as a gift to the forest, he would collect more honey than ever before. So he went to a young lad and told him he'd give him a rupee if he came with him to the forest to help gather honey. The boy agreed and went to tell his mother. His mother told him, "Listen! I am not your only mother. In the forest there is also another mother, and if you are alone or frightened in the forest, pray to this other mother, Banadevi, and no harm will come to you."

Off they went to an island, and the man led the boy deep into the forest; then, telling him "Wait here a moment while I look around for honey", he slipped back to the boat and rowed away, leaving the boy alone. The boy was very frightened, and he thought of tigers and spirits, but then he remembered what his mother had told him and he prayed to Banadevi, and he was afraid no longer. Even when a huge tiger came up to him he was unafraid, and the tiger just came up and sniffed him and licked him and went away again. He lay down to sleep at the foot of a tree as night came on, and as he slept he dreamed that Banadevi came to him riding on a tiger, beautiful to behold, and she spoke gently to him and told him nothing would harm him. In the morning the goddess actually appeared and, again speaking gently to him, told him that if he went home and got seven dinghies and filled them with jars and brought them here he would collect enough honey to fill all the jars.

He went to the shore of the island and at length a fishing dinghy came past and he waved it in. The fisherman was very surprised and asked him why he was there all alone amongst the tigers, and the boy explained and asked him to take him back to his village. Back home he told his mother and the villagers his story, and had great difficulty convincing them. "Such things do not happen nowadays," they all said; but at length he managed to gather up seven dinghies and enough jars, and he went back to the island and filled all the jars with honey. When he came back and sold it, he and his mother had enough money to live comfortably ever after. And to this day in the Sundarbans the people pray to Banadevi when they have to venture into tiger country; they say a special *mantra*, and they believe that then the tigers will not harm them.

That evening, in calm conditions and bright moonlight, we carried on to reach our mother ship at nine-thirty p.m. We dined royally off a variety of curried seafoods, including some very large green crabs we had seen earlier scuttling around the bottom of a fisherman's boat. Crab has never been one of my favourite foods and I avoided it, a decision I was not to regret.

Jim was deep in conversation with one of the boatmen, sharing his somewhat limited Hindi with the boatman's even more limited English. The boatman was full of curiosity. What was our country? Was the Government communist or socialist? What were our crops? Were there any Indians there? And then there were questions about our image of Shiva on the side of *Ganga*, for Shiva was the boatman's own personal god. How did we know about him? Who had painted the image? Then on to Jim's own religion. What was the religion of our country? Was it Jesu Christu? Who is the chief god? "And how do your people do *puja* to the god of Jesu Christu?"

Even Jim could not explain Christian services in Hindi.

"And is your god, too, the god of Jesu Christu?"

"No," said Jim, and then hesitated. "My god is Shiva too."

"Are you then a Hindu?"

"Not a proper Hindu; just a little one."

"And do you eat beef?" Another of those unanswerable questions.

"How many gods do you worship?" asked Jim.

"Ahh," said the boatman. "There is but one god."

To find a humble village boatman thus enunciating the great religious truth of the oneness of god pleased Jim so much that, before retiring to bed, he sang his only *bhajan*, a Hindi hymn he had learned in Figi; it was a gesture that cemented one of those strange little friendships that were to bring warmth to our journey throughout India.

Daylight next morning showed us anchored alongside a large village, protected from the encroaching brackish waters of the Sundarbans by a high embankment. Peter and Murray went ashore early to wander around the village, knowing from experience that my own visit would call out a shouting crowd, a feature of our progress that Peter found little to his liking. He wrote in his diary: "Murray and I went ashore to wander around the village before Sir Edmund made his visit. We walked along narrow mud tracks between the green rice paddies, past houses where shy pretty village girls stood nursing their babies on one hip, and children stared at us wide-eyed. Peace blessed the village; all seemed happy, simple and very beautiful. The people appeared prosperous and well fed; there were no cupped hands for alms. There were bright red hibiscus flowers fringing the edge of the bright green rice paddy."

Back on the launch I was just getting dressed when I heard a fearful commotion. I looked shoreward to see a boat approaching, crowded to the gunwhales with a waving group of villagers, all chanting, "Hil-la-ree, Zin-da-bad! Hil-la-ree, Zin-da-bad!"

"They are wishing you long life," said one of our guards.

"Hil-la-ree, Zin-da-bad! Hil-la-ree, Zin-da-bad!"

And then the word changed. "Man-of-iron! Zin-da-bad! Man-of-iron! Zin-da-bad!"

I hastily dressed and waved to them in regal fashion. I had seldom felt more mortal, with a sunburned face, sun-cream on my nose, dirty clothes, and being about twenty pounds overweight. They were soon followed by a much larger boat crammed with children escorted by their teachers. I was presented with a bunch of flowers and we exchanged compliments. I agreed to go ashore after breakfast.

Suddenly there was a loud cry from the bridge and, upriver, we could see a large creature swimming across. It was a crocodile, and even from a hundred yards away we could clearly see the bumps and horny surface along his back. In practised fashion we leaped over the side into the boats and raced upstream. At the noise of the boat the crocodile dived and reappeared an impressively long way off after being submerged for only a few seconds. Twice more we saw him, about twelve feet long we agreed, though Ding, blessed with a better imagination than the rest of us, thought it closer to eighteen. We agreed to put aside for the time being our earlier plans to go swimming. It is possible, we were told, to escape from the jaws of a tiger but never from those of a crocodile.

I then went ashore and had a conducted tour around the village, a beautiful area of green paddy fields and thatched houses, below high-tide level but protected by great earthen banks. There was much shouting of "Zindabad!" as we visited the post office, the school and the dairy farm. The people told me of their problems—the constant battle with salt water; the lack of fresh water, and how some people carried it three miles from the bores. They could only grow one crop a year, and this was during the monsoon when there was enough fresh water around. They felt the isolation—the lack of transportation to Calcutta, and the absence of medical facilities. One could sense a slight resentment over the twenty per cent of land owned by absentee landlords in Calcutta, although I felt this wasn't too terrible a proportion. On this island of sixteen square miles of arable area, there were 10,000 people—a "small village", as they called it. Already this year four of their people had been eaten by tigers but, although crocodiles had attacked goats and buffalo, they had not killed any humans.

We visited the temple to Krishna, Lord of Love and Compassion, and we left some of our flowers as offerings. We were given flowers from the altar in exchange. We asked how they had heard of us on this isolated island, and they said by All India radio. Also there had been copies of newspapers several days old. We had the feeling that our visit had been the only break in their routine for a very long time.

Jim and I mused over their patient acceptance of hardship and problems, and agreed that our jet-boat group was of quite a different temperament. We were addicted to excitement. We needed something stimulating every day in order to enjoy life—and if the excitement didn't appear we tended to create it for ourselves. Perhaps these kindly villagers, despite their poverty, were lucky to be spared the burden of restlessness.

We decided we needed to fake a tiger-sighting for the film. We did this near a village with cows on the bank. Everything was set up, with me, Peter and our guide in the cockpit of the boat. The guide had little English, but we tried to explain to him what we planned to do, and he nodded his understanding. It was all to be live sound. At the signal from the camera-man I spun around to the bank and shouted, "Tiger!" Everyone leaped for cameras and started shouting in great excitement — except the guide who said in a soothing voice, "No, no, sahib, that not tiger. That cow!" It was the end of a good film sequence.

Jim had been fulfilling his role as cultural and religious adviser. He had a deep discussion with one of the boatmen, who had just steered widely clear of the mouth of a certain creek. "This is because spirits are living up this creek," he said. Then he asked Jim, "Which do you think is stronger, manpower or godpower?" Jim thought a while and said "Ah . . . manpower." This was clearly not expected from someone who looked so much like a *sadhu*, and the boatman said rather sadly, as though he was correcting a favourite pupil who had just let him down, "No, sahib. Godpower is stronger."

That night we reached Namkhana and on the twenty-ninth we crossed to Haldia in less than an hour, in very calm conditions. At Haldia we were joined by Harish Sarin.

5

Calcutta

WE WERE UP EARLY NEXT DAY. THERE WAS A SENSE OF GROWING excitement, for after our diversion into the Sundarbans we were back on the main line of our journey. Our destination was Calcutta, a city of eight million people, and I think we were all apprehensive about what sort of crowds awaited us after the size of those in the small villages of the Sundarbans. It was a cloudy, glowering day and the weather wasn't at all promising — we could see we were in for showers, at least.

A large group of the well-established ladies of Haldia were there to bid us farewell and they sang one of Rabindranath Tagore's beautiful Bengali songs before presenting us with flowers and marking *tilaks* on our foreheads. Rain had begun falling, but Harish Sarin assured us that this was a good omen and would help bring success to the expedition. I felt a note of sadness in our departure, for we had been happy at Haldia.

We waved goodbye to the crowd as we raced down the lock. Behind the dock complex rose the pipes and towers of the oil refinery, with a banner of flame trailing in the wind from a tall chimney. Harish was clearly in good spirits and looking forward immensely to the adventure. His participation had not passed unnoticed amongst his colleagues in New Delhi, for a few days earlier I had been taken aside by the Minister of Energy and Petroleum at a function.

"Is it true," he said, "that Sarin is going with you?"

"Yes, of course," I replied. His eyes widened and he shook his head with a little smile as if he were thinking that perhaps he would be seeing no more of his friend Sarin.

At eight-fifty a.m. we emerged into the Hugli estuary and started upstream. Almost immediately the rain came lashing down and we were soon wet through, our eyes stinging from the raindrops driving into our faces. The river was broad here, almost like the ocean, and there was a nasty chop. Commander Paul had now taken over as pilot and he guided us with complete confidence. Mr T. K. Choudhury,

Assistant River Surveyor, had provided us with a set of notes describing the full length of the Hugli. Somewhere here in the estuary was the Auckland Bar which, he said, "has recently made many people connected with shipping in this port look for tranquillisers". At the head of the estuary we entered the narrower waters of the Hugli River proper. "The pilots cross this Gibraltar of Hugli with their lives just under their tongues," wrote Das Choudhury.

This is the region of the James and Mary Sands, an area of shifting shoals formed by the cross-currents at the mouths of two big tributary rivers entering here, the Damodar and the Rupnarayan. Beneath us, deep in the silt, lay the bones of many a good ship, particularly from earlier times before the Calcutta pilots had formed themselves into one of the most highly skilled pilot services in the world. The position and depth of the shoals can change from one day to the next. If a vessel of any size touches the bottom, she is pushed over by the current with a scouring action that settles the hull deep in the silt. There are tales of nothing but the yards of a big three-masted vessel remaining above water within half an hour of an accident.

A century ago the name of these sands was commonly supposed to be a corruption of the Bengali words *Jal-mari*, "the Waters of Death", but it was subsequently traced to a vessel, the *Royal James and Mary*, "which arrived on September 16th, 1694, with a cargo of redwood, candy and pepper; she fell on a sandbank and was unfortunately lost, being immediately overset, and broke her back with the loss of four or five men's lives." With Commander Paul at the helm and the boat drawing three inches, we felt safe from that fate, anyway.

At this stage most expedition members were looking distinctly seedy owing to the ravages of a virulent form of vomiting with dysentery which had been sporadically picking people off over the last twenty-four hours. I was the only one unaffected.

"What have you been eating?" asked Commander Paul.

"*Chapati*, rice, *dal*, curried vegetables, green salad, raw onion, curried meat, fried *bhekti* [a delicious fish whose flesh is closely woven with minute bones], the big green crabs of the Sundarban . . ."

"It is the crab," interrupted the Commander. "You should eat crab only within a month which has an 'r' in it. Now it is the month of August. I sometimes eat crab at this time, but only if it is prepared by my wife. She washes out the poison from beneath the shell."

It fitted. I was the only one who hadn't eaten the crab and I remained the only person still healthy. The crabs had had their revenge.

As the silt islands and mangroves of the estuary dropped astern, we entered the lush green of the Bengali countryside. Stands of palm

Prayer and peace in the heart of a busy city.

The island temple, Jahngir.

trees and feathery bamboo rose above the bright green of the paddy
fields. Harish and I were in *Air India* with Jon at the wheel. Over in
Ganga, Peter was doing most of the driving and already he was handling
the boat well. After a couple of hours of travelling we were getting
ahead of schedule and so we pulled into a deserted bank to wait out
some time, sharing a little backwater with a tiny fishing dinghy
festooned with a drying net. Immediately people started appearing
out of nowhere, and before long a crowd had gathered. B.B. persuaded someone to bring us some tea, and this we greatly enjoyed.
The sun had now broken through and, though it was humid, in the
warmth our wet clothes quickly dried. After a while we drove on
further and pulled into the bank, where a huge old paddle steamer was
being dismantled for scrap. We wandered around inside the monstrous
hull, clambered up on to the deck and peered down into the water-
filled engine room. It was a rather eerie experience.

As we drove on, agriculture gave way to factories — huge jute mills,
towering brick kilns, cotton mills, the oil jetties of Baj Baj, shoe
factories, paint factories. The massive silhouette of the Howrah Bridge
appeared on the skyline, and we knew we were approaching the
centre of the city. The *Gazetteer* said, in 1886:

> When at length the port of Calcutta is reached, a scene of unex-
> pected magnificence, unrivalled in its kind, bursts upon the eye. The
> long tiers of shipping, with the stately painted mansions of Garden
> Reach on the margin in the foreground, the fort rising from the
> great plain on the bank higher up, and the domes, steeples and noble
> public buildings of Calcutta beyond, gradually unfold their beauties
> in a long panorama. The traveller really feels that he is approaching
> a City of Palaces.

To us that day it was no City of Palaces. The skyline was lined with
giant metal rigs and cranes. Everywhere chimneys belched black smoke
into the air. Rusting ships lined the banks, and we seemed to have left
behind the fishing boats we had grown so fond of down-country. We
wove our way between big iron buoys and lighters, laden with cargo,
ploughing through the brown water. Commander Paul pointed out,
on our right, Man of War jetty, our destination, and we turned towards it just as the rain began to fall from a grimy sky. On the stroke
of one, we raced up to the jetty, three abreast, did a sweeping turn for
effect, and pulled in. We were given a tumultuous reception. On the
bank stood a big crowd surrounding a brightly-coloured tent which
was clearly where we were heading. Running into the river was a narrow

jetty with a barge moored at the end of it. Girls in red and white saris lined the jetty, whilst on the barge waited a crowd of dignitaries and a larger crowd of pressmen jostling for position. The jet boat pulled alongside and, as a forest of hands and arms reached down to help me aboard the jetty, the Press moved in like a well-trained commando unit. Microphones appeared from nowhere and I was showered with questions and commands.

"Tell us about the tiger, Sir Edmund."

"What are your impressions of India?"

"What is the objective of this expedition?"

"Who reached the summit of Everest first?"

A small but determined phalanx of Indian Oil men, who were organising the reception, now moved in to allow it to proceed as planned. A small boy clutching a garland appeared around my knees, and was lifted to place it around my neck. The crowd was forcibly parted for a moment to allow a very beautiful Bengali girl to step forward and press on my forehead a *tilak* mark. I became aware that, behind a camera lens which kept intruding, stood Mike Gill, desperately trying to film what he wrongly thought would be our biggest welcome in India. I was swept up from behind by the crowd, and we surged forward as the two rows of girls lining the jetty blew on conch shells and spread flower petals in my path. Eventually, streaming with rain and sweat, we were all seated beneath the tent for the welcome. A famous *baul* singer, Purna Chandara Das, came forward and with great intensity sang a haunting Bengali melody. There were many speeches and much applause. In my brief reply I tried to point out that we hadn't actually done anything important yet, but my efforts were all wasted—so far as the crowd was concerned we were conquering heroes, and that's all there was to it.

We were driven to the Swimming Club, a haunt of the wealthy élite of Calcutta, for drinks, hand-shaking, autographs and, finally, some food. Then a succession of gifts was presented. Masses of tea, biscuits, travel bags; a case of gin and lots of cigarettes. I don't smoke, but just had to shrug and thank the company on behalf of B.B. and Waka, who did. Waka had sworn a solemn oath a few days earlier that he would never smoke again, but this windfall of cigarettes caused him to modify his oath to the effect that he would allow himself to smoke donations. The whole reception was quite overwhelming and impossible to control. I managed to gather up our team and get them back to the boats by three-thirty p.m. for a formal visit.

At four o'clock the Governor of West Bengal and his lady arrived, and down poured the rain. Fortunately the Calcutta Port Trust were experienced in these matters and, alongside the wharf, they had tied a large boat with an extensive reception deck for V.I.P. functions. While the rain streamed down, we chatted away and I found the Governor and his wife a charming pair. Finally the rain eased to a light drizzle and we took Their Excellencies for a gentle run in a jet boat before returning them to the wharf to make their departure. As the rain had now stopped, we did a whole series of runs for other distinguished guests. There was quite a battle for positions.

Without pause for breath we were snatched from the riverbank to the Grand Hotel for a quick clean-up before drinks with the Department of Tourism at six p.m., and dinner with Air India at seven p.m. By ten o'clock we were close to dropping from exhaustion, but Jon and Jim still had the boats to worry about.

We had decided, after much discussion, to leave them moored at Man of War jetty in the main river rather than go through the laborious process of putting them into an enclosed lock for the night. But we were still worried by the tales of the notorious Calcutta tidal bore. At certain times of the year, high tides come pouring up the wide estuary of the Hugli and funnel into the narrow channel of the river. This concentrated tidal flood runs headlong into, and overrides, the ebbing current of the outgoing tide, and a moving wall of water up to ten feet high roars past Calcutta. It is because of this that the docks of Calcutta are behind locked gates, insulated from tidal fluctuations in general and the dreaded bore in particular. From a maze of conflicting information, a reasonable consensus had emerged that this was not one of the worst times and that our boats should ride out the bore safely while moored at the jetty. But we remained anxious and curious, and so at ten-thirty that evening, Jon and Jim, eyes glazed with fatigue, went back to the jetty to see the bore through with the boats. Jim dozed off in the back of *Ganga*, and would not have been much use if trouble had come; but in fact the change was mild though interesting. With a creaking from the floating pontoons of the jetty, the river rose five feet in a few minutes, jerking Jim into a dazed panic but causing the boats no trouble at all.

I arose next morning to a welter of Press headlines. EVEN THE TIGERS TURN OUT TO SEE HILLARY, said one. Another was to follow me all the way up the river:

FRIEND HAS FORGOTTEN ME SAYS TENZING

Tenzing Norgay, the first man to set foot on the top of the Everest on May 29th, 1953, along with Sir Edmund Hillary, said this when asked to comment on the "Ocean to Sky" expedition launched by the latter. "*Sathee ley ta birsyo* – the friend has forgotten me . . ." Tenzing said he had read in the newspapers that Hillary was now fiddling with boats instead of running after the mountains . . .

The truth of it is that Tenzing and I have not been on an expedition together since Everest, although we have travelled and attended functions together many times in various countries. It is sometimes hard for people to understand that Tenzing and I have each followed our own paths, but that we still remain good friends. When we had met in Australia a few months earlier, I had told him of my hopes for the Ganga but the idea of sharing such a journey had not entered the minds of either of us, or of Mohan Kohli, our host at the time, a fellow Indian and a fellow Everester.

At seven a.m. I climbed out of bed and gathered the gang together in my room for a briefing session. We had exactly twenty-four hours before leaving Calcutta, and I knew that this was my last chance to get everybody together as a group before they went their separate ways. Our major appointment for the day was a reception given by the Governor of West Bengal at Government House at five p.m. This was a very great honour, and we had to be sure to fit all our other activities around that. Mike Gill was to visit the bank to collect two thousand dollars in cash for expedition living expenses on the next 1,000 miles of river. The film crew wanted to film a typical Calcutta scene, and had chosen the busy area around Howrah Bridge. Jon, Jim and Mike Hamilton were giving joy-rides on the river for the friends in Calcutta who were doing so much to help us.

Murray and Peter, having decided to adopt the dress of the country, went out into the bazaar to buy *lungis*, a sarong-type garment which looks something like a skirt. Peter wrote in his diary: "We left the main thoroughfares to see what we could find down the backlanes. Walking was made awkward by the many people who were packing up their beds on the pavement. On beds of ragged clothes, pieces of sacking made do for mattresses and sheets. We went down one narrow street and then along a few more. Seeing an alley to one side we bowed low and made our way into it. Off to one side were small hollows in which very poor people were huddling beside a small ditch running beside the wall, full of open sewage. Then we entered a small courtyard where women washed dishes and children were being gathered together. On all sides there were dilapidated buildings and it was impossible to understand why they didn't all fall into the courtyard in one large heap.

"Retracing our steps over sleeping people, cows and mangy dogs, we returned to the air-conditioned superficial luxury of our hotel and felt a sense of embarrassment walking from the street into that great hall of prosperity. It's a contrast I find hard to philosophise away!"

Almost from the time of the city's founding in 1690, visitors to Calcutta have looked into their consciences when they see the city's great wealth, side by side with what must be the most desperate poverty on the face of the earth. Even if you wish to avoid the poverty there is no way of doing so. The road from the airport starts off well enough as a motorway of sorts, but suddenly it ends in the packed chaos of the streets of central Calcutta, where the planners have abandoned their motorway in despair. Rutted winding roads full of potholes, pools of mud, heaps of rubbish; solid moving masses of people in battered cars; ox-carts and hand-carts, rickshaws and scooters; buses dense with clinging humanity; trucks, crows, cows and dogs. You emerge from this on to the edge of the Maidan, an expanse of grassland and trees surrounded by the decaying buildings of British Calcutta and the new high-rise business buildings of Bengal's industrial centre. And although the Grand Hotel is on the edge of the Maidan, it is a rather grubby edge, populated with groups of beggars. There is no way of avoiding these, either. Give nothing and they still trot beside you plucking at a sleeve; give something and the pursuit is increased and intensified. Like everything in Calcutta, it is an insoluble problem.

For a couple of centuries writers have exhausted themselves trying to describe Calcutta. From the beginning there has been a central area of wealth surrounding the Maidan. Outside this the "native quarter" grew and spread. A traveller from the late eighteenth century describes the "native quarter" thus:

It is a truth that, from the western extremity of California to the eastern coast of Japan, there is not a spot where judgment, taste, decency, and convenience are so grossly insulted as in that scattered and confused chaos of houses, huts, sheds, streets, lanes, alleys, windings, gutters, sinks, and tanks, which, jumbled into an undistinguished mass of filth and corruption, equally offensive to human sense and health, compose the capital of the English Company's Government in India. The very small portion of cleanliness which it enjoys is owing to the familiar intercourse of hungry jackals by night and ravenous vultures, kites and crows by day. In like manner it is indebted to the smoke raised in public streets, in temporary huts and sheds, for any respite it enjoys from mosquitoes, the natural production of stagnated and putrid waters.

The *Gazetteer* tries to soothe its English conscience a century later by saying that "the old contrast which travellers have recorded between European Calcutta as a City of Palaces, and native Calcutta as a city of filth, is not *quite* so strongly marked. On the one hand, the English houses are less splendid; on the other, the native *bastis* are *somewhat* cleaner and more commodious." Even the *bastis*, "the native hamlets of mud huts", were "the despair of municipal reformers and of the sanitary authorities". They still are. A group of British and American urban experts visited Calcutta in 1966 to study the city, and concluded they had "not seen human degradation on a comparable scale in any other city in the world".

The one scrap of comfort for the Indian Government of today is that Calcutta is none of their doing. It is a legacy of the British. In 1690 it was a tiny native village called Kalikat with an agreeably large and shady banyan tree; it had the River Hugli on one side and a festering swamp on the other. The English settled there because the Moghuls had driven them out of the better trading sites upstream. It had a good anchorage and could be defended with relative ease. There was an element of luck in this choice of site, for Calcutta has never suffered the fate of all major deltaic trading ports, that of being silted out of existence, or being deserted by the tributary on whose banks it stands. During the sixteenth and seventeenth centuries, the upper end of the Hugli had been steadily silting up from the top down. The death-blow for the upper reaches came when the Damodar tributary in the eighteenth century jumped its banks one high monsoon to choose for itself a more westerly course, eventually opening into the Hugli sixty-three miles lower down, where it created the James and Mary Sands. Calcutta survived with a reasonable depth of water, but the other trading stations, those of the Portuguese, French, Danes and Germans, were all silted out of existence. Thus Calcutta became the major trading outlet, not only for Bengal but also for the whole Gangetic Basin as far up as Delhi, the capital controlling the legendary wealth of the Moghul empire; and this was systematically pillaged by the East India Company, to be exported, through Calcutta, back to England. In the nineteenth century the wealth of the city depended more on such products as jute, tea, opium and indigo, and in the present century vast coal and iron ore deposits and other minerals have provided the industrial base for the whole of India. Regrettably none of this wealth has helped solve Calcutta's problems, and Rudyard

Kipling's often-quoted lines are probably as true today as when he wrote them:

Chance directed, chance erected, laid and built
On the silt
Palace, byre, hovel—poverty and pride—
Side by side;
And, above the packed and pestilential town, death looked down.

As strange as anything else about Calcutta is the endless fascination it has, whether for visitors or for those who live there. It is very easy, after you have driven in from the airport, stumbled over the beggars of Chowringhee, and read a few of the more apocalyptic accounts of Calcutta, to characterise it as a city beyond hope. Yet the great majority of people one sees on the streets are not pictures of despair; they amble along, many of them, chatting to each other and looking reasonably contented. I remember sitting in a car in a crowded poor area watching a young woman dressed in rags squatting amongst the filth of the streets. She was holding her baby up so that their faces touched; for as long as I watched they were laughing and playing together. In their circumstances one felt the mother should have been despairing to the point of suicide, yet they looked as happy as any other mother and child I have seen anywhere. They keep clean, for washing is part of the Hindu religion. Only the most destitute of Indians ever seem to get dirty, even when living in unspeakably filthy houses and lanes. The women in their saris are always graceful, often beautiful, and the colours of the city, the browns and ochres and greys, with splashes of colour from saris or piles of fruit and vegetables, are in their own way beautiful, especially in the soft light of early morning or evening.

The locals remain patriotic. They would not, they assured us, want to shift to Delhi or Bombay or any of the other cities. Calcutta, they say, has more vitality and personality than any other city. When I first went there more than twenty years ago I tended to believe those who said it would collapse within ten years. But it hasn't. It seems no different, in fact. "Admirers fondly call it an eternal city," wrote my old friend the Assistant River Surveyor. Perhaps he is right.

★   ★   ★

That last day in Calcutta was for me a long and hectic day of preparation, talks, interviews and functions. We had to buy and sort gear; pay off our shipping agents; and be presented with even more gifts by manufacturers—not that we really needed the gifts, but they just kept coming, anyway.

I had asked Mike Gill to arrange transfer of two thousand dollars from New Zealand to India for me, and I now needed this in cash. I had assumed this would be in travellers' cheques, but at this point Mike sprung on me one of those little surprises that make him an unpredictable travelling companion. The money was in the form of a bank draft. We looked at it. It was made out to the Bombay branch of one of the banks of India and signed by the Assistant Manager of the Town Hall Branch of an Auckland bank.

"It's like going into a bank at home and asking them to cash a two-thousand-dollar I.O.U. from the Calcutta Hawkers' Association," I said. Mike looked a bit crestfallen. He said that he'd try, anyway, and that sometimes patience and courtesy could work miracles in India. He was away most of the morning. He said he had worked his way down five queues in three separate buildings—patience and courtesy personified. Finally he came to the desk of a cheerful little man in a room piled high with dusty files. He looked at the bank draft. "We will have to see if we have this man's signature in our files," he said. "There is no other way." The last remnant of Mike's optimism ebbed away. Clearly cashing the draft was going to be impossible. The cheerful little man called over an underling, handed the bank draft to him and then called over another minion to bring a pot of tea. For half an hour he and Mike sat together discussing life. "Life is more than eating and drinking and sleeping. If it is just this, we are no better than insects on a dung-heap. No, we must be always searching for the divinity, and this is where our country has a message for you, because this is a very old country."

India is full of philosophers. And patience and courtesy can work wonders: after half an hour the underling returned bearing two thousand dollars worth of rupee notes in wads.

Meanwhile, with B.B., I was having further talks with Indian Oil about the organisation for refuelling on our way upriver. I was beginning to realise that in getting B.B. as our liaison officer we had really struck gold. He was not only efficient in organising our movements; he also had our interests at heart in all our dealings, and on our behalf he could drive a hard bargain. I was also beginning to realise more fully the depth and extent of the Indian Oil involvement. They were providing the petrol, selecting the refuelling sites, providing a car to travel with us to carry extra baggage and passengers—we had seventeen people, but room in the boats for only fifteen—and, as we later discovered, at each refuelling there was a reception and lunch awaiting us.

At three p.m. the jet boats set off upriver with the film crew for what I had assumed would be a few brief shots of the boats travelling under Howrah Bridge, three abreast, the bridge having been chosen because it is probably the most prominent landmark in Calcutta. Murray Jones offered to climb one of the girders of the bridge to get a high shot, but this was firmly vetoed. It would only need the word to go about that a foreign spy was taking photographs from the bridge, and he would have a million people crying for his blood, with a few thousand swarming up to bring him down. I told Murray I needed him on the expedition.

It was a drizzling, overcast day, with smoke hanging in the air and the brown Hugli, in flood, pouring under the bridge. As the camera crew landed, a crowd formed around them, but the Department of Tourism had arranged a police escort to cope with this. The crew filmed the boats from water-level, with the bridge towering overhead. Then they left the jet boats waiting while they moved inland to find a building from which to film the bridge end-on, with the crowds and traffic moving across as the rush-hour approached. They shouldered their way through crowds, splashed through pools of mud, down an alley to a crumbling five-storey tenement building. Into its darkness they went, across the slippery floor, the air stale with the smell of garbage and urine; up the dark stairwell, to emerge five storeys up on a narrow balcony hardly more than a foot wide. There was no room to pass. They stood in a long line, Mike Dillon at the working end with camera and tripod, then Waka, Peter, Mike Gill, Ding and finally an unhappy-looking policeman. He was beginning to realise that if we collected and passed on vital military information about the Howrah Bridge, he would be responsible. He tapped Ding on the shoulder. "No structural details!" The word passed down the line to Mike Dillon. "No structural details!"

Mike is no hit-and-run photographer. The minutes ticked by as he carefully set the camera on its tripod, took light-readings and composed the shot. The policeman was beginning to sweat now, and a crowd was gathering in the stairwell. "No structural details!" he shouted. Mike was by now concentrating fiercely, one eye applied to the viewfinder, the other tightly shut. Waka tapped him on the shoulder. "No structural details!" "No structural details," repeated Mike, turning for a moment, then reapplying himself to the viewfinder.

It was four-thirty p.m. by the time they had gathered together their gear and raced back to the riverbank. There was not a sign of the jet boats. At five o'clock they took stock of the situation. It was drizzling again. They turned to the policeman, who was happy again now that the cameras had been packed away.

"How far is it to the Grand Hotel? Can we get there in ten minutes?"

He smiled and shook his head from side to side. "One hour," he said. "It is a busy time. There are many traffic on the road. No taxis now. All are full up with people."

"How far is it to Government House?"

The policeman no doubt thought the question was irrelevant, but he replied, "Government House is closer. Only half an hour."

"Come on," said Peter. "Let's walk it." They shouldered the camera gear and set off briskly down a road lined with warehouses. Trucks and cars lumbered past down the rutted street, showering them with mud, and soon they were streaming with sweat. At half-past five an empty taxi pulled up alongside.

"As fast as you can," said Peter, "to the Governor's Palace."

The grey-bearded Sikh driver looked them up and down, and with a jerk of his head motioned them to get in.

Meanwhile the three jet-boat drivers had arrived back at the Grand Hotel, muttering abuse about film crews with no sense of time. They had decided that three out of eight at the Governor's Reception would be better than none at all. We dressed in our best clothes. At five-thirty our cars swept up the drive to the foot of the huge flight of steps rising to the pillared entrance of the Governor's Palace. Inside, a banquet was spread in the vast central hall. The distinguished people of Calcutta were there. The Governor and his lady were at their most gracious as we sipped drinks together.

It was about then that a very battered taxi pulled to a halt at the foot of the steps. As the occupants got out, I realised that here were the missing five of the expedition. They were covered in mud and steaming gently in their wet clothes. They looked as though they should have been dropped off at Mother Teresa's home for the destitute poor, not at the Governor's Palace. There was a brief exchange with the Sikh taxi-driver as they discussed the fare. Carrying tripod and cameras they advanced up the flight of stairs. The Governor, to give him his due, appeared unflinching. I introduced them. "This is . . . ahh . . . my son Peter." My son Peter had on a pair of briefs so short as to be almost indecent, but he was obviously in high spirits at having reached the banquet almost on time. He extended a wet hand to the Governor, who showed just the slightest flicker of distaste as I moved on to the next introduction. "This is Dr Gill, the Deputy Leader." An impeccably dressed Indian at the Governor's side looked stonily at Dr Gill as if contemplating immediate despatch of a telegram to the Disciplinary Committee of the New Zealand Medical Association. "And Mr Michael Dillon, our film director." I was pleased to see that Mike had the sensitivity to disappear quietly into the background, where he spent the remainder of the evening lurking behind pillars, trying to keep out of sight.

Ding had been growing a beard for just over a week, and the sparse stubble of this did nothing to improve his appearance. "Mr Dingle runs an Outdoor Pursuits Centre," I added during the introduction, as if that somehow explained his appearance. Finally came Waka who had shoulder-length hair and generally looked like the sort of person that a Customs Officer would go over with great care.

I was glad when the introductions were over. A genial Indian clapped me on the shoulder. "It is a first for Government House," he said. Jim came over to sympathise with me. "Wonderfully tolerant people in India," he said, and I certainly couldn't disagree with that.

We returned to the hotel to relax over a cup of coffee in the restaurant before the mad rush of our final packing. During the day, I had been walking through the hotel lobby on the way to an appointment when I was accosted by two young men in the garb of Hare Krishnas. One was a Caucasian—a tall, pale young man—and the other was an Indian. The American (for so he proved to be) started talking to me about something they wished me to do in support of their faith—I didn't really listen too carefully as I was in a hurry. Now I saw them approaching the restaurant, and groaned deeply, as I knew they were planning to renew the discussion. Jim Wilson sprang to my aid. "I'll talk to them," he said. "After all, I'm your religious adviser. Your religious development is entering a critical phase and I'm not going to have it mucked about by a couple of Hare Krishnas." He got up and, strolling along the passage, leaned one hefty arm against the wall. With the other on his hip he effectively blocked their entrance. The two didn't give in easily—for fifteen minutes they talked to a firm but sweetly reasonable Jim, and odd bits of the discussion came drifting back. I couldn't quite see myself with an orange robe and shaven head, dancing down the road and strumming a guitar. I ate my meal in peace and quiet, content not to be blessed or saved or converted. Finally the two young men admitted defeat and went away, leaving us alone. I was very thankful for Jim's help.

I went to bed at midnight after packing and letter-writing. At one-thirty a.m. I was awakened by several loud voices. I staggered out of bed and opened the door, to see two Indians standing there, one looking wild-eyed, the other a somewhat bovine character. The excitable one said he must talk to me for five minutes about a most important topic. I said I was tired and must sleep—he could meet me at the wharf in the morning. He persisted; so I said "Goodnight", and made to shut the door. He pushed out his hand and held the door open. Restraining my rising wrath I said once again, "I am tired and I wish to be alone." He gave a wild laugh and said, "So you are like Greta Garbo—you wish to be alone?" I once again said "Goodnight". It all seemed like a mad dream, and I started closing the door against the pressure of his hand and his foot, which was now across the threshold.

"Would you use force?"

I decided I would. I opened the door wide, stepped up to him until we were almost touching, and looked him firmly in the eye. "Will you kindly take a step back out of my room?" I said. He must have sensed my anger. After a second or two of hesitation he stepped back, first one step—I followed him—and then two. I retreated inside the door and closed it firmly. That was the end. I never did hear his important story. I fell back into the sleep of exhaustion.

6

Up the River

I WAS UP AT FIVE A.M., GETTING THE GEAR ORGANISED AND DOWN to the docks, where there was a small but friendly crowd to see us off. Shortly after seven o'clock we unhitched from our moorings and headed out into the main stream. A drizzling rain fell from a grey sky as we planed out on to the flood tide, mottled with the bright green of water hyacinths torn away from backwaters upstream. We threaded our way between buoys, past what looked like an immense floating haystack, and in line abreast we swept beneath the shadow of Howrah Bridge. A roar of traffic came down to us, the rumble of trucks and buses, the sounds of a city on the move. People leaned over the rail high above and waved. The end of Calcutta, we thought. The big crowds we had feared had never really materialised, and despite the headlines we had been receiving and the daily radio reports, it seemed that the great mass of the population was unmoved by our presence.

When we saw a crowd on the bank a short distance further up, we drove over, curious as to what they were doing. We roared in, close to shore. To our surprise the crowd leaped with excitement, waving and laughing, and I could hear my name being shouted. On the next clear space on the bank we came to another crowd; anchored offshore was a boat packed with people bearing a banner saying, "Welcome to Hilleri's Troupe". Grimy factories lined the banks on either side, but wherever there was a clear space there were people—it looked as though the people of Calcutta knew about us, after all.

We called at the temple of Ramakrishna, led in by Jim who had been wanting to visit the shrine ever since he left Varanasi fifteen years ago. He padded around the temple in his bare feet, obviously very happy to be there, and moved by the image of the goddess Kali in the shrine itself. Prem and the other Indian members of the expedition were puzzled by these acts of Hindu devotion on the part of Jim, as we all were to some extent, though we grew more used to them as we ourselves became absorbed, to a varying extent, in the religious manifestations of Hinduism along the banks of the river.

Just beyond this point, we were given a reception by a combined gathering of the Police Training Centre and the Indian Army – a huge crowd and much bigger than we had been led to expect. It was organised with the best of military discipline, enabling us to keep exactly to our scheduled half hour. We were taken to a carpeted area surrounded by the many trunks of an ancient banyan tree, spreading so wide that the whole crowd was able to stand in its shade as we were plied with tea and cakes and delicious Indian delicacies. Again I was struck by the contrast between my own bizarre group, clad in old hats, *lungis* (which only a lower-caste Indian would wear in public), and with bare feet, and our hosts, immaculately dressed in uniform, with their wives wearing exquisite saris. The only ones amongst us looking even remotely respectable were myself and Harish, who had the Indian knack of remaining clean and well dressed, no matter what the conditions. We paid our respects to the senior officers and their ladies, waved at the huge crowd of active-looking young trainees, and were into the boats and away.

That really was the end of Calcutta, I thought, but I could hardly have been more wrong. The crowds seemed if anything to get bigger rather than smaller. The earliest European settlements were on this part of the river, and amongst the trees were fragments of old European architecture with pillared façades and statues, the whole of it now transformed by age, and swarming with the people of India who had come to see us. They were crowded on the *ghats*; they were in the trees; on boats; leaning out of windows; packed on to wharves; swimming in the water; crammed on balconies. As we approached they would wave, and as we waved back we were greeted with an answering roar of welcome, all of them laughing and shouting, their arms high in the air as they surged towards us. We were first astounded, then exhilarated by this mass emotion, something completely outside the experience of most of the group, beyond anything I had met, even after Everest. Never have I felt such spontaneous warmth and excitement radiating from a crowd.

We responded wholly to the emotion, swinging as close to the bank as we dared and weaving from one side of the river to the other to where the crowds had assembled. We waved until our arms ached, smiled until our jaws stuck open, and waved again until our arms fell. In a morning we seemed to have seen more people than the whole population of New Zealand. It was an unending triumphal procession. I doubt whether I shall ever see its like again. The climax came at our refuelling stop at the township of Nabadwip. We saw it ahead; a sea of human heads surrounding a small cleared area on the bank, under a striped canvas awning for our reception. Holding the crowd back were a flimsy bamboo barricade and a few unhappy-looking policemen. As we approached, I spared a thought for the unfortunate senior officer of the Bharat Petroleum Company who was organising the refuelling. Somehow he had to get us ashore, make a speech of welcome, give us lunch, manhandle the 44 gallon drums of petrol alongside our boats, and pump their contents into the tanks—all this with a volatile crowd of 30,000 Bengalis pouring down the banks, threatening to drive him and his men into the river even before we arrived. Harish leaned across to me. "We will need to be careful here," he said. "Bengalis are very, very emotional people."

When we came in and tied up, I was welcomed with flowers and a *tilak* and conducted over to the awning, although I was somewhat reluctant to be separated from the boats and my group. Immediately I had autograph books thrust forward for me to sign, and a great sigh went through the crowd outside—they wanted autographs, too. The bamboo fence restraining them started to shiver and buckle, and the awning was shaking too. A line of policemen moved in to push the crowd back, and one over-zealous officer used the butt of his rifle on a particularly eager young man, one of the largest Indians I have seen. His reaction was frightening. Foaming with rage, fists shaking, he began to shout his anger at the police and at the official party who were gathered under the awning.

The Oil Company man gave his speech, but not a word could be heard above the din. Then he called on me, and though I spoke slowly and clearly, nothing could penetrate the noise. The young man had now worked himself up to fever pitch. His eyes protruded, black pupils surrounded by big circles of white, and his anger was beginning to spread through the crowd around him. I made a quick military appraisal of the situation, working out the route I would take to the boat if the barriers broke. Retreat would be the order of the day, not an attempt at a gallant defence against overwhelming odds. Provided I was fast off the mark before the crowd swept us into the river, I thought I probably had the size and strength to get through into a boat and be off. At this point the organiser, who could see himself losing his job, and perhaps his life as well, had a bright idea: would I go over to the irate young gentleman and shake his hand in an attempt to calm him down? With a little trepidation I pushed my way over to the wall of the tent and grasped the man firmly by the hand. Immediately his anger evaporated; he broke out into a broad smile, and shook my hand vigorously in return. But the forward pressure was too great to stop now, and the bamboo framework was steadily disintegrating.

The pressure inside the tent increased, and I could feel myself getting tangled in a chair and so I shrugged myself clear. The District Magistrate quietly commented that he felt we should retreat on to the pontoon barge where the boats were refuelling, and where he could use his police more effectively to protect us. Surrounded by a heaving though smiling mass, I retreated on to the pontoon, and a line of policemen immediately closed off all access. It had been a tricky ten minutes, and I was glad to be close to the boats again.

I asked the District Magistrate why there was so much excitement. He shrugged his shoulders. "Nothing like this has happened in Nabadwip in living memory," he said. "At school, we all learn the story of how you and Tenzing climbed Everest. We all know what you look like. Many people regard you as more an Indian than a New Zealander. Now the radio has been telling us that we have the chance to see a famous man with our own eyes on the banks of Ganga. Some of these people have come from fifty miles away. They have been waiting here since yesterday."

"They do not know what they are going to see," said Harish. "Some of them think they are going to see Mount Everest itself come down to the river."

Still the crowd was pressing forward, and the suggestion was made that I should head off upriver in the first boat to complete the refuelling. This would take the pressure off the situation. I was glad to agree and, after a tumultuous farewell, I sped off upriver where we were soon joined by the other two boats. Our lunch was on an old tug, slowly making its way upriver. We swooped down on it, hitched the boats alongside and then clambered up. Safely in midstream, relaxed at last, we enjoyed a delicious meal. Then we said our last goodbyes and headed off upstream. I shall not readily forget Nabadwip

There was no time to waste, for we still had close on 120 miles to travel before reaching our destination of Behrampur. The industries of Calcutta were now far behind us, and we were into the rich green landscape of rural Bengal. Villages stood amongst groves of mangroves or the tall palms of coconut and toddy trees. There were stands of jute and sugarcane, and fields of rice paddy—emerald green, or yellow as they approached harvest, and rippling in the monsoon breeze. Women working in the fields stood as we approached, sometimes smiling, always attractive and graceful in their bright saris, a sight that kept our drivers steering close against the banks.

The black humps of fresh-water porpoises surfaced ahead of us, though, unlike their sea-going brethren, they would appear once only, and we never had schools of them playing around us. We passed a

eserted palace of a thousand doors, former seat of the Nawabs of Bengal.

Ancient carvings in the granite flanks of Jahngir island.

line of buffaloes swimming across the river, only their noses, eyes, and bony rumps showing. Small boys rode on their backs or were towed behind, hanging on to their tails and carrying their umbrellas tied to the turbans they were wearing.

The afternoon wore on. We were getting tired now, and concentration was harder to keep. In the opaque muddy water we found it very difficult to judge depth and the lie of the channel. The river bottom was smooth and the current even and any surface indications were very inconspicuous. Suddenly Jon ran hard aground on a shallow sandbar and we were all thrown violently forward. Harish gave his knee a sharp crack and was in pain. We climbed out of the boat and tried to move it, but with only one crew this was impossible. I saw the other boats approaching us from downstream. *Kiwi* was in front, driven by Mike Gill, who was gazing absent-mindedly at a group of women standing on the bank. By the line he was taking, he looked as though he was not only going to join us aground but also to ram us amidships. Just in time, Mike Hamilton wrenched the wheel unceremoniously from his hands and turned hard aport out of trouble. The other boats edged over towards us, and when they reached shallower water their crews waded over to help. We had inflated rubber rollers and began slowly heaving the stranded craft on to these. I called out the old Sherpa battle-cry that I've used a thousand times in the Himalayas when hauling logs or rocks. "Sho-ni sho-ni sho-ni so-o-o-ooo!" Everyone heaved together. As the boat climbed on to the rollers, the friction fell away and soon we had it afloat again. The others piled into their boats and we headed off upstream.

We hadn't gone very far before we ran aground again, and again it was *Air India* in the lead, with Jon at the wheel and myself, Harish, Commander Paul and Prem Vaidya as the crew. Jon had the handicap of having four captains in the boat, and when he asked for an opinion as to which way the current ran, he would get three of them, of which only Commander Paul's was likely to be right. Harish and I were in danger of laying each other out as our arms rose sharply to the horizontal, in opposite directions. All through the day the Hugli had been dwindling in size, emphasising that we were travelling on just one of the numerous distributaries of the Gangetic Delta. Even the name Hugli had dropped behind us, for here the river was called Bhagirathi and would continue to be thus called until we joined the main flow of the Ganga next day. A few centuries ago the Bhagirathi-Hugli had carried the main flow of Ganga to the sea, but no longer — though still, for pilgrims, Bhagirathi-Hugli is the true Ganga.

We picked ourselves up out of the minor shambles of our second grounding, rubbed a few bruises and checked to see that no joints had been dislocated; then we went through the same laborious procedure of dragging off. "Sho-ni sho-ni sho-ni so-o-o-ooo!" It was to become a familiar cry throughout our journey.

The sky behind us was turning black, promising a rainstorm before we reached Behrampur, and the light was fading. Commander Paul pointed towards a section of riverbank which looked no different from any other. "That is Plassey," he said. It was one of the few names I could recall from my scanty knowledge of Indian history, and the Assistant River Surveyor, in his invaluable notes, had described the Battle of Plassey:

> On these fields were fought the grim first battles of Indian independence in the year 1757 between the army of Nawab Siraj-ud-daula and that of Robert Clive, the English Commander. The Nawab lost the battle because of the outright treachery of some of his closest lieutenants, who had been bought over by the Englishmen.
>
> Thus the sun of the Indian independence set for nearly two centuries beyond the muddy water of the Bhagirathi, turning it into crimson red.

Siraj-ud-daula, described as having an ungovernable temper, was only 19 years old when he became the Nawab of Bengal in 1755. By all accounts he was a difficult person to live with, and when the English East India Company offended him, he retaliated by sacking Calcutta. Most of the English were wise enough to flee down-river but the 146 who remained were imprisoned in the small military jail known to history as the Black Hole of Calcutta, and when the jail was opened the following morning only twenty-three were still alive. When Clive sailed from Madras to attempt a punitive expedition, the odds appeared heavily weighted against the English. A few cautious enquiries, however, showed that the Nawab was not by any means universally beloved, nor the English universally despised. The merchants and bankers of Bengal had found the English to be a most useful source of income, and there were some older contenders for the throne of the Nawab, who was probably regarded as an insolent youth. Amongst them were three generals in the Nawab's army, including Mir Jafar, and it was to him that Clive promised the throne if he assisted him to overthrow Siraj-ud-daula.

In the monsoon month of June 1757, Clive, with an army of 880 English soldiers and 2,000 Indian troops moved up the banks of the Hugli. Facing him at Plassey was the Nawab, with an army of 50,000

men. The day began badly for Siraj-ud-daula when the Court
Astrologer predicted disaster, though he too was probably in the pay
of the English. All morning there was an exchange of artillery fire
between the small English army and the vast array of the Nawab's
army, with its glittering cavalry and troupes of elephants. Clive
realised that he had no chance against such an army unless Mir Jafar
openly deserted the Nawab; but Mir Jafar, for his part, was having
second thoughts as he looked at Clive's tiny force. Maybe the Nawab
was going to win, anyway. Mir Jafar decided to sit back and await
developments before making a rash decision as to which side he should
join.

As the artillery duel between the two armies continued, Clive
decided that his best course of action would be simply to try to survive
the day, with the chance of launching a surprise attack that night. But
then the monsoon joined in on Clive's side. A torrential rainstorm
burst on the battlefield at midday, soaking the ammunition of the
Nawab's gunners but not that of the English, who had brought
tarpaulins to keep their powder dry. With the enemy's guns silent,
Clive launched an attack against the headquarters of the Nawab, who
already must have smelled treachery in the inactivity of Mir Jafar. Late
in the afternoon, with the battle turning against him, Siraj-ud-daula
fled, with his huge army in disarray behind him. The Battle of Plassey
was over. Mir Jafar was installed as the new Nawab, after paying Clive
two hundred and thirty-four pounds as a small token of his esteem.
For the Moghul empire it was the beginning of the end. From being
no more than the masters of a prosperous trading post at Calcutta, the
English had become masters of Bengal, a supremacy they were later
to extend to the whole of the Gangetic Basin, including Delhi, after
the Battle of Buxar in 1764.

I certainly had no ambitions to go ashore to see what remained of
the battlefield. It was dusk now, and we were still a long way short of
Behrampur. We passed a burning *ghat*, a macabre sight, with the
relatives squatting around the burning corpse, the fire crackling away,
and the flames leaping up bright orange in the failing light. A row of
vultures sat hunch-shouldered on the bank, watching a dead cow
below. Dusk changed to night, and still there was no sign of the lights
of Behrampur. It had been an exhausting day, and we were tired and
irritable. To compound our misery, the promised rainstorm caught up
with us, reducing our poor visibility to almost nothing. Harish
reminded me that bombers flying missions at night can always see
water below them, even in the dark. I wondered if they could also
see floating mines, for if we came suddenly on a floating log or a boat

it seemed probable that the driver would hit it before he had time to react. Petrol consumption had been heavier than anticipated and all fuel tanks were showing empty. Finally, however, before any of these catastrophes struck us, we came round a bend to find the flashing lights of Behrampur ahead of us. It had been a long tough day of 187 miles, the longest we ever did on the whole journey.

Despite the darkness there was a big crowd which had been waiting all day for us. With some reluctance I agreed to the request of the District Magistrate welcoming me that I should show myself to the crowd. I climbed on to the top deck of his launch, where they shone spotlights on me as I waved in the direction of the riverbank. An enthusiastic response came back to me out of the darkness. Obviously there were a lot of people out there, and I wondered how we'd get through. Our escape was well organised, however, and with Harish and Jim beside me I pushed through the cheerful jostling mob to a waiting car and drove off to a secluded bungalow, to be joined there by the rest of the crew when they had lashed the awnings over their boats.

Although we were all exhausted from our day, there was still the social programme ahead of us. At seven-thirty I was taken to a youth function in the bazaar, more or less expecting some trouble, but it didn't work out like that at all—the youth leaders did their own policing and the whole programme was carried through in the best of humour. Dinner at the District Magistrate's residence, a small palace by the look of it, was a pleasant occasion and we all began to unwind.

"How fast do you travel?" asked one of our hosts.

"Up to 70 km per hour," I said.

"What is the use of going so fast? At this speed you see nothing. It is the same as going by plane." Another philosopher. We laughed together.

I was in bed about eleven p.m. It had been an astonishing day—the vast crowds of people and their enthusiasm. I am unlikely ever to see anything quite like it again. I kept wishing we weren't attracting quite so much public attention. It was a strain not only for me but for the other members of the party as well, and there was a danger that we would lose our feeling of expedition unity, that feeling of working together and taking pleasure in each other's company, which is one of the joys of being on an expedition, particularly with old friends. Inevitably most of the attention had been focused on me, and I hoped the others hadn't been feeling left out. In many ways Peter had the most difficult position of all, for there were many people, particularly young people, curious to meet him simply because he was my son. It was not the sort of attention that Peter enjoyed and I had seen his mood grow darker as the day went on. Prem, who was unaware of all this, had made the mistake of pointing out Peter to a group of autograph hunters on our arrival in Behrampur. It was like putting a match to a charge of explosive on a short fuse. I talked to Peter about it all, and there was a brief flare-up of the family temper. I sympathised, but there was not much I could do about it. There was nearly always stress in the towns and cities. Perhaps without it we should not have developed such an affection for Ganga herself.

The following day was September 2nd and we left Behrampur at the gentlemanly hour of eight a.m. We waved politely to the crowd who had come to see us off – "Queen Elizabeth hand-swivels" was the phrase Peter used to describe our developing technique. Three miles on, we came to a boat-load of youths frantically pointing ashore to the right bank, where an unscheduled welcome awaited us. Beneath a banyan tree stood the familiar line of girls in red-bordered white saris; the sound of conch shells came echoing across the water, and around an elevated platform with microphone and speakers stood a crowd of several thousand people. Harish and Commander Paul advised me against going ashore, but I could hardly refuse when the people had gone to so much trouble with their welcome. I went ashore with the sturdy Commander Paul in advance, and a group of vigorous young men to escort me. A girl placed a *tilak* mark on my forehead, while others festooned me with garlands of flowers – Ding told me I looked like a flower stall. A band was placed on my wrist and another girl touched my feet, bringing her hands together and bowing her head. The rest of the expedition received the same welcome and I noted with interest that even Peter was happy to be welcomed like this by a row of beautiful girls. Shaking hands furiously, I moved up to the dais. There were short speeches, a presentation, and I said a few words. Then it was time to return. My protectors were superb. We charged through the cheering and clutching crowd like a hot knife through butter, and duly arrived safely back on the boats.

It was an overcast morning, but even in this subdued light the countryside glowed as we drove on. We had been told that ahead of us, on the right bank, lay the Palace of Murshidabad, the seat of the Nawabs of Bengal over the past 300 years, but I was hardly prepared for the size of it when it came into view a few miles on. It looked like Buckingham Palace: a huge building 400 ft long and 80 ft high, with a sweep of steps rising to a long façade of fluted pillars. It was made of brown stone, with a blotchy appearance in parts, as if someone had been attempting to camouflage it.

"It is Harzadwari," said Commander Paul, "which means it has a thousand doors. Since 1947 the Nawab has not been able to afford to live there and the Government has bought it from him. They cannot afford to live there either."

The three boats nosed into the bank, where we had a discussion on the merits of an expedition visit. Most of the party were indifferent. Mike Gill reminded us of the man who said that if we drove upriver at 70 km per hour we might as well be in a plane. Harish was concerned that we might fall behind schedule – there was nothing of the timeless East about Harish, or any of our Indian members, for that matter, for they were all a good deal more punctilious about time than was the New Zealand contingent. In the end a few dedicated antiquarians went in for a flying visit. It was like a huge unlit museum, deep under layers of dust. There were thrones, acres of Victorian furniture, racks of armaments. A chirpy little guide led them to a huge black oil painting, where he stood to attention and solemnly intoned the words

> Not a drum was heard, not a funeral note,
> As his corse to the rampart we hurried;
> Not a soldier discharged his farewell shot
> O'er the grave where our hero we buried.

"It is burial of Sir John Moore," he explained with a grin. He moved on to one of the innumerable paintings of the Nawabs who had inhabited the palace. "Special thing about this painting is that cushion on toe always points towards you no matter what side you are standing." Without pause he moved on to a six-foot-high painting of two children. "Special thing about this painting is that girl is always looking at you no matter what side you are standing."

At the end of the palace was a high-ceilinged room packed with hand-painted Islamic books, beautifully illuminated. Eddies of dust swirled down between the rows of shelves, as a breeze blew through the palace. It was all fascinating and all decaying. There was the feeling of an army of microbes and fungi at work to return the palace and its contents to the silt of the holy river on whose banks the palace stood. It was worth the visit.

Our next official appointment was with the Brigadier in charge of the Farakka Barrage who was to meet us at Jangipur, where the diversion canal from Farakka joins the Bhagirathi. On our way we saw two figures in the distance who appeared to be riding a bicycle in tandem across the river. As we drew closer we saw that the bicycle was mounted on pontoons, and that the pedals were connected through a drive-shaft to a small propeller astern. The mechanism looked about as efficient as an egg-beater. The older of the two cyclists was smiling broadly, obviously delighted to see us.

"I am a truck owner," he said, "and he is my employee." He pointed at his companion, a young man who looked as though he was praying. "He is very worried because he cannot swim. We are making a trial run. It is very fast downstream but a little slow upstream." We waved goodbye as they bent to their work again, continuing their steady drift down towards Calcutta.

At Jangipur we climbed aboard a river launch to be joined by the Brigadier, who had arranged for us cups of tea and dishes of *rasgulla*, delicious Bengali sweets made from cream cheese rolled into a ball the size of a walnut and soaked in syrup—it was a dish I had been developing an increasing weakness for.

We raced on up what was left of the Bhagirathi, here confined between narrow banks, and all the way porpoises were leaping out of the water. Suddenly the banks fell away on either side. Ahead of us stretched a vast sheet of brown water, blown into steep waves by the wind and studded with the sails of country boats. The far bank was miles away and yet, in spite of the distance between the banks, we could feel beneath us the power of the current and see on either side the boils and waves and eddies of a great river. It was like moving on to an inland sea. We had reached a milestone on our journey. We had joined the main flow of the Ganga.

Downstream from the Bhagirathi, the river is known as the Padma, for the name Ganga, if it is applied to anything from here on, is reserved for the Bhagirathi-Hugli on which we had been travelling. Somewhere not far east of where we were, the Padma entered Bangladesh, fanning out into the great leash of distributaries that form the delta. We refuelled at a town called Dhulian on the south bank, shook hands and signed autographs, and moved on in the direction of the Farakka Barrage looming up in the distance, a colossal structure stretching right across the river. Like any barrage, it has a series of gates all the way across, 102 of them in the case of this one, and these can be set at varying heights as required to divert water into the feeder canals upstream, such as the one used to keep the Bhagirathi-Hugli open in the dry season. Earlier we had been warned that we might have to drag our boats round the end of the barrage rather than drive through it, but our fears of a hot haul were laid to rest when the Brigadier directed us to the far side, where gate number 92 had been opened for us. There was an enormous flow of water. The Brigadier said that at present 1,600,000 cusecs were coming through the barrage, bubbling under the half-lowered gates, but in the dry season the flow could drop to as low as 55,000 cusecs, only one-thirtieth of what we were seeing now—no wonder that India and Bangladesh had been arguing about the control of the Ganga in the dry season.

I expected a pretty fierce rapid through the opened gate but, although the water was fast, it was relatively smooth, and we shot through with no trouble at all. Traversing back across the face of the barrage, we eased up to a small landing-stage at the foot of a curved concrete bank. A brief welcome from some delightful schoolgirls, and we grabbed our gear, and were driven off to a guest house forming part of the new township of Farakka which housed the staff who maintain the Barrage. So far we hadn't camped once, which was not the way I'd planned it.

Late that afternoon I visited the local High School, an impressive occasion with thousands of bright-eyed faces, full of vitality. As I looked around me, it was difficult to feel pessimistic about the future of India. The same school invited us to a cultural show put on that evening in a large hall. We had no sooner taken our seats on the front row than a strange figure came on stage and began an impassioned speech. We assumed that he was the head master, though he looked odd, to say the least of it. His hair and clothes were dishevelled, he wore thick glasses, and he had wild staring eyes. He appeared to me to be speaking in either Bengali or Hindi. I bent over to B.B.

"What is he saying?"

"You should know," said B.B. "He is talking in English."

"That's not English," I said. "What do *you* think it is, Jim?" Jim listened intently. "I think it's probably Hindi," he said, but B.B. just laughed.

Having wound up his speech with a fine peroration the dishevelled gentleman came down to us, shook hands and distributed copies of a pamphlet, and a book entitled *Unification of Physics and Metaphysics*. B.B. tapped me on the shoulder. "They do not know who he is, and they think he was speaking in English."

I began reading the pamphlet:

Sir Edmund Hillary is that noble of the history who subdued the overbearing peak of Mt Everest on 3rd May 1953.

This evening, on 2nd September 1977, at Farakka, on his mission from "Ocean to Sky" I take the opportunity of presenting this unique person of the race an unique culmination in the history of human understanding, *Unification of Physics and Metaphysics* . . .

The terminal concept is not of any freakish origin nor it is going to retire from the enclave of human knowledge without performing its deal within the global expanse of time and space, but the world of knowledge is so absolutely involved in committing priggish follies in all through its pursuits. The charge of committing priggish follies is no abuse but fact stated curtly. With that crying objective in mind, I have no hesitation in qualifying this presentation to the hands of Sir Edmund Hillary.

Let the patronage of a first order man of the race expediate the real valuation of the obstruse concept, indispensable for the salvation of mankind from the vortex of woeful distress and fulfill its term as quick as possible. I as humble author, shall remain an instrument in his hand, most faithfully . . .

P.S. Little printing lapse and short of expressional clarity in the delineation of a new born concept is regretted.

It could only happen in India.

The official welcome followed in impeccable English. We settled back to enjoy one of the most delightful social occasions of the whole journey. There was some exquisite dancing by girls ranging in age from six to twenty, I suppose. It was difficult to imagine European children ever achieving the rhythm and grace of these girls, even the little ones, all with exquisite hand and body movements. A group of four men sang to us, the main singer being, we were told, a telephone operator on the Farakka Exchange, the others clerks on the Barrage project. They sang songs full of beauty and melancholy.

"It is the song of a fisherman," said B.B., "singing to Mother Ganga how kind she is to him and how beautiful."

At one stage there was a commotion at the back of the hall and I asked the Brigadier what it was all about.

"People are pushing in," he said. "They want to share your *darshan* — they feel they will gain merit from being in your presence."

I wished I could dispense with my *darshan*. I could hardly explain my lack of faith in my own *darshan*, or my feeling that it was too small a return for the warmth and generosity of the welcome given to me by these people and the thousands, or even millions, we had passed on the banks of the river.

September 3rd dawned fine, as if the monsoon had suddenly come to a halt. We said goodbye to Commander Paul with a mixture of regret at losing a staunch and knowledgeable friend and pleasure at the thought that we would now be relying on our own resources. It was the end, too, of the river notes written by my good friend the Assistant River Surveyor. From now on it would be up to us to find our own

way, and that's the way we liked it. Buoyed up by this sensation, we
made good speed against the current, looking eagerly around for the
right channel. Almost immediately we ran aground. Murray was
driving, but again the boat was *Air India*, whose crew was by now
bruised all over. The pattern of our groundings was establishing itself,
but it made prevention no easier, for it was difficult, travelling at speeds
of over 30 km per hour—and the boats would not plane at less—to
decide and act fast enough to turn out of trouble a second or two
before hitting the silt concealed beneath the brown water. The driver
and crew would realise that the texture of the water had changed, that
the channel had veered off to right or left, but before they could take
some sort of evasive action, the boat had struck. It was like running
into a vertical clay wall. There was nothing gentle about it. The silt
here was soft, terrible stuff in which we sank thigh-deep before hitting
a firm layer on which we could push. We were thankful for small
mercies: that at least we were far enough from Farakka not to be
clearly visible. We drove on in bright sun. All around, the horizon
was flat except to the south-west where a range of low hills showed in
the distance. The sky was a pale blue bowl across which sailed the
monsoon clouds. towering to over 30,000 feet, higher than the tallest
peaks of the Himalayas.

All day we passed fleets of country boats moving under sail. They
were superb craft, with heavy black wooden hulls whose design must
have been established centuries back. On the stout wooden masts they
carried magnificent square-rigged sails, dyed dark orange or red or
blue, the colours muted by the passage of time and the texture
variegated with patches—any dress-conscious teenager would have
given a month's salary to achieve such an effect on a skirt or a pair of
jeans. Despite the strong set of the current, there was enough wind to
drive the boats upstream, their sails billowing in the warm breeze.

A few miles beyond Farakka we crossed the border between the
provinces of Bengal and Bihar. At Farakka we had been told to beware
of the crowds in Bihar. "In Bengal people are emotional. In Bihar
they do not get excited, but they are violent. You will need to be very
careful in Bihar."

We had no problems when we refuelled at the town of Colgong.
The crowd was small, hardly more than a couple of thousand, and
they were certainly quieter than the Bengalis had been—only about
two hundred autographs, handshakes and photographs sought, and we
moved off again. Half a mile offshore, two islands of granite, like big
beehives, rose out of the river, the current surging around them. It
was difficult to work out how they got there in the first place, for they

were the first natural rock we had seen since our arrival in Calcutta. Even the metal for roads in Bengal comes from hundreds of miles away, and we had grown used to the feel of silt between our toes wherever we went. These were magnificent islands, each partially clothed in trees beneath whose shade we saw the cells and caves of holy men who, at the time of our visit, were not in residence. I climbed up steps hewn in the centre granite to the summit of the larger island, and from it we took photographs while the boats drove through the surge of current between the islands, and Murray and Peter wrestled with a difficult climb up an overhanging crack on a cliff below.

We carried on for ten miles to where we found a beautiful terrace amongst mango trees, between two small villages. Harish asked some of the villagers if we might camp there and was told we were most welcome. We pitched a comfortable camp with a large tent for storage and cooking in bad weather, and a number of smaller tents; the jet boats were securely lashed to tree trunks, with each captain sleeping on board—and very comfortable they made themselves, too. The tents had fine screening, but in any case we had very little trouble with mosquitoes, for there was usually a breeze off the river and this kept the insects away. We each had a foam mat to sleep on and a sheet bag, for we had no need of sleeping-bags at this stage. A few hundred people gathered around as we settled in, but they were no problem, as they were firmly controlled by the senior villagers. Later they disappeared.

Dusk in India is the best moment of the day. The bright light faded to the warm glow of evening. Beyond the river the fiery orange disc of the sun sank below the horizon and the dark closed around us. Pemma fed us well, and we talked easily amongst ourselves. We seemed to have found at last the Ganga we had dreamed of—gentle, soothing away the tensions of the past few days. As if to emphasise the point, a boatload of girls sailed slowly past, unseen in the dark, but sweetening the air with their singing. I crawled into my tent with a great feeling of contentment.

7

Rural India

THE SUN ROSE AS IT HAD SET, A HUGE DISC, BRIGHT ORANGE THROUGH the haze of the plains. Village life was starting around us: people carrying water, cleaning their teeth with frayed *nim* sticks, and walking upstream away from the village with *lota*, the brass pots they use to assist themselves in their morning ablutions. The sounds of cattle and dogs and the chatter of human voices came from the houses nearby, and a couple of girls in crimson and blue saris flitted through the trees, watching our movements. Pemma gave us cups of tea, followed by breakfast of omelette, *chapati* and vegetable curry. We packed the boats, our camping gear being lashed into the bow under the foredeck, whilst cameras and other gear required during the day were packed in the rear of the boat around the engine housing. Of the five-man crew, four would sit or stand on the side-to-side seat amidships, whilst the fifth either sat behind on the engine housing or in front on the foredeck, a pleasantly cool position with an excellent view, but dangerous because of the metal fittings situated here; these could do terrible damage to an unprepared expedition member suddenly thrown forward during a grounding, and groundings were a daily occurrence.

It was a magnificent day on the river, as it had been yesterday. We never grew tired of watching the country boats under sail being guided on the river by the cumbersome wooden rudders attached to their high sterns. Along with the film crew and Harish, I boarded a handsome boat with two great patched sails. It was delightful on board, with the creak of ropes through their blocks and the gentle swish of the water rushing along. The owner at the helm said he had a load of seventeen tons of sand on board, and for transporting this a distance of twenty-five miles he received four hundred rupees ($47); he did this once a week. When he had bought the boat ten years ago it had cost him three thousand rupees ($355) but it would now cost seven thousand rupees ($862).

"Will you sell the boat to us?" asked Mike Dillon, jokingly.

"At no price!" he quickly replied. He looked happy and contented.

I thought of the hundreds of thousands of unemployed villagers forced into the towns and cities each year in search of work, and I could understand his certainty.

The river here was as wide as we would see it, a complex array of channels winding between huge silt islands, uniting and dividing in an unpredictable fashion. Some of the islands covered several square miles, with herds of white cows grazing, and semi-permanent villages of thatched huts. I doubt whether we were ever completely out of sight of human beings; there was always somebody: a fisherman perched on a bamboo frame, like a spider in his web, sweeping the water below with a net; a lone herdsman with a few buffalo; or even sometimes a solitary figure with nothing to suggest an occupation of any sort. We were baffled by the way a seemingly important channel dwindled into still shallows or marshes. Once we drove deep into a narrowing waterway which ended in a lagoon surrounded by marshes, with stands of tall rushes. There were always birds in these sequestered places — cranes standing four feet high; squat pelicans stomping around; storks, egrets, ibises. A flock of unidentified birds whirred upwards, wheeling and turning, and a straggling ribbon of geese flew across the bright clouds of the monsoon sky.

Towards mid-morning we turned south at a bend in the river, to see before us a small island of granite, breasting the full force of the current, and the white towers and stone stairs of a temple climbing up it. It looked like the palace of a princess in the fairy tales I had read as a child. This was the Island of Jahngir, with the town of Sultanganj on the bank a quarter of a mile away. An old wooden craft, packed with pilgrims, was rowing across to the island. We nosed into a channel between an outlying granite pinnacle and the main island. The granite flank beside us had been carved with elephants and gods, and women with slim waists and high, rounded breasts. The carving was at least a thousand years old, they said, but the present temple was built less than a hundred years ago. We climbed up steep stairs, peering at shrines about which we understood so little. Pilgrims sprinkled flower petals on images, kneeling before them. Ashore in the town the temperature must have been roasting, but on the island we bathed in the warm breeze blowing off Ganga, which stretched to the horizon west and north of us, like the sea.

The photographers drove ashore from the island to the town of Sultanganj, which was as drab and dirty as the island was beautiful. At the embarkation point for the ferry, some young women were collecting Ganga water in large containers for ritual purposes, and they were immersing themselves in the holy river. "They looked like temple goddesses," Mike Gill said later, "as they rose from the water with wet saris clinging." He'd taken photographs to prove it. So had Ding, though, according to Mike, he had been moaning softly throughout and was unlikely to have set the exposure correctly. I looked carefully, later, but never saw any photograph answering to Mike's description. Perhaps they'd imagined it all. It was an unreal place.

As we travelled along, Mingma spotted an island with some piles of dry timber by a village, and we went ashore and bought some for the evening. We shot under the mighty bridge at Mokameh (two layers with rail on the bottom and road on top), and then into the refuelling depot.

They had two barges, a large one connected to the land by a gangplank controlled by a few policemen, and a smaller one on the riverside. It was to this that we moored our jet boats. Their plan for refuelling was a sound one, but it failed in the execution when, after the first ten minutes of discipline, the police allowed everyone to stream aboard. It became almost impossible to move, and I was constantly being dragged into sweaty photographs with gorgeous ladies. The smaller barge started tilting dangerously. Capsize that and we would lose not only a large part of the crowd but also our three jet boats. With some frantic signalling I was able to attract the attention of the drivers and get them to cast off. We had all been warned of the procedure to follow if we happened to be on a loaded boat that accidentally tipped over. We must dive deep; then, before surfacing, swim underwater until our lungs were nearly bursting. This would take us clear of the main mass of passengers, mainly non-swimmers who would grasp at anything afloat. Jim, during his years in Benares, had worked it out in detail.

Refuelling completed, we departed upriver with the cheers of the crowd ringing in our ears. In Bihar, no less than in Bengal, the warmth of our reception was incredible and I found myself feeling a sense of loss each time as I left friends behind—friends I'd known for only half an hour or less.

A few miles upriver I found a lovely green spot for a camp, amongst a grove of trees. Harish said to the Headman of the village that we would like to pitch our tents there. The Headman replied,

"Where have these foreigners come from?"

"From 5,000 miles away," replied Harish.

"Then they are our friends," said the Headman. "We would like to stand and watch them." So they did, but only about 200 of them—and by our standards that was complete solitude. Jim entertained the children with one of his acts. Diving into the Ganga from a position upstream, he swam underwater until opposite the children, then emerged on to the bank in front of them with a roar, a terrible bearded monster who had them scattering and shrieking in all directions. Even after he had done it a dozen times, the little ones were unsure whether he was man or demon.

Mike Gill did an equally fast exit from a swim in the Ganga, but for a different reason; he claimed to hear a heavy exhalation of breath, and over his shoulder he saw a green head the size of a fist, an apparition which was variously attributed to his imagination, a water snake, or a tortoise.

Harish returned from drawing water at a nearby well. It was a task he had allotted to himself at each of our camps, and one we greatly appreciated. With an abundance of firewood, Pemma soon had a fire blazing and a meal ready. It was a happy evening.

Somewhere during the past hundred miles we had passed the junction where Ganga joined with the Kosi from the north, the river draining Mount Everest, the river of our jet-boat expedition of 1967 with Jon, Jim, Mike and Mingma. In Nepal they call it Sun Kosi, the Gold River, but in India it is simply Kosi, the River, and it has an evil reputation as a river which wriggles back and forth across its alluvial fan as it debouches into the plains, always ready to find a new river bed, and leaving a trail of destruction in its wake. To the Indian peasant his rivers mean life itself, and he names them accordingly—Old Twister, All-Destroyer, Forest King, Lord of Strength, The Flooder, Queen of Death. And for more benevolent rivers—Streak of Gold, Goddess of Flowing Speech, River of Pools, Glancing Waters, Dark Channel, Sinless One, Golden, Stream at Which the Deer Drinks, Forest Hope, Silver Waters.

The next morning was September 5th, and our run for the day was a short one of two and a half hours to Patna, a city of a million people, the capital of Bihar, the poorest province in all India.

Jim wrote in his diary, "Woke after a refreshing night on the boat, Codeine phosphate and Lomotil holding the gut on a tight rein." Everybody suffered from dysentery in varying degrees, though until I read people's diaries later on I was hardly aware of it, with the exception of universal catastrophes like that of the Sundarbans crab. I suffered less than anybody, the result no doubt of the extensive exposure over many years which gave me a high degree of immunity. The way to avoid this particular form of suffering lies in immunity more than in careful selection of one's food, for we discovered repeatedly that we were as likely to pick up a bout of dysentery from a grand banquet at an expensive hotel as from a grubby little curry shop by the side of the road, where the food had been prepared hot as we waited.

While we were getting ready to leave next morning, one of the sailboats we had passed yesterday, easily recognised by the pattern and colour of its patched sails, cruised gently against the current, with its crew either asleep or eating breakfast. They were obviously doing as well as we were in all respects. It reminded me of the fable of the hare and the tortoise.

As part of a deliberate policy, I had been travelling in different boats, and for this day I moved into *Kiwi*. At the wheel was Mike Hamilton, who had proved himself a shrewd and careful driver and to date had an unblemished record so far as groundings were concerned. Within an hour he had joined Jon's club, which was becoming less and less exclusive as the days went by. Mike Gill was seated on the foredeck with Mike Hamilton; Waka and I were in the seat behind, and we were trying to work out the nature of a red object in the river as we drove upstream between it and the bank. Suddenly, with a crash of moving gear, we ran aground on a sandbar with extreme abruptness. Waka and I jackknifed forward, while Mike Gill was left hanging in the forestays running from the awning overhead to the bow. He was bleeding from rope burns on both forearms but relieved that the damage had been no worse for, on the bow of *Kiwi*, someone had placed a six-inch high brass goddess with her arms and sharp brass fingers extended above her head, and the only thing to save Mike from sliding forward across the arms of the goddess had been a four-gallon plastic jerry-can of water which had made him take off upward as well as forward.

"It's not your lucky day, is it, Mike?" said Waka. "If it hadn't been for that jerry-can you could have gone to a Family Planning Clinic in the nearest village and claimed a free transistor radio."

The red object proved to be a sari wrapped round a corpse also aground on the same sandbank. As we drew closer to Patna the corpses became more common, a feature we eventually grew used to as we approached all the big cities on the river. Usually a corpse could be recognised by the crows strutting back and forth on it as if contemplating the destiny of their craft. The Hindu custom is to burn their dead and scatter the ashes upon a river, Ganga being by far the most holy for this purpose. A corpse in the river usually meant that the family had been unable to afford firewood for the funeral pyre and, though I realised that Ganga can purify even the unburnt dead, it was a custom I never quite got used to. It made us disinclined to linger on the river as we approached Patna, and we arrived there a couple of hours ahead of schedule, to the consternation of the local organisers, and we agreed to fill in time on a silt island in the middle of the river before making our formal arrival in an hour's time.

An enthusiastic welcome at the water's edge.

Jet crew forging ahead, Peter, Mohan and Jon in *Air India*.

At Varanasi the author takes to *lungi* and beads.

As we made our way across, a huge paddle steamer loaded with people pulled out into the current and made its way slowly upriver, the huge paddles on each side splashing and threshing the water as they whirred around. Smoke billowed from its funnel and the high-pitched whistle sounded out across the river. "You wouldn't believe you'd find a boat like that in 1977," said Peter.

The silt island had not long since emerged from the Ganga, for the grass was sparse and there were no trees. Scrawny cattle grazed in the intense heat, while the herdsmen squatted under scrub shelters away from the midday sun. They looked very poor; they must have wondered what we were doing there. Downstream someone had come to me with a petition, thinking I was the new Commissioner for the area, but for peasants as close to subsistence level as these were, a visit from a Commissioner was unlikely. Perhaps they thought we were a medical team there to do vasectomies: there was no way of knowing what was passing through their minds. It was so hot that we joined one of them under his shelter. He grinned at us, opened a leather pouch and offered the contents to us: a black ball of unleavened dough. It probably made a sizeable proportion of all his worldly wealth, and yet here he was offering it to us, the well-heeled owners of three extraordinarily expensive-looking boats.

Time passed. Harish brought up a matter that had been troubling him; he felt that the Indian involvement in the expedition was not receiving sufficient publicity. Although not a word of criticism had reached me, there were people, he said, who were asking why the Government of India was giving us so much assistance. At least one journalist, writing in Bengali, had been openly critical, saying that even the most senior government officials would not have received such treatment. The same journalist had said that my own reason for embarking on the expedition was to make money; that C. W. F. Hamilton Ltd were paying me a handsome commission on all jet boats sold in India; and that I would be making huge profits from book, magazine and film rights.

"That's good news," I said to Jon Hamilton when I had first heard the report. "What percentage am I getting?"

"Well," said Jon, choosing his words carefully, as always, "the directors had thought that your reward would be mainly in heaven, but we could consider offering you the usual three-fifths of five-eighths, with payment to be indefinitely deferred." I had vaguely thought of seeking out the journalist concerned and offering him a half share in the profits from the media rights, providing he would pay a half share of the expedition's expenses. I saw Harish's point, however, and we agreed that we would try to keep the Indian members of the expedition as much to the forefront as possible. It was not easy for, when we arrived at any destination, the pushing and crushing crowds made it impossible for me to ensure that I always had an Indian team-companion near at hand. The other New Zealand team members, with the exception of Peter, were left pretty much alone while I was engulfed by the crowd, making my movements unpredictable. We set off for Patna at midday with a determination to do better.

The Patna waterfront is an unlovely place, its sloping banks lined with bricks to prevent the city sliding into the river. There are no sacred places here; we saw no temples, and there were no steps of bathing-*ghats* going down to the water. The strong current made our landing difficult as we pulled in against the brickwork in front of the Bankipore Club, where the well-to-do people of Patna had gathered to welcome us.

It was into another strenuous round of autograph-signing, Press hustle, and a succession of no less than three evening receptions. But the next morning we had a memorable experience when we visited J. P. Narayan, one of the great figures of twentieth-century Indian politics, and a man held in the highest respect throughout India. He had worked with Mahatma Gandhi and had spent many years in the cause of land reform. His imprisonment during the recent Emergency had brought down a storm of protest on the previous government, leading to his eventual release. He was an old man and unwell, with a kidney ailment requiring weekly dialysis. Nevertheless, when I met him in his modest but comfortable home, I was deeply impressed. He had an air of serenity and incorruptibility; there was something saintly about him, not a common quality in Western politicians. We chatted about ordinary things; the villages we had visited, the virtue of adventure, his health after his recent spell in jail—nothing of great importance, but I left feeling that we had met a great man. Peter asked for his autograph, something I have never seen him do before. B.B. was moved close to tears.

Murray, a passionate socialist, somehow contrived to see J. P. Narayan by himself later. He wrote in his diary: "I entered his white-washed room with a neat bed and a kidney machine in one corner. Feeling most humble I clasped my hands in the traditional Indian greeting and said *Namaste*. For the first time on this expedition I found my tongue and we talked. Small and frail but alert, he sat erect in his bedside chair. I asked him about his friendship with Gandhi.

" 'We were not really close friends,' he said. 'I was older than he was but when I was studying in America my late wife lived at his

Ashram. He had no daughters, only four sons, so he always regarded my wife as his daughter. I learned my Marxism in America,' he said with a smile.

" 'Are you still a Marxist?'

" 'No, not now. I follow Satyagraha, Gandhi's way.'

" 'Are you happy about the reforms you fought for and initiated? Have they gone far enough? Are they effective?' He thought for a moment and replied slowly.

" 'No. On paper they are there, but still in the villages they have not been implemented. Land reform is still the problem and, of course, the caste system.'

" 'How long will it take to change this?'

" 'A long time. Everyone talks. The Prime Minister talks. There have been many reform movements on land, on caste, on economics, but they have not worked.'

"And so we talked on, unhurried, uninterrupted for half an hour. He is undoubtedly as impressive a man as I have ever met."

The shambles of our departure began before lunch. I was carried off to the Bankipore Club "for a quiet beer", but really I was over-whelmed by crowds asking for autographs. I escaped back to the hotel for lunch with Indian Oil and that too was packed out. Sweating and frazzled, we pushed our way through a traffic jam of rickshaws down to the departure point, where a huge crowd awaited us. Time was running out. The press of humanity was closing in on us and soon, by the look of things, they would be on to the boats.

"Forget about packing the gear properly," I said. "Just throw it all aboard and we'll fix it up later."

This was misinterpreted, and a moment later someone had cast *Kiwi* adrift. The boat moved swiftly downstream, tangling with the steel hawser of a moored barge as it went and wiping out one of the awning uprights. Mike Hamilton was frenziedly searching for the key to get the boat started before he ran under the overhanging bow of a large steamer which could have destroyed the boat altogether. Just in time he had the engine going and was out and away, safely into mid-stream. Our hosts, as worried as we were, were shouting, "Go out into the stream, please! You must go out into the stream!" A moment later *Ganga's* bow rope was cast off and swinging violently on her stern rope she was nearly pulled under. It was one of the worst moments of the whole expedition.

My main aim now was to camp as soon as possible. Jon and Ding were both sick, with high temperatures, and I was feeling tired. We were now in a wide complex area where three great rivers joined, and shoals and sandbanks abounded in slow-flowing water which was difficult to read. We had two more groundings before I found a pleasant spot on open grass, but then Jim arrived, lamenting the lack of trees. When I waved him on, somewhat tersely, to find a better place, he led us across to a clump of trees on the far bank, only to haul up by a very large village which quickly brought a veto from the rest of the gang. As we crossed the river yet again, we drove into our third grounding of the afternoon, finally after two hours returning to another treeless place about a mile above my original spot. By this time I was not in a good humour.

As darkness fell, we erected the tents, and Pemma and Mingma got on with the food in their usual indomitable fashion. I was fed up with Ganga, India, and all the members of the expedition, and retreated to my tent very grumpily. However, Mingma and Pemma (and Peter) duly fed me and I went off to sleep in a slightly better frame of mind. I woke early and started work on the damaged boat awnings. I was determined not to be at the mercy of hotels again and in a couple of hours had the awnings adjusted so that we could quickly lower and zip up the insect netting or the waterproof canvas sides, thus enclosing the boat in a comfortable rectangular tent. We had breakfast and departed at nine a.m. After a couple of hours' travelling, we pulled into a village where we were welcomed with a quiet warmth, in striking contrast to the frenetic welcomes in cities. Here the mania for hunting autographs was blissfully absent. We were given tea under a colourful awning near the river, and we talked with the village Headman and the school teacher, surrounded by a friendly crowd. As in all the villages we stopped at, there were children everywhere—not the starving pot-bellied infants we had half expected to see, but healthy, cheerful children full of spirit.

"They are not nearly as shy as they were two or three decades ago," said Harish. "Independence has been good for them, but there are too many children. We have made great strides since 1947. We have built steel mills and factories. We have more than doubled the size of our economy, but at the same time our population has increased from 300 million to 600 million. Somehow we must slow down our population growth."

I wondered what the future held for the children on this great crowded plain we were now crossing, its countryside already filled to capacity. We had been told something of the early history of the Gangetic Basin. 5,000 years ago, the valley had been clothed in forest, populated with dark-skinned aboriginal tribes. Until recently it had been assumed that these were a Stone Age people, but in 1926 the Indus Valley Civilisation was uncovered, sophisticated cities dating back 4,000 to 5,000 years – the time of the earliest known civilisation on earth, with paved streets, water supply and drainage systems, granaries for storage of food, and all the trappings of government of an ordered city. No comparable cities have been found in the Gangetic Basin, but geographically it is close to the same area of the sub-continent as the Indus Valley and it seems likely that the people inhabiting the Ganga came from the same origin.

In 1500 B.C. the Aryans swept down from the north, the pale-skinned warlike people who at the same time were spreading westward out of Central Asia into Europe – for Aryan blood and its language, Sanskrit, are important elements in both Indian and European civilisations. From the Indus Valley the Aryans moved east through the forests into the upper part of the Gangetic Basin, particularly the long strip of land known as the Doab, between the Ganga and Jamuna Rivers. The area around Delhi, in the Doab, has been the site of great cities since at least 1000 B.C., the time when Hinduism was being crystallised into its present form and recorded in the myths and legends of the Mahabharatha and the other repositories of Hindu philosophy and folklore. The caste system was established then, with the two highest castes, Brahmins and Kshatryas – the priests and the warriors – being drawn from the Aryan conquerors, while the dark-skinned aboriginal people formed the lowest caste.

Already in those times Ganga was a holy river and the sacred places had been identified – Varanasi, Prayag, Hardwar, even Badrinath, our destination in the Himalayas – and all are described in the Mahabharatha. In civil administration, in the arts and in philosophy, Hinduism reached a high degree of sophistication, further enriched by the contribution of the Buddha in 600 B.C. The kingdoms of the Aryans spread eastwards into Bengal and beyond. In 250 B.C., the Buddhist Emperor Asoka united almost the whole of India into a vast empire, ruled from his capital city of Pataliputara on the site of present-day Patna.

Buddhism declined over the centuries, to be replaced by a resurgence of Hinduism, particularly under the influence of Shankaracharya in A.D. 800, a great teacher who returned to the ancient sources of Hinduism in the Mahabharatha and other Sanskrit literature. We were to hear more about him on our journey into the hills later on in the expedition, as we journeyed into the mountains at the headwaters of the Ganga.

From about A.D. 1000, Indian history is occupied with Islamic conquests from the north and west, culminating in the Moghul empire of the sixteenth and seventeenth centuries. Then came the British. And all the time the population of the valley had been expanding, bringing the enormously fertile plains under cultivation, leaving now not a trace of the original forests except in the hills and mountains. To a group of New Zealanders like ourselves, from a country largely barren of history, there was a fascinating richness in the story itself and in the traces of old civilisations on the banks of the river. It added an entirely new dimension to our expedition experience.

We drove on up the river, heading for a refuelling spot at Buxar. We were again in a broad area of complex channels and shoals, and Jim, who had not yet run aground, did so now with a flourish. The abrupt stop from 30 m.p.h. wrenched the seat from its fastenings pinning Jim, Harish and B.G. under the dashboard. Mingma, who had been sitting on the engine housing, was now lying with his face in the back of the seat, with blood flowing steadily from his mouth. Harish and B.G. had extended the areas of bruising perpetrated on them in other boats. Only Ding was unhurt, and he had been lying on a heap of foam mattresses in the bilges, delirious and with a high fever. While the crews of *Air India* and *Kiwi* heaved the seat back into position and tidied up the shambles of food, stoves and packs in the boat, Max Pearl stood ankle deep in water, putting stitches into Mingma's split lip. Even Jon, with his vast experience, was impressed with the violence of our groundings. A jet boat can run across dry land if it be shingle, rocks, mud or even coarse sand, but when it runs aground on these banks of fine wet silt, the stop is virtually instantaneous.

A huge crowd awaited us at Buxar, lining green banks like an amphitheatre around a bay alongside the old fort. I was relieved to find that the crowd consisted of restrained Biharis rather than emotional Bengalis, and with unaccustomed solemnity we moved up to a large embroidered tent on the hill. Murray and Mike Gill were there to greet us, for they had been travelling by road for the past two days, this being their turn to hold the boat numbers down to fifteen. As the autograph-hunters became more insistent, Mike led me away to the fort on the hill, constructed of red sandstone and surrounded by a moat. I stood on the battlements, surveying the scene, while the crowd shifted to assemble in front of where I stood. Somewhere amongst the gentle undulations of the surrounding countryside the Battle of Buxar had been fought, sealing the fate of the Moghul empire, but even the District Magistrate beside me had no idea where it had taken place. As I returned to the boats I saw a porpoise frolicking around the bay as if giving an exhibition for the crowd. We waved farewell and departed.

A few miles upstream we pulled into a grove of trees and camped. As always, we gradually mellowed under the influence of a lovely evening. A big boat went past, towed by a long line from the mast. An old man came up, insisting that we take him with us.

"How old are you?" I asked. He was stooped, with white hair and a wispy beard.

"Eighteen," he said. Perhaps he meant eighty, but we could not budge him from his original statement.

I went to bed, puzzling over the reasons for the excitement that our journey seemed to be creating. While planning the expedition I had been worried that our boats would be resented as noisy intruders on the holy river, yet everywhere we were welcomed as heroes and accepted as pilgrims undertaking a meritorious journey. The widespread publicity, especially from the radio which beamed news of our movements even into the most remote village, was part of the reason. We presented an unusual combination of circumstances — a text-book figure come alive (there is a chapter on Tenzing and me on Everest in a widely-used Indian school book); a dramatic form of transport not normally seen on Ganga; while the element of holy pilgrimage (however unholy we might be in fact) appealed to the deep religious base of Indian life and culture. Whatever the reasons, the result was this all-pervasive excitement and welcome, moving and yet confusing at the same time, making this expedition something quite different from the journey I had imagined. It was a hot night and I lay awake a long time.

In perfect conditions next morning we drove upriver. Again we were ahead of schedule, and I pulled into a calm bay beneath a village perched on top of a clay cliff. It was no hardship to stop here, for I always enjoyed our village stops. The mud walls of the houses seemed to grow out of the very clay itself and in the distance a white temple rose in a green field. An alley led to a swept courtyard shaded by trees, and here, on seats brought for us, Jim and I spent an hour talking to the village elders in broken Hindi. They were interested in what we were doing, but accepted it calmly. They told us about their village and the local temples. There was an old Shiva shrine a short distance down the river, we were told, and on the far bank, in a grove of trees, another temple where there was a *sadhu*, a good one we were assured, who never sat down but stood all the time. The laughter and goodwill between us were tangible things, bathing us in a warm glow; chatting on, imperfectly, in the cool breeze above Ganga, we felt strangely contented and reluctant to go, but at length we said our farewells. The engines sprang into life and the boats surged on to the plane with the wind whipping spray in our faces. We were close to the mid-point of our journey. Slowly, above the horizon ahead of us, rose the impressive skyline of Varanasi, the oldest city in India and the most holy. Would they, too, welcome us? I wondered.

8

Varanasi – the Holy City

Varanasi — the city that is a prayer. On the banks of the river that is almost a faith stands Hinduism's greatest city: Varanasi, by the flowing Ganga. For several thousand years pilgrims have cleansed themselves of their sins here and sought release from the cycle of rebirth. The Ganga starts where saints meditate, in the high Himalayas; it meets the sea in Bengal, amid the realities of an industrial civilisation. Somewhere between the two lies India's turbulent present — Varanasi, city of a thousand temples, called Kashi or Light by the devout.

Hinduism, deep and mystical, is everywhere. In a decorated doorway, in a glimpse of a glittering temple, in the sound of a sacred bell, in the chant of the priests and the fragrance of flower oblations.

Be still. Come to Varanasi. Open your heart and you will find Varanasi has much to give you.

Government Tourist Brochure

WE EASED BACK ON THE THROTTLES AS WE PASSED UNDER THE BRIDGE AT Varanasi, or Benares, as it is also called. On our right was the crowded skyline of the old city, minarets and domes and towers crowding forward toward the water-front which stretches in a great arc, with its stone walls and steps and temples, layer upon layer of them, rising directly from the broad river which here curves around like the crescent of a new moon. The opposite bank, by contrast, was empty, and green fields stretched to the horizon, except in the far distance, where we could see a great structure which Jim told us was the palace of the Maharajah of Benares.

On the outskirts of the town was a large group of people with flags waving, and a launch struggling slowly against the current. They waved us into the bank. I scrambled ashore, where I was introduced to the Commissioner of Varanasi who said he had arranged a camping-place for us at the other end of town, in the grounds of Chait Singh Palace. He invited me to join him on the roof of his launch for the journey, and so I clambered up. We were immediately followed by all the surrounding officials, the Press, and anybody else who could scramble aboard. The boat staggered out into midstream, rolling drunkenly from side to side. "Dive deep and swim until your lungs burst." I remembered Jim's words, as if they were some sort of prayer or *mantra*. Jim drove alongside.

"There are strong religious reasons why you should enter Varanasi aboard *Ganga*," he shouted up to me, adding under his breath, "and you're more likely to survive the journey." I agreed wholeheartedly. Taking the Commissioner with me, I clambered down into *Ganga*, and we raced up past the *ghats* and the handsome buildings crammed together, to draw up before the imposing façade of a sandstone structure that had obviously started life as a fort. Turrets flanked a high stone wall, pierced in the centre by an entrance at river level with steps climbing steeply to the centre of the building.

We pushed through the crowd, up steep stairs which were dark and smelled of bats, to emerge high up in a greasy courtyard. This was the Palace of Chait Singh, who had been King of Benares from 1770 to 1781, when he was deposed by the British. The courtyard was full of people, and by the look of them they all wanted autographs. Chait Singh had been unable to defend his palace and I could see no reason why we should succeed where he had failed. What I wanted more than anything else was solitude, and I should probably have as much chance of finding it, camped here, as I should on the *maidan* in Calcutta.

Jim and I climbed the battlements to scan the horizon for a quiet backwater. Across the river a grove of trees grew out of a cornfield. We drove over. It was peaceful, with a cool breeze off the river and, although we had waded through calf-deep mud to reach it, we decided to camp there. During the afternoon we relayed over food, firewood, water, and officials with whom we discussed our plans. All sorts of engagements were being proposed. Before I'd washed the mud from my legs, I found myself committed to a Lions Club, a Jaycees, a Rotary meeting and a civic reception. I found it difficult to think, surrounded by a milling crowd, and although I had no desire to offend people I had even less desire to spend my days in Varanasi addressing the local businessmen in their social clubs. Above all else, I wanted to see Varanasi and get the feel of the place for myself. I had enjoyed going into villages or meeting young people or talking with the Press. They were part of what I believed in, encouraging people to get out and see their own country. But even my Victorian sense of duty was beginning to desert me with the autograph marathons and business receptions. Eventually the programme was settled in a reasonably satisfactory fashion, for I knew most of the others would leave me to it while they explored the city. I had to admit that they weren't really needed. I envied them their freedom.

As dusk approached, the local people vanished, leaving us to ourselves. Sitting with Jim, I mellowed as a noble sunset lit the western sky behind the city which rose before us across the river. Bells echoed across the still water—the beat of drums, the chanting of priests, the sound of temple music. The burning *ghat* glowed bright as the light faded. I began to see why Jim grew to love the place in his two years there. I asked him to describe it.

"As for Varanasi—how can one describe it? Ramakrishna once said, 'As well try to draw a map of the universe as attempt to describe Varanasi in words.' It is as old as any presently inhabited city on the face of the earth. Already a well-known centre in the days of Gautama the Buddha, and mentioned constantly in the ancient literature, it has been continuously a holy pilgrimage centre ever since. It is built on a curve in the river, facing east so that the rising sun strikes full on the face of the city. And what a face, what a waterfront! The buildings seem to grow out of the river, pink stone and brick and white façade, a profusion of angles and steps and jutting corners and temple spires which no single architect would dare design, but which sits with an air of complete authority, no jarring note anywhere save for two recent hotels. In September the monsoon flow is still high, though dropping; the cascades of steps flowing down below the buildings are mainly under water, and the throngs of pilgrims walking along the sacred waterfront are absent. But at each *ghat*, and especially at the main *ghat*, always moving groups of people bathe and pray and tout and extort and massage and shave and sing and play.

"Varanasi is not at one of Ganga's great confluences. Two small rivers do join Ganga here, the Varuna and the Asi, and between these two tributaries the city lies and from them takes its name. But they are hardly big enough to account for the great and ancient sanctity of the place; indeed, the oldest site of habitation, Kashi itself, lies north of the Varuna, outside the area enclosed by the two streams. I have not heard or read an explanation of the sanctity of the site, perhaps because a city so old needs no explanation. But I am sure an important part of its original appeal, as now, was the way in which, from anywhere along the gently curving waterfront, the sun rises directly and majestically across the river. In the hush of daily transition from darkness to light, a time of special significance for most religions, the two great sustainers of life symbolically join together here in unforgettable splendour: light and warmth from great Surya, the sun, and water for growth and cleansing from Mother Ganga.

"Behind this beautiful waterfront the city teems with its 700,000 citizens and its countless visitors. Traffic ancient and modern copes in dignified chaos with narrow streets and lanes which were built to suit traffic no faster than a bullock-cart and the occasional horse-drawn vehicle. Still competing successfully, these are joined by honking cars and buses, and by uncountable cycles and rickshaws, with bells jangling, and by motor scooters often with an entire family precariously aboard. And of course there are pedestrians in thousands, calmly strolling in death's way as cars bear imperiously upon them, and then swaying gracefully aside just before the last injurious moment.

"But lord of the roads and alleys is none of these. That title goes undisputedly to the cow. There is no swaying aside for these noble beasts, arrogantly sure of their safety in a Hindu land. If a large determined bull blocks a small alley, we humans can but meekly wait.

"All the lanes and alleys of the city are fascinating, by day or by night, even the residential areas having a mazelike charm all their own, and hiding behind drab façades are airy houses opening on to walled gardens. But it is above all in the lane known as Vishwanath Gali that Varanasi behind the waterfront excels itself. It is rarely more than six feet wide, and often less; it meanders into the heart of a maze of alleys between the main road and the river, and it is lined with an array of shops that fill the narrow confines with a blaze of colour and sound and smell. Here is Mohan in his tiny crammed silk-store, and for half an hour he will billow silk after soft silk before your wondering gaze—batik and print, gold- and silver-embroidered masterpieces in a kaleidoscope of colour. And if after half an hour you buy something he is happy; and if you don't he is still happy (though less so) and either way will insist you stay for tea or a cold drink. On the other side, an imposing entrance leads to a magnificent showroom displaying copper and brass and silverware, engraved and enamelled and filigreed, all of superb craftsmanship, for Varanasi brass, like Varanasi silk, is to the unprejudiced connoisseur, such as myself, unrivalled anywhere.

"Between the two, there are tiny sweet stalls; a man on a plank selling wooden biros; a shop with toys of garish bad taste which might with care last a child for a few minutes, and several more fabric shops with their hanging drapes like curtains in a long hall. And this is but the first twenty feet of an alleyway that dives and twists and runs straight again for about a mile. It passes ancient temples, now with a golden roof, now with sandstone carvings, now a simple shrine with Shiva *lingam* or image of Ram. Now an area is all brassware; then comes a section bristling with white and black Shiva *linga*, small and large; now a food area reeking of *ghee* and butter, or fresh with the smell of ground flour. The alley skirts delicately round a huge mosque built on the old site of Vishwanath *mandir*, the main Hindu temple, and always, save very, very late at night, it is thronged with a moving stream of people and dogs and cows, buying, walking, shuffling, talking, the vital heart of a vital holy city."

Next morning was cloudy: for the whole of our three days in Varanasi the weather was indifferent, at best, with the sky darkening at times as showers swept across the camp. I stayed in camp in the hope of finding peace there, but soon the visitors began to arrive, by boat from across the river, or by car along the sixteen miles from Varanasi, across the bridge lower down, ending up with a two-mile walk through the cornfields around us. The local cricket team came stumbling in through a shower of rain, soaked to the skin but cheerful. Two taxation officials, who were probably used to being rejected, followed me to my tent, asking me why I had left Tenzing behind. And I had one moment of wild exultation when a large and wealthy-looking woman, implacable in her resolve to ride in a jet boat, fell backwards on the muddy bank, precipitating herself gently downwards into the waters of Mother Ganga. Guilt rose within me that I should be capable of such unchivalrous feelings, and I sprang to her assistance. Poor woman! She could not even gain merit by thus bathing in Ganga, for the east bank, on which we were camped, is not a holy place like the great waterfront on the west. To die on the east bank means reincarnation as an ass.

Harish solved our problems with the swelling crowd of visitors by summoning a group of police, who thereafter kept our camp reasonably open. I still had no regrets that I had chosen to camp here rather than at the Chait Singh Palace, but some of the disadvantages of our location were becoming apparent. The trees were not mangos or banyans or *pipals*, or any of the other fine trees of India. They were *babuls*, thorn trees which grow like weeds, dropping thorns and leaves where we walked and even into our food or cups of tea as we ate. The river was falling steadily day by day, for we were in the dying phases of the monsoon. As it fell, it left an ever-larger area of deep black mud between our tents and the boats moored at the river's edge. Especially when we left for functions at which we ought to look respectable, our efforts to reach the boats free of mud provided the spectators with considerable entertainment. We were seldom successful, either, and around camp we spent much of our time with crusts of

black mud on our legs, a torment to our Indian friends who were
more fastidious than we dirty New Zealanders. After our traumatic
groundings downstream it seemed perverse, to say the least, that the
banks of Ganga here, where we longed for silt, should consist of mud.
When we drove aground here, the moment of impact was inperceptible,
and with a straight run we could slide the boats forty yards up the
mudbank to the entrance of our tents.

It was at Varanasi that I abandoned Western dress, after having
watched for some days now, with envy, the comfort of those who had
been wearing *lungis*. It took me a while to rid myself of the feeling
that I was wearing a skirt, and I was not entirely appreciative of the
shrieks of laughter greeting me from other members of the expedition,
who looked no better themselves. "Ed Hillary in drag!" said Ding,
and began taking photographs. Peter bought me a set of beads which I
became rather fond of. I wondered what sort of reception I'd receive
from the boardroom of Sears if I attended their next meeting in Chicago
dressed like this.

Jon was still unwell from the mysterious fever he had picked up in
Patna, and it worried me to see him simply resting under the trees,
looking pale and thin. Ding was on the mend, however, and reverting
to his normal boisterous self. As part of his convalescence he had made
a water-ski contraption from a piece of plywood, and with Michael
Hamilton or me at the wheel of *Kiwi* he was soon whizzing around the
river in front of our camp, with the occasional spectacular wipeout at
40 m.p.h. The ultimate achievement was when I towed both Ding and
Mike Hamilton across the river on one board.

A professor of microbiology dropped by one afternoon as he drifted
down-river collecting water samples to test Ganga's famous purity,
physical as well as spiritual. Even the cholera vibrio is said to curl up
and die when placed in Ganga water, and lesser organisms succumb
immediately. Explanations abound for this phenomenon: radium in the
water; minerals, medicines and herbs gathered in its youth in the
Himalayas; the presence of benign microbes eating the malignant
ones; or Mark Twain's theory – "No self-respecting germ would live
in it." The professor confirmed that counts of bacteria in Ganga are
exceptionally low, and that the water beside our camp was safe to
drink. The strength of his convictions was diminished in our eyes by
the death, while we watched, of a small fish swimming in a bowl of
Ganga water beside him. I suppose it was lack of oxygen, and, as
Mike pointed out, the fish did not appear to have dysentery at the time
of its death.

Driving across river to the Varanasi waterfront was a distance of less than a mile, and our jet boats were constantly busy ferrying people back and forth as we explored the city.

On the *ghat* beside Chait Singh Palace, a group of young men assembled each morning, performing yoga, swinging weights, and doing other exercises. The gymnastic instincts of Murray and Peter surfaced immediately and they joined in without discrediting themselves and without concern that they were less expert than the regulars. But then a supple youth began climbing, moving easily from hold to hold up the vertical face of the Palace. Thirty feet up, he hauled himself to the top of a protruding block—not an easy move—and, turning towards the river, jumped far out to avoid the steps below, entering the shallow water with a splash. Murray and Peter responded instantly and they too began climbing. They did it, but came out with respect for the climbing abilities of their Indian friend. When it came to jumping off into the river, that was a different thing again. Murray spent a couple of minutes screwing up his courage while we shouted him on from below. He made a vulgar gesture at us as we became increasingly uncomplimentary.

"When I climb something, I don't usually turn round and jump off it," he shouted. "You ought to see what it bloody well looks like from up here." No sooner had he plunged in than the Indian youth raced to the top of the turret, fifty feet up, and leaped from there. We conceded that he'd won.

The same morning, a pair of snake charmers displayed their skills in the roofed minaret on the turret of Chait Singh. They were two solemn but self-assured little men, and they carried some round earthenware pots, a large basket, a mongoose on a string, and a musical instrument, made from a gourd, with a resonant nasal sound. While one played the instrument, rather beautifully I thought, the other unwound a twelve-foot python from the basket and wrapped it around my neck, its head placed firmly in the grasp of my right hand. As the earthenware pots were opened, a tangle of snakes emerged—little ones, green ones, brown ones, even a dead one; and finally three cobras reared their hooded heads and rose with a slow hypnotic movement, the light shining on their waxy scales and their wicked eyes like bright, black beads. We declined the offer of a fight between the mongoose and the cobra. "The mongoose always wins," said B.B. "It is very bloody if they let it go on, and very expensive, particularly if the mongoose kills the cobra."

In the other turret of the palace, an expert yogi was warming up. We watched him glide smoothly through a series of fantastic postures. At times he looked like one of those amazingly deformed Calcutta beggars whose limbs have been broken and set at right angles during infancy, or like the victim of some terrible car accident requiring heroic orthopaedic surgery to disentangle limbs inextricably knotted together. Even the python seemed impressed.

The whole world of the Indian streets described by Rudyard Kipling seemed to be assembled on the *ghats* of Varanasi. Dancing monkeys performed for us. Cows lumbered past. Mike Dillon had hired one to do a cow *puja* for his film, but she was a recalcitrant animal who disliked being pushed around. She splattered the *ghat* with excrement at the beginning of the ceremony and throughout was vigorously licking her owner's hair, a habit he obviously disliked—he looked to be in danger of damning himself to perdition by giving the holy animal what an average New Zealand dairy-farmer would call "a good hard kick in the slats". Mike Dillon, who tended to be accident-prone, was bitten by a monkey at the Durga Temple where there was a performance of *sitar* music. A baby monkey had climbed his trousers while filming was in progress and removed a handkerchief from his pocket, and when Mike snatched the handkerchief back, the mother monkey flew at him, biting his wrist.

One evening some wealthy businessmen invited us to watch some dancing girls they had hired for the evening. The performance was held only a couple of miles from our camp and we walked there, past cornfields, splashing through puddles in the dark. It was a small house but comfortable, a country retreat. After sipping drinks, we went inside where a rug had been spread on the floor. There was no other furniture. Sitting cross-legged in comfort is a skill I have never mastered and so I stretched out full length, leaning on one elbow, trying to feel like a sultan resting in his harem after a hard day's work. Three musicians tuned up their instruments. The dancing girls, when they appeared, came as something of an anticlimax. Perhaps we had been misled by our imaginations to expect something more sumptuous and erotic; they were three handsome girls, but no more beautiful than thousands of others we had seen standing on the banks of the river during the last 800 miles. As dancers, the schoolgirls of Farakka were incomparably better. As the evening wore on, they varied their routine by doing something approaching a belly dance before selected members of the audience who would eventually, with a show of reluctance, pass across some money. Sociologically it was an interesting evening, but Hugh Hefner would have done it differently.

One afternoon I went incognito a few miles beyond Varanasi to Sarnath, where the Buddha preached his first sermon to five disciples in a deer park, 2,500 years ago. I was fascinated by what I saw here. I

Ganga,, Kiwi and *Air India* circle Jahngir island.

The Ganga sailing *dhows* were endlessly photogenic.

The impressive skyline of Varanasi, holiest city of Ganga.

A *puja* at Varanasi.

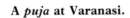

Young men exercising with weights at Chait Singh Palace.

A peaceful temple near Garhmuktesar.

The jet boats approach Deoprayag.

Crowds lined the water at every *ghat*.

End of the jet boat route: *Kiwi* (above) and *Ganga* inspect the seething, boulder-obstructed foot of the waterfall above Nandaprayag.

A mountain village above Govindghat.

The Alaknanda at Badrinath.

High Camp, with Akash Parbat - Sky Mountain - beyond.

was shown the famous lion pillar, whose capital forms India's national emblem. The ancient diggings from 300 years before Christ were strewn with stone remnants of the towns, monasteries and *stupas* that nurtured what is still the world's largest religion, though by now it has almost vanished from India, the country of its origin. Mark Twain wrote of Varanasi that it is "older than history; older than tradition; older even than legend. And looks twice as old as all of them put together." A facetious comment, but as I stood in Sarnath it seemed true.

Each day, for one reason or another, I was across to the *ghats*, usually Dasashwamedh, one of the five holiest *ghats* on the waterfront, and the most central. I was often left there waiting, usually for the film crew, but I liked the place. I would edge the jet boat through the crowd of local craft and tie up to the steps; I became friendly with one of the boat-owners who produced cups of tea for me, and in return I took him for the odd run in the jet boat. There was always a crowd bathing, standing on the stone steps immersed to their waists. Old people come to Varanasi to die and they were always there, performing ritual ablutions; conscious, I suppose, that it might be their last purification in Ganga this side of eternity. Alongside, there might be a young man vigorously soaping his armpits, intent only on getting clean, or a woman dexterously manipulating her sari to keep herself modestly covered while she washed from head to foot.

There was none of the intensity and hysteria of Calcutta. There were beggars at Dasashwamedh, but they were a droll lot, squatting on the pavement beyond the *ghat*, passing jokes along the line. They all looked happy and well fed. *Sadhus* mingled with the crowd, some of them bizarre in the extreme; some were white with ashes; some stark naked or nearly so (there was one wearing nothing but a solitary brass ring); I saw one painted as black as night except for his lips, which were crimson, and he had six arms radiating from his shoulders, so lifelike it was hard to know which set was real. I never felt out of place in my *lungi* and beads—it would be difficult indeed to look strange amongst the inhabitants of Varanasi.

Once at Dasashwamedh a lovely little girl came up to Jim, courage and worship shining in her eyes. She spoke in Hindi. Prem listened, then laughed with delight. "Sir," she had said, "are you the men who went to the moon?"

The occasion I remember above all others was a late afternoon *puja* at Dasashwamedh, performed to help and bless us on the second half of our journey, which would undoubtedly be the most arduous portion of it. Jim preceded us to do *puja* in the inner temple, for they needed one of us to confront the goddess herself. Jim found it a moving ceremony as he made offering of flowers, and did *arati*, a circular waving of a tray of lighted oil-wicks. The altar had a profusion of flowers and fruit and sweet-smelling incense, surrounding a beautiful porcelain image of Ganga herself, the holy river personified as a goddess, for this was the chief Ganga temple on the waterfront.

Jim was then led outside to where Harish and I waited, for only three of us were to take part in the *puja*. Harish was impeccable in pressed trousers and white shirt; Jim looked like a *sadhu*, wearing nothing but his *lungi*, with a rope of beads emerging from beneath his great beard to rest on the hair of his chest; I, in my *lungi* and beads and shirt, occupied some sort of middle ground. The young priest was a striking young man wearing yellow robes, with long black hair surrounding a handsome face. Standing at the water's edge, he beckoned us to him. In front of him, just out of the water, stood a worn grey wooden platform heaped with flowers, with conch and other shells, with rice and coconuts and fruit, and with a brass tray with bright red and orange powder on it. Beside it stood a magnificent brass *arati* lamp, two feet high, with tiered layers of wick-holders which we had to light in the wind, wick after wick, some hundred or more in all. Jim, Harish and I all took turns, while the priest began to chant his *mantra*, to blow his shells, to break his coconuts and lave all with Gangapani. Under his direction, we held our hands to receive flowers, masses of crimson petals and yellow garlands and, as gracefully as we could imitate him, we threw them into Ganga. Behind and around us the beat of drums and clashing of cymbals and chanting of *mantra* rose and fell on the wind, and to our side another acolyte lit tiny oil lamps in earthenware dishes to float them on the water, a raft of small flames amongst a sea of petals. Then, magnificent in a wild disarray, eyes flashing, the young *pujari* turned to take up the burning *arati* lamp, and as the drumming and chanting rose to a crescendo, waved it with abandon, chanting still with unabated vigour his prayers of praise to Ganga and his prayers for the blessings of Ganga and Saraswati and Kali and all the gods of the rich Hindu pantheon — a climax of sight and sound and mythological allusion which was profoundly moving. When the final *mantra* died away and some offerings of food had been placed in our hands, we knelt with the priest on the banks of Ganga, touching our foreheads on the wet sand.

For me it was one of the most impressive religious occasions that I had experienced. Jim wrote in his diary: "It clinched in my mind the realisation that this was no stage act but a *puja* they were most happy and honoured to do — Hindu priest at Hindu shrine welcoming the latest in the long line of great men verging on deity in the all-embracing Hindu sense, simple New Zealander turned into a symbol of the greatness of humanity, its potential divinity. This theme had been expressed in flowing words at countless functions—but it was profoundly more moving to have it expressed in symbolic acts at the holy *ghat*. Not only in sophisticated city minds and newspaper columns, but also here on the Varanasi *ghats* Ed was welcomed, and we as his retinue welcomed and taken to their hearts. I suddenly realised why no bathers had objected to our noisy boats and splashing waves—arrogant though it may sound, they felt we were blessing them with our presence, and they welcomed us and showed us round and co-operated with us as fellows in the same faith."

We left Varanasi on the morning of Monday, September 12th. The overcast weather of the past few days was now clearing, with the sun shining through in patches and in its warmth we drove upriver to the palace of the Maharajah of Benares, with whom we were to have breakfast. One of his large retinue showed us over the palace museum, the most interesting part being the armoury. It seemed that generations of Maharajahs had been obsessed with the problem of how to combine a sword and a gun in one weapon, and there were some wonderful variations on the theme. From there we were taken to meet the Maharajah himself, in a marble hall filled with photographs of this and earlier Maharajahs meeting Tzar Nicholas, Edward VII, Marshal Tito, Queen Elizabeth II, and a host of others. Prem squeezed my elbow. "Next week you will be up there," he said.

We sat down to breakfast on a great balcony high above the river. The Maharajah himself ate nothing, for he was of too high a caste to eat even with his own family, let alone a bunch of heathens like us. He was a charming and attentive host and kept us well entertained with anecdotes and history, and he listened thoughtfully to what I told him of our journey. Only half in jest, he tried to persuade Harish that one of the jet boats should be donated to him for transport of tourists across the river from Varanasi to his palace. When we took him for a ride, the crowd of retainers from his palace cheered him with obvious love and pride.

We drove off into a strong wind. The river was rough and we hunted back and forth from one bank to the other, seeking patches of relative calm to avoid the terrible pounding we received in these conditions. An hour upriver we saw on our left the high walls and battlements of a great fort, built on a hump of rock two hundred feet high, protruding into the mainstream of the river. It was the fort of

Chunar. There was no scheduled stop here, but a huge crowd lined the banks, and they had built a high podium shaded with awnings. We argued at first whether I should go in, but finally I decided what the hell! They'd made their arrangements. I decided to accept them. I was taken up to the podium, where all the important people of Chunar were lined up with speeches ready—an hour of them at least. I knew how to cope with this situation, and as soon as the first speech of welcome had been completed I strode up to the microphone myself, warmly thanked the first speaker, made a few remarks of my own and added a few words of gratitude. "I would like to see the fort," I said in conclusion.

We followed a foot-track to where the fort rose from the surrounding countryside. A steep ramp led up between high stone walls, its flagstones worn by the passage of innumerable feet for at least four hundred years. It was built by the Moghuls, but like everything else it fell into the hands of the English. Warren Hastings fled there during the briefly successful revolt of Chait Singh, former owner of the palace we had visited at Varanasi. We strolled along the battlements to the highest point of the fort, where the headland pushed into the river. It was like being on a mountain. We stood on a broad stone platform with pillars supporting a shady roof. Below us swirled the brown waters of Ganga and on either side its broad ribbon stretched to the horizon, to Prayag in the west and the spires of Varanasi, that we had left, in the east. The General in charge of the fort stood beside me, talking. It was cool up there, with a breeze blowing across. I liked the General, who looked a hard, tough soldier, but he talked only of Ganga, which he did with great warmth, and of the Hindu myths. And again I was moved by this river that inspired such affection in so many people. History, there in the fort was a living presence, and I left Chunar reluctantly.

We drove on up a choppy river in bright sun. Our refuelling stop was forty miles on at Mirzapur, but before then we were overtaken by a monsoon storm forming behind us. It looked like the end of the earth, a wall of cloud, black as night, bearing down on us with parts of the horizon blotted out by sheets of rain like thick curtains lowered from the sky. Lightning flickered, and we heard the roll of thunder. The darkness grew closer. The boats, lit by the sun, seemed unnaturally bright; there was a moment of transition as the brightness faded almost to dusk; and then the rain burst like the opening of a dam. The drivers shielded their eyes and sunburnt lips as best they could, for we were driving at speed and there was no way in which our awnings could keep out anything.

At last we saw Mirzapur, a cluster of houses on top of an eroded bank sixty feet high on the outside of a curve in the river. Most of the town was hidden from view. On shore, an awning was being whipped around by strong gusts of wind. Our Indian Oil hosts and the crowd, soaked, like us, to the skin, were intermittently sliding into the river, for the bank was of steep mud, greasy in the rain. Standing on the bank was a splendidly painted red bicycle, decked with flags and equipped with flotation chambers and paddles on wheels. After raising his hand in salute, the owner, who must have dreamt of this moment for weeks, rode down the bank in triumph and, to the cheers of the crowd, plunged into the water with a splash.

We were conducted to a nearby house. Our host for lunch was Raj Dutt, who proved to be an important local businessman involved in the carpet trade for which Mirzapur is famous. We were ushered inside, taken to a comfortable lounge, and given a beer. Out on the balcony, where the rain had now stopped, there was a tremendous view of the river. We descended to meet briefly a hundred or so guests in a tent, and then we returned to the peace of the house. We had intended to camp further on, but our host pressed us to stay the night; we thought of our damp gear and changed our minds. It was Indian hospitality at its best, relaxed yet providing for our needs in a way that no expensive hotel could. We bathed and fed well, and when night came we slept in communal fashion on our foam mats on the floor. Raj and his brother had an excellent library and were well travelled; we enjoyed chatting with them. There were no autographs and no photographs — a merciful release for which I could thank one of Raj's retainers, an extraordinarily tough-looking little man with a scarred face. He looked like a thug, I thought, an unintentionally accurate impression, for as I learned later, Mirzapur had been a centre for the activities of the original Thugs, a cult of religious fanatics who practised ritual strangling with a knotted handkerchief on passing travellers. Before the Thugs were exterminated in 1840 they were said to be strangling thirty thousand travellers a year, burying them in mass graves.

The Dutt carpet business was organised in the same way, I imagine, as many Indian handicrafts are. The weaving was done in villages by peasants in their spare time, something to be done when work in the fields was over. They had over 400 weavers working for them around Mirzapur, all with their own looms. The Dutts supplied wool, guided the weavers on colour and patterns, and finally did some clipping and finishing before marketing the carpets abroad, mainly in the U.S.A. Raj showed us a superb silk carpet, thick-piled, with the soft texture and sheen of silk, and woven in brilliant colours to the design of a contemporary abstract artist. The price in Mirzapur was 400 dollars, rising to ten times that amount by the time it reached some penthouse in New York.

Late that afternoon, a famous local yogi, Pandit Raj Bali Mishra, sought us out. He practised *hatha-yoga*. By breath control and meditation he had developed magical powers, which enabled him to stop his heart, bend iron spears with his eye and halt cars or elephants or trains. He would like to give us a demonstration. Although he claimed to be 68 years old, he looked younger, for his face was strong and hardly lined; his skin was golden brown, his eyes bright, and he had a full beard and a shock of grey hair. His smile was quick and warm, showing teeth stained red with betel-nut juice. We all liked him immensely. He began by stopping his heart, with Max Pearl holding a finger on the pulse of his left wrist. The pulse stopped. Pandit Mishra was less enthusiastic when Max tried checking the right wrist as well. This time the yogi's pulse stopped for ten seconds only, before resuming, though weakly. "Valsalva Manoeuvre," said Max, "with the left radial artery smaller than the right. He holds his breath, and that affects his heart."

To prove the point, Mike Gill stopped his own pulse with the same manoeuvre, the main point of difference being that Mike turned dark purple in the process, whereas the Pandit had been able to achieve the same effect almost without effort.

The Pandit now changed his orange robe for a bizarre strong man's outfit, consisting of a dirty white singlet, a pair of yellow silk shorts covered in stars and moons, and a pair of loose elastic knee bandages. He then took a couple of tablets containing herbal medicines, said a brief *puja*, and gave the audience a short speech about his god-given gift. Placing a folded handkerchief in his eye-socket, he took an iron spear six feet long and close to half an inch in diameter. Placing its point against the handkerchief and the other end on the ground, he leaned forward. The shaft bent, slowly at first and then with a rush until it was bent double. A roar of applause rose from the crowd. At this point Jim stepped forward.

"It is my turn," he said. Consternation spread along the ranks.

"Don't do it," said Max. "We haven't got an eye surgeon with us."

"You might be able to give lectures with one eye, but you won't be able to drive jet boats," said Jon Hamilton.

Jim ignored them. He picked up the bent spear and proceeded to straighten it with surprising ease—it was made of iron, but soft iron. The Pandit quickly took over, ensuring that the spear was absolutely straight before Jim proceeded to place the point against the handkerchief he had placed in his eye. He leaned forward and strained down on to the spear for almost a minute. Nothing happened. He paused for a moment, removed the handkerchief from an eye now looking bleary, and he meditated for a few moments. He followed this with some breathing exercises and a *puja*, conducted with the utmost solemnity. This time he repeated the Pandit's act exactly. The spear slowly buckled until Jim had the shaft looped hard against the ground. The Pandit laughed and applauded as loudly as anybody.

"Have a go," said Jim, taking the handkerchief out of his eye, which appeared intact. "You take the force of the spear here," he said, indicating the bone round the upper part of his eye-socket. None of the rest of us had the faith in our eye-sockets that Jim had — and you could never be quite sure that Jim had not absorbed, insensibly, during his years in Varanasi, the magic powers of *hatha-yoga*. It wasn't worth losing an eye to find out.

That was the end of the performance for Jim, but for Pandit Raj Bali Mishra it was no more than the preliminary warm-up. For his next act he lay across two chairs, shoulders on one, knees on the other, with his body held rigid between. A sharp spear was placed upright in the ground, its point protruding into the small of his back. Two men lifted a huge slab of sandstone on to his belly and a sledge hammer was handed to Harish, who proceeded to lay into the rock in an attempt to break it. It didn't break, but neither did the yogi; nor were any of us prepared to take the risk of being impaled. A similar act followed, this time with the yogi lying on the ground, his back arched over a pile of broken glass, while on top of him was piled a colossal rock, so big that it took four men even to move it. Two men stood on the rock and then all was removed; the yogi had only a minor scratch on his back. Then came a pulling competition between the jeep and himself. I watched his preparations with the greatest interest, for he had already said he would like to try to stop a jet boat. His preparations showed that more than the power of *hatha-yoga* was involved, for he began by hammering some substantial iron stakes into the ground. A six-foot railway sleeper was placed against these, and the yogi sat behind, a loop of rope passing around his back, around the ends of the sleeper, and forward to the towbar of the jeep. He braced his legs straight forward on to the sleeper and signalled for the jeep, driven by Harish, to start moving, which it did, tightening the rope before coming to a halt with its wheels skidding helplessly. Before finally committing himself to combat with the jet boat, the Pandit went for a ride "to feel its *darshan*", and presumably to get the feel of its horse-power rating. Jon was worried, and Max with him, not because a defeat might discredit Hamilton jets but because of the uncertainty of the outcome. It all depended on the strength of the yogi's knees and hips, for if they buckled he would be shot over the top of his sleeper and iron stakes, like a stone from a catapult. The yogi was satisfied that he could handle it, however, and the time was fixed for next morning.

The news spread, and half Mirzapur assembled on the riverbank to watch the contest. The yogi prepared his stance as he had done for the jeep. Jon was in *Air India*, fifty yards offshore, far enough for the jet plume not to dowse the yogi. The crowd fell silent as the rope went taut and the pitch of the engine rose steadily. The yogi's legs began quivering, the thick muscles standing out in cords and knots and shaking under the tension. His face, too, showed that he was using all the powers he possessed, both spiritual and physical. After fifteen seconds the roar of the engine reached a plateau, indicating full power. A shout of triumph went up. Jon turned off the engine and the yogi leaped to his feet laughing with delight. We shook hands and congratulated him, as pleased as he was, for although I was impressed by his strength, it was the courage of the man that I admired above all else.

The story of the success of Pandit Raj Bali Mishra followed us all the way upriver, not as a feat of strength and courage but as evidence of the magic powers of *hatha-yoga*. The iron stakes, the sleeper, the friction of the rope and the quivering muscles were not reported, and most of those who heard the story believe to this day that our boat was stopped by the powers of magic. For us the significance of the occasion extended further than we had at first realised for, though our boats had been subdued by Pandit Raj Bali Mishra, they were, unbeknown to us, acquiring the reputation of being magical craft themselves, capable of ignoring earthly obstacles, as if they were chariots of the gods. The realisation, in the rapids of the upper gorge, that our boats and their owners were mere mortals obeying laws of gravity and susceptible to the power of a big river of falling water, came as a profound disappointment to thousands or even hundreds of thousands of people longing to believe that they had shared the *darshan* of supernatural beings.

Before leaving Mirzapur, Prem, Jim, Mike and Max visited the Temple of Vindhyachel Devi. "It is famous," said Prem. "If you have troubles you come here to pray for assistance. People come from all over India." The temple was away from the river, approached by a narrow lane lined with shops selling garlands, coconuts, coloured powders and the other requisites for making *puja*. Like most famous temples, it was old, at least 600 years, said Prem. The temple itself was small, confined in a courtyard surrounded by a high wall from which grew a banyan tree casting its shade from one side to the other. Even at the early hour of six a.m. there were people everywhere, walking, praying, prostrating themselves on the ground or against the wall of the temple with their palms raised in supplication. In the heart of the temple lived the goddess, in a cramped windowless cell approached through a series of corridors and iron-barred gates. They joined the queue to make their offerings. In front of the goddess there was room for at most three people at a time. Garlanded with flowers, they cracked coconuts on the worn stone pedestal, pouring the milk over the feet of the goddess and praying for their greatest need, presumably survival during the six weeks to follow. On either side stood harassed, shabby little priests collecting money, and moving supplicants through as quickly as possible. Vindhya-Devi herself, made of black marble clothed in silk, was two feet high with staring silver eyes; her foot rested on a black rat. It felt like a descent to the underworld: Vindhya-Devi was said to have been the patron goddess of the Thugs, and it was not hard to believe.

We were told that the famous Hindu temples of India are often owned by Brahman families and that the offerings made there go to the owners, who can easily be millionaires. The history of famous temples is replete with tales of unholy wrangles between members of the family or between rival families, though we were told that these in no way detract from the holiness of the shrine itself, which is something quite separate.

At ten a.m. we left Mirzapur, bound for Allahabad some eighty miles distant. There was still wind on the river and rain in the sky. After five hours we saw ahead of us the river forking into two branches of almost equal size, with a spit of sand reaching forward between them at the confluence. Behind was the red wall of the fort of Allahabad. This was Prayag, the junction of Ganga and Jamuna, comparable in sanctity with Varanasi, and another landmark on our journey.

9

To the Gate of God

At the confluence of the two rivers, every day there are many hundreds of men who bathe themselves and die. The people of this country consider that whoever wished to be born in heaven ought to fast to a grain of rice, and then drown himself in the waters. By bathing in this water, they say, "All the pollution of sin is washed away and destroyed; therefore from various quarters and distant regions people come here together and rest. During seven days they abstain from food, and afterwards end their lives."

The Chinese Pilgrim Huan-Tsang, Seventh Century A.D.

... the tongue of land at Allahàbad, where the Jamuna and the Ganga join, is the true Prayag, the place of pilgrimage to which hundreds of thousands of devout Hindus repair to wash away their sins in the sacred river. Here is held every twelfth year, the great Kumbh fair (Mela), when the planet Jupiter is in Aquaries and the sun in Aries ... The most strict observers keep the whole month as a period of sanctity, bathing daily at the confluence of the two rivers, fasting by day, and altogether abstaining from all but the commonest food.

Imperial Gazetteer, 1886

WE WERE APPROACHING PRAYAG IN SEPTEMBER, NOT JANUARY, and not even the annual Mela was in progress, let alone a Kumbh Mela. We would have loved to see one of these great religious gatherings, though whether we would have been able even to land is doubtful, as the crowd at the last Kumbh Mela was estimated at ten million, probably the largest assembly of people gathered together in one place in the history of mankind. Even in the less crowded conditions of late monsoon, the Prayag was an impressive and beautiful place. According to religious belief three rivers mingle here, but one of them, the Saraswati, is subterranean, or mythical, according to your belief. The Saraswati is celebrated in Sanskrit literature. The Aryans settled on its banks and the *Vedas* were revealed and written there, but subsequently it disappeared and no substantial river of that name exists. Hence the popular belief that it took to itself a subterranean course. Above Badrinath in the mountains we later encountered a tributary of the Alaknanda called Saraswati which was said to be larger at the upper end of its gorge than at the lower, the remainder having entered an underground channel connecting it with Prayag. Whatever its course, it was certainly not visible to ordinary sinners like ourselves. But the two we could see joining, still swollen with the monsoon rains, were a tremendous sight — Ganga on our right, Jamuna on our left. Between the two we saw the Sangam, a spit of white sand, and in a backwater were crowded many boats and bathing pilgrims. Above this, stretching for some distance up the Jamuna, loomed the massive bulk of the Allahabad Fort, a huge Moghul structure with walls of red stone, and massive rounded towers and battlements.

A strong wind was lashing the turbulence of the mingling waters into large waves, and we splashed and crashed as we approached the junction, where we were met by an official launch and were joined, in *Ganga*, by a senior police officer. Directed by him, we drove up the Jamuna beneath the high walls of the Fort. Under a threatening sky we approached a crowded wharf, where I stepped ashore. After being greeted by some officials, I was asked to take part in a *puja*, and I sat on the edge of the wharf with my legs dangling towards the river, with the priest chanting and throwing flowers into the river and breaking a coconut to pour its milk into the water. But the rain closed in on us, soon becoming torrential, scattering the crowd and bringing our welcome to a hasty conclusion.

My original plan — to spend only one night in Allahabad — had dismayed our Indian friends, for it seemed to imply too casual an approach to one of the great holy places of Hinduism. So we spent two days and two nights there at the government tourist bungalow. During the afternoon I had a number of visitors, but Jim Wilson kindly acted as a buffer for me in most cases. I gladly accepted the invitation to a civic reception, but other functions were kept to a minimum. Half a dozen self-assured students from a private school were unusually persistent in their demands, concluding with the promise from one that he would get his father to shorten the civic reception by half an hour if I would come and address their school. I could hear the steel creeping into Jim's voice as he firmly made it clear that there would be no visit to their private school nor any other, regardless of what enticements they might offer.

We dined at various times with Indian Oil and with Rotary, and at the home of B.B.'s sister — superb Indian meals all of them, for by now we much preferred Indian cooking to our own. B.B. came from a most prolific family, with relatives wherever we stopped, but he had praised the cooking of his sister at Allahabad above all the others. In the cool of her home we ate the most delicious *masala dosa*, a South Indian delicacy of finely spiced vegetables folded inside a crisp pancake made from rice flour. It was true Indian domestic hospitality and a pleasure for us all.

In Allahabad we received our first big packet of mail from home. I had been expecting news of the birth of my first grandchild, and it was here that I received the following telegram: "Boys both well". I took it to Max Pearl for some medical advice. "Can the medical profession usually anticipate twins, or do they just stand by and count them when they're born?" I asked. Max assured me that the medical profession never makes a mistake, or hardly ever, and after puzzling over the telegram for a while re-worded it to read "Boy. Both well" — the correct interpretation, as I later discovered.

Waka was shattered by a letter from his girlfriend saying that she was tired of living in solitude at home while he enjoyed himself in distant parts, and that it was all off. The only way out of this impasse seemed to be a toll call to New Zealand, but this had to be deferred until Delhi, three days later. My mail always contained letters from people living on the banks of Ganga requesting that we visit them. I regretted that I could seldom reply to these letters, let alone meet their requests, but they gave me some sort of understanding of the thoughts of the crowds of people we passed on the banks.

Mike Gill had a pile of mail from home. "Dear Daddy ... when Mummy tells me to go and do a pee, the pee always comes. Why is she always right?" ... Mike read to us a story about his four-year-old daughter, a vigorous child known to most of us. Mike's wife Linda wrote, "Caitlin and I had a long chat, begun by her, about robbers and jail. I explained how people who took things belonging to other people were caught by the police and sent to prison, where they stayed for a few weeks or months or even years.

"Silence.

" 'But *look*,' she said in her most exasperated voice, 'robbers have to take things?'

" 'Why?'

" "Coz that's how the world's made. People have to do what they want to do.'

"Silence, this time longer, then she said, 'Let's talk about something else.' Later I found a ten-dollar note and some silver in a hiding-place in her room. What are we rearing, do you think, a thief or a philosopher?"

The following morning Peter and Murray went early to the Sangam —which literally means "gathering place"—the triangle of sand at the confluence of the rivers. With the river still high, the sandbank was cut off from the shore by a narrow channel across which boats were ferrying pilgrims. The Sangam was empty except in one corner, where a few hundred people were bathing, or preparing themselves by shaving their heads, leaving only a single wisp on the back of their skulls and a little pile of hair on the sand. Women were holding aloft wet saris which blew gently in the wind like bright banners. Peter wrote in his diary: "Murray and I walked to some small platforms built out into the water at the furthermost point of the spit between the two rivers. Here we sat, dangling our legs in the water, washing off the mud through which we had been wading. As we waited, two boat-loads of pilgrims came alongside the platform and tied on: they talked of the three rivers before bathing in the holy water, sweeping their hands over their freshly shaven heads. It was so peaceful sitting there in the sun, the holy waters of Prayag sweeping beneath us and the glory of blue above. I felt good there, thinking of India and what we had seen, then thinking about what lay ahead. White water and mountains to climb. I looked forward to the mountains."

At the great annual religious gathering of the Mela, the Sangam, all seventy-five acres of it, is crowded with people. The great Kumbh Mela of 1954 was held in a year more auspicious than any other this century. Access to the Sangam that year was by way of a single ramp, broad enough for normal times but potentially dangerous if used by five million pilgrims. On the day of Amavasya a million pilgrims bathed in the dark hours before sunrise, and this was followed by processions of sadhus passing down the ramp to the Sangam. There are innumerable sects of sadhus, but on that morning there were some old-established sects with fiercely militant traditions, and they marched in massed array carrying tridents, swords, lances and fire tongs as well as drums, bugles and gongs. Some were naked; some rode on elephants, horses or camels. At the foot of the ramp cars stalled and these, along with some elephants, blocked the way forward. The press of the crowd from behind disrupted the procession of sadhus who, resenting the intrusion, fiercely stabbed at the pilgrims with their tridents. Panic spread through the vast crowd which surged forward, the pressure from behind forcing them in the only possible direction — off the ramp, into a ditch muddy with rain that had fallen during the night. The situation was by now beyond control. People were trampled under foot, driven into the mud, or forced into the river to drown. Hundreds or even thousands died. It must have been some consolation to those with them to know that they could hardly have met their death in a more auspicious place or at a time better calculated to ensure eternal bliss.

Our civic reception by the city of Allahabad was held in the grounds of an old museum. We drove there down the broad and tree-lined streets of the uncrowded, restful city. Amongst the trees of the museum grounds a raised platform had been prepared for us, and before it a large crowd of distinguished visitors had gathered. The welcome of the Chief Justice of Allahabad High Court, Mr Chandrashekhar, was interrupted by one enthusiast from the crowd who insisted that he should speak in Hindi rather than English. The Chief Justice, in laconic tones, apologised, saying that he came from South India and spoke no Hindi. This was followed by a superb speech from Mrs Rajen Nehru, a member of the family of the great Pandit Nehru. She had the golden tongue of that great family and we listened to as stirring a piece of oratory as I have heard for a long time.

This inspired me to raise my own standards. The gathering laughed cheerfully when I apologised for speaking in English rather than Hindi, and I apologised, too, that my English was less perfect than that of Mrs Nehru. I spoke of the opportunities of adventure for the youth of India, and how important it is that they should be encouraged. And I spoke about the warm and generous welcome we had received throughout India. In conclusion Harish gave a fine speech in Hindi.

We left early the next morning, for during the next four days we had long distances to travel before reaching Garhmuktesar, near Delhi. We had said our last farewell on the banks of the river, and were turning out into mid-stream, when Mike Gill announced that he'd left something behind.

"What is it?" I asked.

"A sound recorder," said Mike, trying to avoid the black looks being turned on him, for we were impatient to be off.

"Is it important?"

"Well, it's worth four thousand dollars, and we can't really do the rest of the film without it . . ."

"Where is it?"

"In the boot of a car."

"Whose car?"

"I don't know."

At this last reply, a great groan of despair rose from the group, as from one man. It was one of the few moments of absolute unanimity we had achieved so far on the whole expedition. Only B.B. could save us now—and he did. In an hour he was back with the lost recorder.

The river above Allahabad was smaller, probably a fifth of the size of the river we had first met at Farakka, or less. The great northern tributaries draining the Nepal Himalaya were now down-river—the Kosi, Gandak, Gogra and Gumti—and the western tributaries, the Son and the Jamuna. The banks of the river had changed, too. Gone were the palm-fringed paddy fields of Bengal, for now the country was less fertile, with long stretches in grazing rather than crops. We saw herds of cattle and goats and buffalo tended by children, a wild free life that Indian writers have often captured so well. There were trees, too, giant peepuls and banyans, groves of mango and guava, as if we were travelling through a vast area of parkland.

Although the flow of water was less, the river was still broad, not as in the dry season when it is a desert of sandbanks with skeins of water winding through them in narrow channels. Now the sandbanks were covered in brown water, sometimes only an inch deep, and our newly acquired ability to read the currents was taxed to the utmost. In each boat there were always three people in the front seat scanning the water ahead for the boils and smooth bulges marking deep water, or the shallow ripples and stranded twigs of shallows. Usually there was someone sitting on the foredeck reclining against the windscreen, for it was cool there, with a fine sensation of water speeding past on either side.

Late in the day, with our tanks almost dry—we could manage just over one hundred miles with a full load of fuel—we pulled in to our loveliest refuelling spot yet, the pink steps of a *ghat* near Fatephur. We stayed longer than we should, for we always enjoyed the hospitality of Indian Oil, but at length we drove on into the black sky of a rainstorm. Soon we were drenched, but not cold, for even here, a thousand miles from the sea, the air and rain were warm. It was difficult finding a channel, peering into the blinding rain. Jim and I in *Ganga* were leading the fleet at this stage, and we felt pleased with ourselves when we emerged through the far side of the rainstorm without grounding. The warm breeze dried us then as we raced into the setting sun, with low grass banks on either side, green against the black sky and slashed with gold where pools of water caught the sun.

On a wooded point we found the perfect camping-spot: grass under low trees, the river confined beside us in a deep channel. The people from a small village nearby gave us leave to camp, and brought firewood, refusing payment—typical of the warm and generous hospitality we were receiving throughout from the people of the villages. It was a happy evening and it darkened into a perfect Indian night. The sky was ablaze with stars, washed clean by the departed storm; all around thousands of fireflies flashed from tree to tree, and crickets boomed loudly. The temperature was cool but without chill.

As we woke next morning, the sun rose like a ball of orange fire from across the river. By eight o'clock we were away, picking our way up the current by the tell-tale boils and smooth mounds. Tall chimneys, factories and a bridge appeared on the horizon, for we were approaching Kanpur, a rapidly growing industrial city of more than two million people. We had no plans to stop here and, wrinkling our noses against the smell of the tanneries and other factories of the city, we drove on a few miles to the steps of a Shiva Temple at Bithur, where we refuelled. Harish left us here to return to Delhi, for he had work to attend to, and his expedition to Gangotri and Gomukh had yet to be organised. Bithur, we were told, is the site of a city older than Kanpur, and in 1857 it was the seat of Nana Sahib, the Maharajah of Bithur, who became the leader of the Indian revolt against the British in Kanpur during the First Indian War of Independence, formerly known as the Indian Mutiny. The uprisings against the British, which were never co-ordinated and for that reason ultimately doomed, occurred from one end of the Gangetic Basin to the other. But no incident was more famous, in the eyes of the British at least, than the siege of the British garrison at Kanpur (or Cawnpore) and their subsequent massacre.

In February 1857 there had been an abortive and bloodless protest in Behrampur, where we had stopped our first night out of Calcutta – but the main uprising occurred in May and June, spreading like bushfires in a drought eastwards from Meerut, near Delhi. It was mainly a revolt of the sepoys, the native soldiers employed by the East India Company. The mass of the Indian population in the villages were probably not greatly affected by the increasing presence of the British during the eighteenth and nineteenth centuries; they had always been exploited by somebody and very likely the British were no better or worse than anybody else. But for the sepoys it was a different matter. They were in close contact with the foreigners, under the rule of a small group of officers arrogantly sure of their superiority. In 1813 India was open to Christian missionaries and, as the British settled in, there was increasingly a threat to the traditional Hindu caste structure and religion, and to the Moslems too. The sepoys were more aware of these attitudes than most, but the situation might never have erupted into violence had it not been for the incident of the greased cartridges.

In 1856 the new Enfield rifle was introduced into the Indian Army, replacing the old musket. It used a new form of ammunition, each shot

Bathers at Varanasi, the city that is a prayer.

The view from the Maharajah's palace.

Everywhere there were people wanting to shake hands.

an individual charge of gunpowder wrapped in a cylinder of paper heavily greased to keep the powder dry. Before using it, the sepoy bit the end off the cartridge, grease and all. A rumour spread that the grease was fat from cows or pigs, the one intolerable to Hindus, the other to Moslems. A Brahmin sepoy was said to have been told this by a worker in the arsenal at Dum Dum near Calcutta, where the cartridges were being made. "It is difficult to convey," wrote an observer, "an adequate idea of the force of the shock beneath which the imagination of that Brahmin must have reeled when he heard those words. It was all true, then, he must have felt. The Government was really bent upon ruining him. They had devised an expedient which, under the specious pretext of putting a better weapon into his hands, was to destroy his caste, his honour, his social position, everything that made life worth having, and to pave the way for his perversion to Christianity ... For him to be told that he was to touch with his lips the fat of the calf was as appalling as it would have been to a medieval Catholic to listen to the sentence of excommunication." The revolt was set alight in Meerut in May 1857 by a British colonel, who must have been insensitive even by army standards. A group of sepoys who had refused to handle the offensive cartridges were publicly humiliated by being stripped of their uniforms, chained in fetters, and sentenced to ten years' hard labour. Next morning the sepoys rose against the British, and within twenty-four hours the revolt had spread to Delhi and beyond.

The situation of the small British garrison at Kanpur was an unenviable one, to say the least. The sepoys outnumbered the British soldiers overwhelmingly—without the native army India could never have been subdued in the first place—and now the sepoys had turned against their masters. The British retreated into the military barracks of the city, and for three weeks held off the siege of a huge but disorderly army. It was at this point that Nana Sahib sent a truce-offering, allowing the garrison to vacate Kanpur by boat down the Ganga to Allahabad. The offer was accepted, and next morning the exhausted remnants of the garrison climbed aboard a collection of country boats. No one knows whether what happened next was a deliberate act of treachery or an accidental shot which rapidly developed into a pitched battle. The British were in a hopeless position. One boat almost got away before running aground on a sandbar, and four survivors swam down-river to tell the tale. The men were killed in the river or on the bank. The surviving women and children, about three hundred of them, were kept as hostages for three weeks, but subsequently they were put to the sword at the approach of a British relief column advancing towards Kanpur, killing and burning all in its path with a ferocity equal to that of the sepoys themselves. These events took place exactly one hundred years after the Battle of Plassey. If they did nothing else, they served notice to the British that their hold was a tenuous one. The Year of Independence, 1947, came only ninety years later.

*   *   *

We were running north as much as west for, from Allahabad on, the river sweeps northward in a huge arc parallel with its lesser twin, the Jamuna, and is separated from it by a long, narrow strip of land known as the Doab, meaning "two rivers". Delhi, which is on the banks of the Jamuna, lies in the upper Doab, and we expected to reach Garh-muktesar, eighty miles east of the capital, in three days' time. Often we passed ancient ruins. There were big mounds eroded by the river, displaying the crumbling brickwork of buildings which must have been covered by wind-blown silt during the course of centuries. The area has been inhabited at least since the tenth century B.C. when the invading Aryans founded the city of Indraprastha close to the present Delhi; it was the centre of the Moghul empire, and since 1911 Delhi has been the capital of all India. We stopped at an old ruined mosque decorated with enamelled mosaic in brilliant turquoise; it was at least seven hundred years old, according to a herdsman grazing his cattle through the deserted building. Further on were two fine Shiva temples. It may be extraordinary elsewhere, but in India it is the norm to find architectural masterpieces in the midst of sparsely inhabited grazing land. The setting was exquisite. A *ghat* led from the river up to the temples. Central in each, under the single spire finely carved in stone, was a black Shiva *lingam* with Nandi, the white bull, carved in marble. On the walls were white sculptures of Ganesh, of Shiva and Parvati, of Vishnu and Lakshmi. They were three hundred years old, deserted, but not completely so, for around the *lingam* was a garland of fresh marigolds.

Although the channels and sandbanks were as complex as ever, there were no waves to contend with, for there was less wind, and the river lacked any long fetch of water on which waves could build up. Sometimes the channels would seem to run out completely, leaving us lost in a world of sandbanks and driftwood, in water of unknown depth, across which we drove with bated breath. The edge of the Doab was often a high bank of clay riddled with the holes of nesting birds. Clouds of these would whirr out and fly with us for a distance — brilliant green and crimson parakeets, flocks of grey pigeons and big golden owls, frowning at us from trees or silent on their broad soft wings as they flew beside us.

We refuelled at a *ghat* near the ancient city of Kanauj, renowned two thousand years ago in Europe for the steel of its swords, but now for its perfumes. The stops blur together in my memory. Mike Gill wrote of this one in his diary: "Ed in good humour. Stepped ashore off the bow of *Ganga* with one fist raised saying, 'Once more into the breach, dear friends . . . or close the wall up with our English dead . . . or whatever it is.'" The hospitality continued to be overwhelming – delicious Indian meals, beer and soft drinks, and often gifts as well. At Kanauj we were given small phials of perfume, some of them subtle and attractive, others with a strange musky odour which B.B. said was an aphrodisiac. Mike Gill smeared himself, with no effect, except to make people keep to windward of him, and, as Waka said sadly, there was no way of testing its aphrodisiac properties, anyway. Some of the gifts were huge figures, earthenware vases, alloy imprints of gods and warriors – and when we ran short of space on the boats we were left with no option but to consign the larger ones to the purifying waters of Mother Ganga, consoled as we did so by the thought that their donors could hardly have wished for them a more auspicious destination.

We pushed on through a late afternoon rainstorm, "I'm glad the monsoon finished yesterday," said a dripping Dingle – the official end of the monsoon is September 15th – and still in pouring rain we pitched camp at a lovely spot in a tiny inlet, a grass bank below a grove of trees with a huge mango dominating the scene. A few villagers arrived, squatting inquisitively around our tents. Across the inlet, which was only ten feet wide, three little girls sheltered from the pelting rain beneath a sheet of bright blue plastic, laughing at the strange people who had suddenly arrived from the river.

In the quiet before dark, we heard voices calling to each other from the middle of Ganga, and far out we saw a raft of floating debris. Then we picked out turbaned heads. It was a mob of water buffalo being driven across the river, only their eyes and noses and a bit of backbone showing above the surface of the water; in the quiet air we could hear them breathing heavily as they swam, sounding like porpoises. In the swift current they must have ended up miles downstream from where they started.

While Mingma and Pemma prepared the evening meal, I retired to my tent to write up my diary for the day. Two dogs from the nearby village approached and began scrapping and snarling at each other. "Would someone get Mingma to hit those dogs between the eyes with a couple of rocks?" I called out. Mingma's footsteps approached, and he peered inside my tent.

"No rocks having, *Barah Sahib*. One bottle giving," he said. There was the whistling sound of a bottle revolving through the air, followed by an agonised crescendo of yelping from two dogs, fading as they retreated into the distance. Mingma poked his head into the tent again. "One bottle, two dogs," he said, beaming, pleased to have used the throwing skills of a Sherpa yak-owner.

We woke to a gloomy but beautiful morning, with a band of orange light across the horizon between river and black clouds. Our next refuelling stop was at Fatehgarh, where a whole military garrison had turned out to welcome us. Crowds of young Sikhs lined the low grass banks, and they wore brilliantly coloured turbans: crimson, turquoise, emerald, gold – in the dull light they glowed like jewels. They had been there the whole of the day before, for the forward information about our arrival had been wrong, as it often was. There was not much we could do about these inaccuracies, for invariably a dozen people would put forward their ideas about our arrival, and usually the earliest guess was the one accepted. It didn't seem to matter much. Everyone accepted a long wait and an extra day's holiday in the best of humour. While the rest of us ate, drank and signed autographs, Jim dived beneath the boat to clear the water-intake gratings of the jet units, which had been losing power. There was a tangle of grass and sticks, and one stone which puzzled Jim – how a stone in this river of sand? We received gifts of printed silks and cottons made at the nearby city of Farrukhabad, an important centre of the Indian textile industry. When I returned to New Zealand, I realised that half the women of Auckland were wearing skirts made of Farrukhabad cotton, or with designs like it.

Early in the afternoon, Ding chalked up a magnificent grounding after turning up a narrow channel not much wider than the boat. He describes it in his diary (which by now had sunk to the level of pure farce – "rising to fresh heights of eloquence", was his own description): "I seized the wheel from Hamilton. The throb of the quadraphonic V8's with the overhead hub caps put me in paradise and I forced the jet to its limits. In the lead boat Hillary and Wilson faltered and unflinchingly I shot into the lead, ruthlessly overcoming problems at each turn. The other boats followed me without hesitation or question. We had covered at least eight hundred metres when I shot at tremendous speed, unintentionally, up a narrow channel. I calmed my terrified companions. 'Courage,' I said. 'The Ganga can only be conquered by sheer guts.' At that point Jon Hamilton, sleeping in the back, woke up and saw tall grass going past overhead. He sat up with a cry of terror. 'Go left,' he shouted. I went right. We ran aground at 40 m.p.h. Jon congratulated me on the brilliance of my driving.

Inspired by my example he took the wheel himself for the rest of the afternoon."

By now the only two members of the expedition who had not taken a turn at driving were the two Indian camera men, Prem and B.G. Prem described how he had his first drive on the river that afternoon: "Twenty-two days of constant travelling made me impatient to lay my hands on the steering of *Air India*. I diplomatically moved into the front seat and told Jon, 'You must be very tired by now.' He gracefully gave me his place, and now I was the driver of *Air India*, following tips here and there from Jon. What a change from the road drive to the river drive! No traffic, so no traffic police; no horn; no bumpy and jerky road, no gear to change the speed. It was just one accelerator under your right foot, and the steering wheel. It was like skating smoothly on greasy water. Jon was happy with my new assignment and said at dinner, 'You are a good driver.' I felt I had scored over my colleague B.G.!"

The bridge at Soron, our next refuelling place, loomed up unexpectedly, and we pulled into a shallow bay, grounding gently twenty metres offshore—an ideal refuelling spot, for the water kept us clear of the crowds which usually clustered around us.

I exchanged a few words with the Press.

"Which place has given you the best reception?" they asked.

"Everywhere," I said, and there was loud applause.

Ding chose this moment to turn on one of his acts with Jim. After a preliminary show of anger, they hurled themselves at each other, Ding finally throwing Jim across the stern of the boat. The crowd watched horrified as Ding picked up an ice-axe and plunged the shaft into Jim's back—actually through his armpit—and then walked off leaving him slumped over the stern, the ice-axe apparently protruding from his back. In an amazingly corpse-like fashion Jim slid off the stern to lie floating face down in the water. The police were not sure whether to ignore this, to laugh at it, or to mount a *lathi* charge to club Dingle unconscious and arrest him. He was saved in the end by Jim being forced to come up for air—which he did briskly, waving to the crowd who were by now laughing and waving.

I moved up to the dais where the official party and microphones were waiting. It was the biggest crowd for some days, even though we could see no town large enough to warrant such an assembly. I delivered my speech of greetings and thanks, now polished by much repetition. I told them that for me the Ganga was proving to be one of the most memorable experiences of my life. I thanked them for what they were doing: their welcome, the generous assistance of Indian Oil and the Government of India. I doubt if many people understood in detail what I was saying, but they caught the sense of it. I ended with a single word of Hindi—"*Dhanyabad!*"—thank you —and as that single word rang out from a dozen loudspeakers there was an answering roar of approval and applause which cheered me immensely. Despite all the barriers of language and culture, I felt I was sharing our adventure with these people and that they were glad to be part of it.

Beyond Soron we drove between areas of bare silt, with swamp and grasslands receding into the distance on either side: if there were any trees or villages here, they were well back from the river. The dull sky turned to black and rain began. Finally a village came into view hard on the banks of the river. As we drove nearer, we saw that the village was not merely close to the banks; it was falling into the water, and even as we watched, the dividing wall of a house split off, crashing into the river whose main current here was sluicing away the bank.

We camped in a cornfield just upstream from the village under the gaze of hundreds of peasants held back by a barrier rope. The village was called Mahmudpur. At the beginning of the monsoon there had been three hundred houses; now there were one hundred and fifty.

"When Mother Ganga calls," said one man sadly, "you go." The Government had said they would put up a stone embankment, but it seemed likely that the whole village would have gone before that happened. Even the temple had gone, and by now those who had lost their homes were rebuilding them a mile or so inland. Somewhere further downstream the walls of Mahmudpur were reforming into sandbanks and fields that would soon grow grass for grazing and, eventually, for crops, perhaps even for a new village. I wondered who made legal decisions about the ownership of land so casually destroyed and created by the river on its journey to the sea.

Before we pitched our tents, B.B. checked on the rate of erosion— about three feet per day he was told—and we moved our tents well into the cornfield. The owner came forward with his sickle and cleared his corn from the land for us, refusing any payment in recompense, an attitude so foreign to what we are used to in the West that it seemed like some form of madness. "You are our guests," he said. "It is my pleasure to help as I can. Your houses are better than ours," he added, looking inside my tent. Mingma was already laying out his bedding inside the tent he shared with Ding. "Dingle sleeping that side," he said pointing towards the river and laughed. We were right on the edge of the village and, singly or in groups, most of the party wandered down wet, dirty lanes separating the mud walls of houses roofed with thatch—poorer than any village we had seen and yet the inhabitants offered us food as we walked around, peering at what was left of their village. Jim, Peter and Mike were offered a smoke from a clay pipe by a bleary-eyed gent squatting on a platform outside his home. "Strong stuff," said Jim, coughing gently and passing it on to the other two. "Smoke enough of that and you could make a Holden V8 sound like music of the gods."

Prem was questioned about us. "Who are these Mahatmas on Ganga Yatra [Pilgrimage]? We have heard of them on our radio. We have had important people to our village before, but never have we heard their arrival announced by radio." Prem told them who we were. "And have these men been to the moon, too?"

Peter and Murray were invited into a house, "because," said the owner, "your feet will bless my house. Do you go barefooted out of respect for Mother Ganga?" An old villager came up to them and briefly knelt to touch their feet, almost furtively, before moving on without even looking up.

"He hopes to share the merit you will acquire through going on this pilgrimage up Ganga," explained Prem. "He could never afford to go on such a journey himself, but in this way you can do it for him."

"It is a mark of respect, too," said B.B. "Whenever I visit my father I kneel and touch his feet. Peter, whenever you return to your father after a period of absence you should kneel and touch his feet."

I had the impression that this was a habit Peter was unlikely to slip into easily.

We retired to bed with the periodic splash of silt falling into the river, reminding us of the fate of Mahmudpur. By the time we left in the morning, another four feet of village had vanished.

We were now less than a hundred miles from Garhmuktesar. In these upper reaches, Ganga was a lonely river with areas of tall sedges and marshland stretching off on either side, and birds more common than human beings. There were tall grey storks, white egrets and cranes rising heavily into the air and flapping off with measured wing-beats.

A few miles on, Mike Gill ran aground for the first time, leaving Waka and Peter as the only ones with unblemished records. Mike had cunningly been doing as little driving as possible, but Jim and I in *Ganga* felt the time had come to stop him looking so smug, as each day the groundings continued. The place selected by Mike was in a complex area of shallows, and *Air India* and *Kiwi* were reluctant to come too close to render the usual assistance in lifting the stranded boat off. Ding and Max, 400 yards short of the stranded boat, hopped overboard in what was at first knee-deep water, but soon they were up to their necks in the brown water and feeling the pull of the current. The grounded boat was still 300 yards away when debris began to float from Max's pocket. Ding came to the rescue, recovering a comb, a letter from home, and a silk tie presented by a Lion at our last re-fuelling stop. By now the pair of them were in deep water, travelling downstream at about five knots with the three jet boats slowly vanishing on the horizon. A roll of dental floss emerged from another of Max's pockets and gently trailed itself for a hundred feet along the surface, eventually tangling itself around Ding's feet. "If I drown now, Max, you can tell my next of kin that at least I didn't have any decaying food matter between my toes."

Their cries for help brought no reaction from any of the jet boats and so the two of them kept swimming, wondering where they'd fetch up, glad the river wasn't infested with crocodiles, and grateful that they had a comb, a silk tie and 500 metres of dental floss. Part of the problem was that Jon, at the wheel of *Air India*, was feeling desperately unwell and in no condition to take note of what had happened to his passengers. Meanwhile the rest of us were involved in the usual desperate manoeuvres required to move a one-ton jet boat off a sandbank. By the time we were afloat and aware of our diminished numbers, Max was starting to go under for the third time, or so Ding claimed when we at length hauled them aboard.

We refuelled at Narwa Barrage, which channels water into the Lower Ganga Canal built a hundred years ago. Before we arrived, we were told that the Barrage gates were closed, which would mean dragging our boat up the embankment past the Barrage and down the far side. Opening the gates, they said, would flood one hundred villages and, although they had discussed whether this should be done for our convenience, they decided that such an action would be received unfavourably by those flooded out. They apologised and hoped we would understand their predicament ... But, as so often happens, the information was wrong. The water levels were the same above and below the Barrage; they opened one gate for us and we drove through without problems.

Shortly after two p.m. we reached Garhmuktesar, on the road to Delhi, which was two hours' drive to the west along a main road. We were met by a large emotional crowd and, for the first time since Calcutta, did a few television interviews both for the Indian channels and for foreign networks. We spent four days at either Garhmuktesar or Delhi, for this was a period of re-organisation for the mountains and for the white water of the gorges that lay ahead.

I was disturbed by Jon's health, for he had not been well since Patna. "Jon very thin looking, always sick, not now strong like on the Sun Kosi," said Mingma, as worried as I was. For two weeks now he had suffered from a recurring fever, weakness, and a persistent cough, and the pills Max had given him made no lasting difference. It became serious that first night in Garhmuktesar when Jon, after an exhausting afternoon repairing a leaking seal on the driveshaft, went down with severe pains in his belly. Max and I got together and agreed he should spend a few days in hospital in Delhi for investigation and treatment. He was put on intravenous fluids without food, and we were told there was no chance he could rejoin us before Hardwar at the earliest, and there was even a chance he would have to pull out altogether.

To lose Jon's driving skills would be a disaster of the first magnitude for, although anybody could drive on the flat water of the plains, the white water would be a different matter altogether. But I had to do something. I moved the boat teams around so that *Air India* now had what I called the Kamikaze Kids—myself, Peter, Ding, Murray and B.B. There was no protest from B.B. at being included in what was clearly a suicide squad, though perhaps this explained why he broke out in a nervous rash a few days later. Peter and Murray accepted their new role almost with enthusiasm, for both had been feeling increasing frustration at their so-far insignificant roles in the expedition. Already they had suggested that they should set off into the mountains direct from Delhi, to make a reconnaissance of the mountains we were heading for, and to choose a route. Either of them could happily face snowstorms, ice-walls or sheer rocks and enjoy it. But to sit through a series of receptions and live in expensive hotels was more than they could bear.

There was still the question of who would become chief driver of *Air India* if Jon was definitely unable to continue. Murray drove jet boats the way he climbed mountains, straight up the middle and fast, but he had yet to prove that his skill in driving approached that of his climbing. Ding also was inclined to be dashing rather than circumspect, though his instincts for survival were strong. Peter had quickly taken to driving, helped by having recently learned to fly—a different skill, but related in some ways. Of the three I was inclined to back Peter, but learning to handle big water would not be easy, and there was not much time left. Usually the first bad error of judgment in these rivers is the last—the crew might float free but a jet boat sinks like a stone. The best plan, meanwhile, was for us all to pray that Jon's health would return.

Others were busy in Delhi. Mike Gill was trying to extricate five thousand feet of movie film from the Customs, assisted by an employee of a firm called Jeena & Company who specialised in freight forwarding. He was a gloomy man, as might be expected in someone who had spent his life wrestling with the Indian Customs, and when Mike left to return to Garhmuktesar he was still empty-handed.

"I will bring it to Ganga," said the man from Jeena & Company with a melancholy smile.

Waka, desperate by now, had decided to put through a toll call to his girlfriend in New Zealand, even if it took him all day, which it did. He began at midday. Around four p.m. he was briefly connected to the hill station of Darjeeling in sight of the snows of Kangchenjunga, a romantic destination but not what he wanted. At seven p.m. he made contact with a small town in Greece. Finally, and literally at the eleventh hour, he reached New Zealand, and all was well.

I was welcomed again by Miss Vatsala Pai at the Department of Tourism, who had been helping us through their branch offices all the way up the river, and I received my accustomed mail from a host of well-wishers. One offered me his four-hundred-page thesis proving that Ganga is a canal made by man in antiquity. Another enclosed a chart of the river beyond Garhmuktesar:

Respected Sir Edmund,

I could guess from your talks that the high officials in New Delhi could not give you correct information about your voyage from Rishikesh through the Bhagirathi Ganga. You, of course, know the flowing stream of Ganga carrying all the waters of different rivers with different names coming down from the Siwalik Ranges of the Himalayas meeting at the confluence of Devaprayag. I place herewith a rough chart of the region for your scrutiny. I humbly state that I have my fifty-four years of intimate experience about these rivers' flowing courses.

I may submit here with an open heart that I have never heard of anyone in this century who is bigger and greater explorer, adventurer and a hillclimber than you are. I spent so many sleepless nights when my restless mind followed you on your track of great explorations including the South Pole. The world will never forget you as the most indomitable, energetic and eternally young man in its history of exploration.

I express my best wishes to your partymen who are with you in your Ocean to Sky adventure.

Your most sincerely . . .

Back in Garhmuktesar, Jim was staying in a rest-house with little to make it memorable apart from an immense banyan tree in the front courtyard, surrounded by a raised circle of bricks and swarming with monkeys.

"The monkeys have returned from their morning stroll," wrote Jim in his diary, his Hindu tolerance extending to all living beings, "and one was in *Kiwi*, calmly eating biscuits out of the front pocket. One had Ding and I on, making threatening dashes towards us, to which we replied with enthusiasm till an impasse was reached and the monkey withdrew with dignity. What marvellous creatures, and how great to have them round us free rather than in a zoo."

The monkeys were less in favour with Mingma after they had burgled his room. Murray wrote: "The place where we are staying is overrun with hundreds of small monkeys. Screeching little bastards who grit their teeth if you go too close." Ding, too, had something to say in his diary: "A crowd of monkeys also gathered to see the jet boats arrive, but none asked for our autographs. I was so grateful that I gave one an apple. The rabid little red-arsed bastard took it with a growl. This rest-house is guarded by armed men — against the monkeys, I presume."

★   ★   ★

On September 22nd we resumed our journey up Ganga, leaving Garhmuktesar at seven a.m. Harish was back in Delhi, organising his expedition to Gangotri and Gomukh, and now Mohan Kohli and Joginder Singh had joined us for the journey up the gorge. Also with us was Dr Colin Aickman, High Commissioner for New Zealand, who was travelling to Hardwar and Rishikesh with us. To show the new-comers what jet boating was all about, we ran hard aground twice in quick succession, for we were back on a wide deserted river, studded with sandbanks like a minefield.

Waka's grounding was a fast one and secretly pleasing to those of us who were feeling envious of his increasing cockiness about his un-tarnished driving record. He was following the other two boats, but about twenty yards to one side of their line. The river was so shallow here that even a minor deviation could mean losing the channel. Mike was sitting on the foredeck; I was behind. We all saw it at once, the ominous fading of the current marks, and made our preparations. I braced myself against the windscreen rail; Mike raised his body off the deck, leaving himself suspended between his four limbs like a spider. Waka had about three seconds in which to take evasive action. With the rashness of youth he decided to risk all on an increase in speed, a manoeuvre which can put the boat higher on the plane, decreasing its draught. A moment later, travelling at 40 m.p.h., we struck. The others came back to congratulate Waka. It was our last grounding, and Peter remained the only one with an unblemished record.

We had lunch upstream from Bijnor on the riverbank, by courtesy of a wealthy industrialist who owned a glass factory there. Like our carpet-making friend in Mirzapur he was a Punjabi called Dutt and his lifestyle was similar, like that of a nineteenth-century English industrialist. The food they gave us was as good as any we had in India, and our standards by then were high. The founder of the business was our host's father, who had seen the land by moonlight while crossing Ganga on the nearby railbridge; although there was no source of raw materials nearby, all of it having to be brought by rail, he liked the place so well that he settled and built his factory. Their glass is still hand-blown, for the old man disliked machines, both in themselves and because they displaced men, of whom they employed up to two thousand, from their jobs. By a strange coincidence they had a daughter living in Auckland, my home town in New Zealand. They had always owned powerboats and knew the river well, right up to Hardwar.

"I would have warned you of the rocks and fast water," said the head of the family, "but now I have seen what your boats can do. You will have no problems." We parted as though we had been friends for years instead of hours.

When we carried on, the nature of the country changed considerably. For 1,300 miles, Ganga had sprawled across a flat plain of silt, with only an odd rolling swell of hills in the distance for relief. But now the river changed. The silt vanished. Fast water came sweeping down gravel beds with increasingly lively rapids. This was real jet-boat country, and we side-slipped round the corners with a new exhilaration. We were driving uphill, up a huge fan of shingle carried down from the mountains and spilling through the narrow gap in the hills at Hardwar. Crops had vanished from the banks, which were now wilder, with forest and pampas grass. A terrified herd of white cows, the holiest of all animals, plunged into the river beside us in a shower of flying water. In the mists ahead we could see hills rising, and even mountains — and we knew we were approaching Hardwar, the "Gate of God", gateway to the mountains.

White Water

As we approached we could see that Hardwar was a true gate into the hills. The river emerged from a gap between steep forested spurs dropping from the Siwalik Hills on either side. The town appeared as tops of temples showing through trees on our left, whilst other temples higher up nestled into the slopes of the hills. We came sweeping around a fast-flowing corner and there, on the sloping banks on the town side, was a huge crowd waiting to greet us. Half a mile up-river we could see the giant Hardwar Barrage. Jim pointed out the topography.

"The town's not on the river. It's on the banks of the Ganga Canal over there," he shouted, pointing to our left towards the temples. "The main river used to flow over there, but when they built the Canal they had to use that part of the river bed for it. Spiritually disastrous, I would have said, transforming the sacred banks of Ganga into a man-made canal, but that's what they did. The Barrage diverts waters to the Canal from the river." I steered in the direction of the crowded bank, but Jim called out, "Let's bypass the welcome for five minutes and see if there's any way through the Barrage." And, turning away from the official group standing at the water's edge, with girls holding garlands, he swept off upstream followed by Michael Hamilton. With some reluctance, for it seemed like discourtesy, I followed suit. The stream became increasingly violent as we drew up in front of the Barrage, whose left half consisted of an imposing concrete spillway — almost dry, for the series of iron gates at its head were closed — while the right half was a fixed weir over which the river poured in a long smooth curtain of water, the upper level being about eight feet above us.

"There's no way through that lot," I said. "What would the spillway be like if they opened the gates?"

"Brisk, I would think," said Jim. "Very brisk."

We swept back down the river and over to the landing-stage where we stepped ashore and were formally greeted. I was pleased to find no concern at our bad manners, for the welcome was as warm as usual, with garlands and *tilak*. The two Mikes wanted to film our arrival again, and set up their cameras on the banks. We went back down-river and then swept into the landing-stage for an even warmer second welcome under the eyes of the camera – to the officials' obvious delight.

I met the Chief Engineer of the Barrage – a kindly man ready to help in any way. What could he do for us? Anything that was possible would be his pleasure.

"Could I see the spillway with the Barrage gates open?" I enquired, with little confidence either that he would do it or that it would be worth doing anyway.

"Of course. In half an hour."

We drove back to the Barrage and tied up in a protected backwater. Slowly the gates opened, the air filled with the thunderous roar of white water, and we watched in horror as the whole of Ganga swept down the confines of the spillway, smooth, green and powerful at first, but irrupting at the bottom into an immense stopper wave curling back on itself, and below this a surging mass of tumbled white water – a quite impossible place for our boats.

It seemed clear that we would have to haul the boats out of the water and drag them overland above the Barrage. But the Engineer was not to be beaten as easily as that. He suggested that we investigate an alternative route up an overflow channel joining the river to the Canal. Michael, Jim and I walked up the almost dry channel, which led to a weir separating us from the Canal which flowed past from right to left. Even as we watched, the water level was falling, for, with the spillway newly opened, most of the river was flowing there rather than down the Canal. The weir was not fixed but made of wooden flaps, four feet high and hinged at the bottom so that they could be lowered, forming a free communication with the Canal. The Engineer waved us on to the bank. At his command a troop of extraordinary river-men did a quick *puja*, then leaped at the flaps, knocking out some wooden struts and tripping the chain which held them up. Water poured down the almost dry creek bed, but not enough for our boats.

"I will close the spillway again," said the Engineer.

By the time we were back in our boats, now emptied of gear, the side-stream was flooded from side to side and we drove up in a slashing run. We reached the breach in the Canal barrier, but the water had risen at least four feet and was now a terrifying prospect.

"I will open the spillway gates," said the Engineer. I wondered what the villagers down-stream were thinking, with the Canal rising and falling in this unpredictable fashion. Eventually the breach became navigable, neither too swift with too big a fall nor so shallow that we

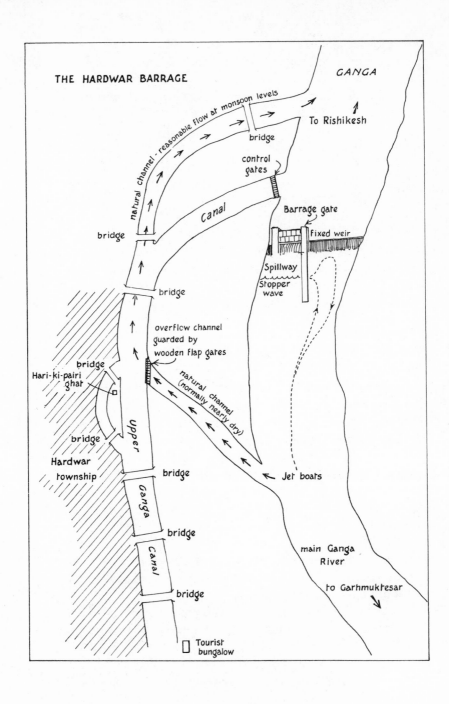

THE HARDWAR BARRAGE

GANGA

natural channel - reasonable flow at monsoon levels

bridge

To Rishikesh

control
gates

Canal

Barrage gate

bridge

fixed weir

Spillway
Stopper
wave

bridge

overflow channel
guarded by
wooden flap gates

natural channel
(normally
nearly dry)

bridge
Hari-ki-pairi
ghat

Upper

bridge

Hardwar
township

bridge

Ganga

Jet boats

bridge

Canal

main Ganga
River

to Garhmuktesar

bridge

☐ Tourist
bungalow

Away from the crowds, contemplation.

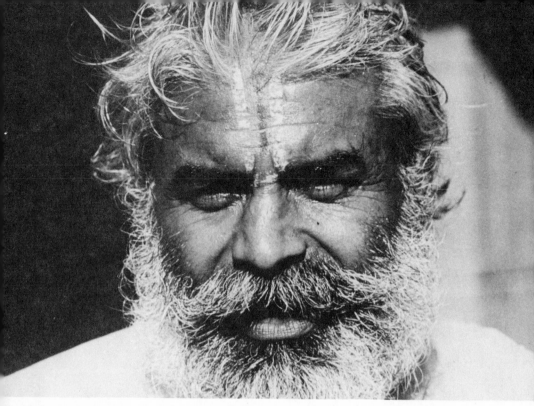

The yogi who won a tug of war with a jet boat at Mirzapur.

People waited all day to greet us at Rudraprayag.

might hit bottom. Michael moved first, driving with great force straight at the tongue of water; he hit it a little off centre, made a violent lurch, and then was up and over into the Canal. Jim made his preparations, taking time to get into the right position, and then set out on his run, striking the tongue in a better position and crossing into the Canal in a very smooth fashion. I had already decided that my driving skills were not up to handling this tricky place, and so Michael came back to take *Air India* through.

By this time the water was significantly shallower and Michael's line of approach was different. As the boat leaped over the curling wave and on to the sweep of water surging down from the Canal, the bow dug in and struck the sharp steel edge of one of the lowered flaps. The boat stopped dead. Michael was flung into the windscreen, his knee snapping the ignition key off flush with the dash, and the engine was wrenched off its mounts. Gallons of water poured over the deck and the boat drifted helplessly down-stream. Fortunately, there was a spare key screwed under the deck and the engine was still functioning; in a few minutes the boat was going again. Michael got into position for another run, and this time came through perfectly to the cheers of the crowd of onlookers.

I could see now the layout of the township. The Canal was about fifty yards wide, running straight and swift between concrete banks, with the main township and waterfront squeezed against the hill, and bridges arching across from one side to the other. There was at least as much water here as in the main river—in the dry season the Canal takes off almost the whole flow of Ganga for irrigation purposes, though never all of it. As Jim pointed out, the religious implications of drying up Mother Ganga altogether would be catastrophic. The Canal was a bad place for boats. Jim was nearly beheaded by a wire hanging low across it, and here and there iron poles just broke the surface of the water, enough to punch holes straight through our hulls if we struck one at speed. Along the flat promenades on either side, *sadhus* in orange robes walked or sat cross-legged, and on the main *ghat*, a small, flat island called Har-ki-pairi—"the footprint of Vishnu"— visitors and pilgrims crowded round a most un-Indian looking clock-tower. The tall façades of the pilgrim rest-houses, known as *dharmshala*, rose here and there from the water's edge. We drove carefully upstream to where we could re-enter the Ganga above the Barrage to satisfy ourselves that it was navigable, and then returned to our rooms at the government tourist bungalow.

We had a very pleasant and relaxed dinner with some of B.B.'s relations, but I was happy to escape to what I felt was a well-earned rest. I found Peter, Waka and Jim deep in philosophical discussion in my room. Peter wrote in his diary that night: "Much philosophising and verbosity this evening with Jim and myself concluding that our beliefs are basically the same. We now call ourselves 'Physical Monists', which means that the body is one physical piece and there is no separate entity that one might call a soul. We agreed that the body is a complex network of biochemicals, molecules interacting in marvellous ways which result in the human body. The brain is an even more incredible product of nature's evolution. We agreed that when you die there is nothing left; the body is dead, all is finished. What remains is what is in the hearts of friends and family, for there a semblance of one's past life continues."

This was stimulated by a meeting between Peter, Waka and Jim and two disciples of The Mother, a lady *sadhu* who ran an *ashram* at Hardwar. One disciple was a Bengali, one an American, and they tried to persuade our three to place themselves under The Mother's guidance so that they could be helped to "find themselves". Peter, Waka and Jim said that they preferred to continue their discovery of themselves as captains of their own ships. "It's just a cop-out, handing over your life and decisions to someone else," Waka insisted. The other two agreed. They asked me what I thought. "I'm not sure I'm all that keen on knowing more about myself," I said wearily. "I know a good deal now, and most of it's bad." It had been an exciting day with plenty of action, but I was tired now and happy to escape to sleep.

I woke early and scribbled a list of things to organise. Outside, there was quite a crowd, even by seven a.m. They surged forward with demands for autographs each time I appeared. I skulked in my cell like a bad-tempered bear and snarled each time an autograph-hunter appeared, saying, "Just one more, please, please, please!"

That morning, to my immense relief, Jon arrived by train, weak but cured of his illness and ready to resume his position as lead driver in *Air India*. He joined Michael who, since first light, had been assiduously repairing the damage done to *Air India* during our dramatic ascent into the Canal the previous day. A large chunk of fibre-glass had been gouged off the keel near the bow when the boat struck, and this had to be made clean and dry before repairing it with new fibre-glass and resin. Their first attempt to get it dry after driving the boat high on to a sandy bank foundered when the Canal level rose suddenly, floating the boat free. But with a kerosene heater augmenting the heat of the sun, the bow was dry enough to repair by about midday.

A *puja* had been arranged for us by the Har-ki-pairi Ghat Committee.

It seemed the proper thing to do. The invaluable *Gazetteer* said: "The town is of great antiquity, and has borne many names. It was originally known as Kapila after the sage who passed his life in religious austerities at this spot. When Huan Tsang, the Chinese Buddhist pilgrim in the seventh century A.D., visited the area, he found a city some three and a half miles in circumference, enclosing a dense population. The existing ruins strongly confirm his account. Tamerlaine plundered and massacred a great concourse of pilgrims at Hardwar shortly after he had seized Delhi in 1398.

"As the spot where the Ganga issues forth, Hardwar obtains the veneration of each of the great religions of India, and preserves the memorials alike of Buddhism, Shivaism and Vishnuism, and of rites perhaps earlier than any of them ... A great assemblage of pilgrims takes place on the anniversary of the day upon which Ganga first appeared on earth. From Hardwar the pilgrims often proceed to visit the Shivaite Shrine of Kedarnath and the Vishnuvite temple of Badrinath, worshipping on their way at the five *prayags* or sacred confluences."

Mohan Kohli assured me that Hardwar was the holiest place on the river, the third point on our journey described thus. But then I discovered that all the Press and their cameras were going to be present at our *puja*. It sounded more like a Press conference, and I decided not to go after all—the rest of the expedition could do *puja* on my behalf.

At this the Secretary of the Har-ki-pairi Ghat Committee grew angry. Without me, he said, there would be no *puja* for anybody, nor any photographs of the *ghat* either. Mohan stepped forward to pour oil on the troubled waters—would I do *puja*, he asked, if the Secretary would promise to keep the *ghat* free of pressmen? To this I agreed, though with little conviction that the *puja* would be held in privacy, even though the *ghat* was a small island reached by an overhead bridge which could easily be closed off. As I had feared, it was largely a publicity stunt. I had the impression that the Press, instead of being excluded, were probably the only people allowed on to the *ghat* apart from myself, and I advanced across the footbridge amidst a jostling throng of reporters and photographers. "What has been the highlight of your journey so far, Sir Hillary? ... What are your impressions of Hardwar? ... Who first set foot on the summit of Everest? ..."

At length I found myself seated on the concrete steps of the *ghat* with my feet in the sacred waters, a priest beside me and a barrage of clicking cameras and flashing lights going off all around me. One gentleman of the Press took grave risks when he waded thigh-deep into the water, only three feet in front of me, taking pictures with a telephoto lens. What was he trying to get? Close-ups of the Hillary teeth? The Hillary tonsils, perhaps? I was sorely tempted to place the size thirteen Hillary foot in the centre of his abdomen, and give him a quick push into the deep and fast-flowing waters of Mother Ganga behind him. The whole performance was of little merit so far as I was concerned and it was with some relief that I escaped. The waterfront at Hardwar is very beautiful, and a *puja* done there under peaceful and natural conditions must be a memorable occasion.

By three p.m. the fibre-glass patch on *Air India* was pronounced hard enough for us to get under way. We loaded up and were ready to go, a big crowd around us to say goodbye, when down came torrential rain, driving hard from the mountains and sounding like showers of pebbles drumming on the awnings and decks of our boats. We were soon soaked, even wearing our red rain capes, and for a while we waited, cheerfully swapping jokes with the remnants of the crowd. When the downpour eased slightly, we dashed out, only to have the rain pounce on us again, beating on our eyeballs and forcing us to shelter under one of the many bridges across the Canal. For half an hour we played a cat-and-mouse game with the rain, scuttling from one bridge to the next, where we hovered, clinging to wires trailing down from the bridge. Murray, Peter, Ding and Waka performed some extraordinary feats of rock climbing on the piles and overhangs of the stone bridges to fill in time. It was late afternoon now, and with darkness approaching we had to move if we were to get to Rishikesh that night. Michael Hamilton suggested that it might be too late already, but there was no way I planned to spend another night in Hardwar.

Jim and I decided to get going. We moved up the channel, both of us peering into the driving rain. By a combination of faith and good luck we missed all the obstacles, and as we emerged from the channel into the main river, the rain was easing off.

The river was beautiful – broad and swift with dividing streams and islands clothed in forest, like a giant-sized New Zealand river. As the mist and rain rolled away, we saw forested hills looming up on either side and blocking the way ahead, except where a narrow gap marked the beginning of the true gorge and the site of the town of Rishikesh. Towering storm-clouds edged with silver by the setting sun filled the sky, giving an air of grandeur to the scene. We were wet and frozen, but stimulated by it all, and an air of excitement prevailed.

We arrived at Rishikesh just as dusk was approaching. A huge crowd had gathered and, when we pulled into a bouldery bank for refuelling, absolute chaos reigned. Like us they were cold and wet, for they had been waiting most of the day. By the time the boats were refuelled it was dark, and we had a nervous run upriver through the waves of a sizeable rapid, driving by feel as much as by sight before inching in to tie up by the steep steps of a temple. Then we all ended up in a forest bungalow with a magnificent outlook across the river, gleaming now by the light of the newly risen moon. There was a coolness in the air that made me feel I was really in the mountains now.

Although Rishikesh does not have the sanctity of Hardwar it is yet another holy place of pilgrimage, and very beautiful. It is built where the river finally bursts out of its deep mountain gorges, a town and bazaar area on the true right bank and a very fancy waterfront of temples and *ashrams* on the other bank, the river fast flowing and cold between. High forested spurs enclose the town on three sides, but to the south the view is down sloping valley flats towards Hardwar. Many famous religious sages — *rishis* — and religious movements have their headquarters here and it is a favoured spot for meditation for Indians and foreigners alike.

In the bungalow we ate a meal and read some mail that had arrived. Mike Gill was lamenting the non-arrival of his movie film from Jeena & Company. Ding was writing up his diary as part of a letter home. "Opposite the bungalow, on the other side of the valley, is the *ashram* of the Maharishi Yogi who flies in rich Westerners in search of Truth, by helicopter from Delhi. Crafty old bugger! From tomorrow onward is the bit they reckon is tough." He looked up. "This could be our last letter home," he said lugubriously. The remark struck echoes in the minds of all of us, for we were uneasily aware of the fact that tomorrow we were embarking on the first bad stretch of the river. It turned out that Ding thought that this would be our last despatch of mail, not that we were about to die. But there was an ominous note to his remark, for all that.

I found Jim looking sombrely at a photograph on the wall. It showed the confluence of two rivers with a prow of rock between them, clustered with houses and temples. On the larger of the two rivers was an evil-looking rapid, a stretch of white water foaming down an incline littered with big boulders.

"Where's that?" I asked.

"Rudraprayag, it says," replied Jim, "with the Mandakini joining the Alaknanda."

"Which is the Alaknanda?" I asked, curious now, for the Recce Report had mentioned no rapid at the confluence, and this was a beauty. Jim pondered for a while, looked at the map and back at the photograph.

"According to the map, the Alaknanda is the one with the rapid." He looked worried. "Surely to God we can't have missed a rapid like that on the Recce. Maybe they've printed the photo back to front," he said, aware as he said it that he was grasping at straws. It must have weighed on his mind, for next morning he described a confused nightmare in which he drove his boat into the wild rapid, only to have it break in two, the bow section skidding away from him across the waves. Ashamed at writing off yet another boat, he chased after the bow, despairingly trying to get the two bits together again and struggling in vain with a curious type of clip fitted by Hamiltons to cope with this sort of situation. He never did get it together. He woke, relieved to find it was a dream, but with a lively foreboding about Rudraprayag which was to stay with him up to, and in due course into, the rapid.

I had a good sleep, interrupted briefly in the small hours by a strange apparition. It was raining, but above the drumming on the roof I heard the sound of a man battering at the door and stumbling towards the room where we slept. I sat up with a start. A dark figure carrying a bundle loomed in the doorway.

"I am from Jeena & Company," said the figure. "I have brought the film." And he sank dramatically to the floor.

I awoke feeling depressed and stayed that way all day. I suppose it was the unknown problems and dangers that lay ahead of us. People kept popping in for photographs and autographs—God knows I was really getting sick of it. Everyone had advice to give us about the river above Rishikesh. "It is full of boulders. Even for your boats it is impossible." Some said the river was too narrow. Some said we would get no higher than just above Rishikesh. At the other end of the scale were those who said that, by exercising the magic powers of Yoga, we could overcome all obstacles. Others believed we could fly above the surface of the water, using blades like helicopters for the steep places.

We were told of two previous attempts to descend the river. The first had taken place some years earlier, when a couple of Indian youths had attempted to descend the river in a home-made raft, starting from Birehi, a point deep into the gorge. The raft overturned almost immediately in the wild water and the first of the two soon drowned. The second managed to haul himself on to a rock in the middle of the river. As he watched the raft break apart, he remembered that he had promised his friend's mother that he would bring him back alive, and he dived back into the river in a despairing attempt to save him. He too was drowned and because of this became something of a legend in the valley.

The news of the other tragedy appeared as a brief news item on the front page of a Delhi newspaper we had just received.

"CZECH CANOEISTS DROWN—Two members of the Ganga '77 Expedition were drowned below Birehi today. One was washed ashore unconscious but died before medical assistance could be given. The body of the second canoeist has not yet been recovered." We knew nothing of this. We had heard nothing of an expedition called Ganga '77, and at this stage had no idea whether this was a serious attempt to navigate the river or the tragedy of a pair of inexperienced youths facing dangers they knew nothing about.

It worried me at times that I might kill off some of my friends with my crazy ideas. I felt in all honesty that my own safety didn't matter too much. Dying for me would mean nothing—though the discomfort involved frightened me off—but the others did matter. And yet somehow I kept organising these trips. It was some consolation that my friends would be doing crazy things by themselves, anyway—and I knew they were competent, with strong survival instincts. It was also a help to know that I'd never lost a life on any of my expeditions— but there could always be a first time and that didn't bear thinking about. Maybe I should just leave them alone to live their normal decent professional lives, raise their families, make money, and become pillars of respectability in the community. And yet I knew they loved these adventurous trips . . . they certainly required no persuasion when I invited them to join me.

I put aside these gloomy thoughts and began sorting gear with Mingma. In the hills, Mingma was back in the country he knew and loved, and he had a new gleam in his eye as he set to work with the organising. Above Rishikesh, the Indian Army was giving us vehicle support in the form of a jeep and a three-ton truck with drivers. They were invaluable. We loaded all our spare gear on the truck, bought food, and had everything fully organised by midday. After some discussion, we agreed to move the canopies from the jet boats. There were good reasons for this: they could make it difficult for five people to abandon a sinking boat; they added to our weight, now an important consideration; and they probably had significant wind-drag in places where every bit of power might be needed. But I was sorry to see them go. They had served us well, sheltering us from the sun as we drove across the plains, and from rain when we were not on the move. Without the gay stripes of the canvas awnings and their ribbons flying in the wind the boats looked small and naked.

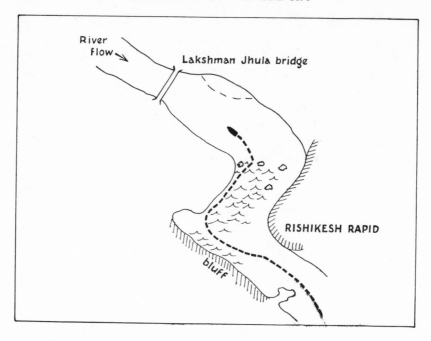

As I came down to the boats at the end of the loading, I was mobbed by a big crowd, and presented with flowers and leaflets by some holy men. I said goodbye to our friends and quickly clambered on board the boat.

Then we were away, and for the first time I felt the familiar grip of fear in my belly. We had been told that the first big rapid was some five miles on, but within half a mile we came round a corner to see a considerable rapid with big waves, and I thought as we plunged in, "My God! If we strike this at the beginning of the gorge, what's the rest of the river going to be like?" The river poured through two right-angle bends in a big S, banking around the first bend to crash down a steep boulder bank to pile up against a steep cliff before easing out down to Rishikesh. We drove close by under the bottom cliff and turned hard right, up boiling but easy water, avoiding the boulder bank, and then we eased out up a steep tongue between big waves. In reality, it was an easy route, but dramatic and exciting so soon after leaving Rishikesh.

At the top of this first rapid above Rishikesh we found ourselves driving through a quiet pool under a high swing-bridge. Legend has it that Lakshman, a brother of Ram—one of the great incarnations of God in Hindu belief—first built this bridge to cross the river when he was searching for his wife who had run away. "Of course the bridge has been renovated from time to time since then," we were assured. It would need to have been, for according to the Hindu mythological timetable Ram and Lakshman walked this earth many, many thousands of years ago.

Then we entered the gorge proper. On either side of us the walls of the valley closed in and steepened, made of grey-black rock worn smooth and clean by the waters of high floods and, above this level, green with moss and vegetation before the tall wooded slopes of the high hills carried on upwards at an easier angle. In parts we could see the line of the road winding and climbing in impossible-looking terrain. For a few miles the current was fast but the surface smooth for the most part, and we planed up easily. Jon estimated the flow at about 20,000 cusecs, small compared with the 1,600,000 cusecs back at Farakka, but still a big river for all that. The noise of the boats reverberated back and forth between the rock walls of the gorge, which would have been silent without us, for the smooth-flowing water made no sound.

But then we heard the distant roar of white water. We rounded a bend to see ahead of us the river steepening into a line of white waves, like huge corrugations on the water's surface, with the flick and toss of spray rising into the air. Jon went first, while we waited at the foot of the rapid: if anything happened to the lead boat he would need us to rescue the occupants as they were washed out into the tail-race. He drove quietly up smooth water close to the bank, looking for a line through, for the big waves could not be climbed direct—somehow they had to be circumvented. Then the note of the engine rose higher as he moved out into the rough water, diagonally across in the deep trough between two waves till he reached a line of better water, hard and boiling but relatively flat. We could no longer hear the engine above the roar of the rapids, but slowly the boat climbed upwards, obscured at times by the toss of waves, but clearly on a good route. And then we saw Jon break through on to the tongue of smooth, steep water falling down from the lip of the rapid, and he was through into the calm pool above.

Jim followed in *Ganga*, with B.B. and me beside him. Waves that look big from a distance are always enormous when moving through them. Crossing the trough was like being in a storm at sea, but then we were through on to Jon's line and climbing up under full power. The waves rose more than head-height on either side and, in areas of turbulence, holes would suddenly appear in the water and as suddenly close over. But Jim drove well, keeping exactly to what seemed a miraculously easy route through very big water. Mike Hamilton followed in *Kiwi*. We felt confident he would have no trouble, and he didn't.

Almost immediately we came on a second very similar rapid. It was late in the afternoon now; the sun had re-emerged after a brief rain shower, and the light was brilliant and clear. Again Jon was ahead. In the immensity of the gorge, and amongst those big white waves, the boat was insignificant; we could hardly have seen it if it had not been for the glowing crimson of the rain-capes of the men crouched on the front seat.

I felt mildly jubilant as we drove through to the top of this second rapid with relative ease, for the drivers were going well and the boats handling superbly. We had not gone much further when we came to a small crowd gathered on a beach. They waved us over. One of the men was a river engineer and he had brought for us a graph of the river, showing the average gradient for each section of the river between each of the *prayags* and Rishikesh. My jubilation began to fade, for the graph made chilling viewing. The section we were now in, with its lively rapids, was almost flat compared with the ever-steeper gradients ahead. The landmarks of our journey from now on were these five *prayags*: the first was Deoprayag, and the second, Rudraprayag, the setting of Jim's nightmare; the third, fourth and fifth were Karnaprayag, Nandaprayag, and Vishnuprayag. The gradient on which we were now travelling was a mere nine feet per mile, increasing to fifteen feet per mile up to Rudraprayag, then twenty-two, thirty-seven, and a final terrifying rise to sixty-two feet per mile on the final stretch between Nandaprayag and Vishnuprayag. This last section was the one described in the Recce Report as consistently rough, though even here Jim and Murray had shown a qualified optimism. Above Vishnuprayag Jim had described the river as impossible – and if there was one thing we could accept with absolute certainty it was his description of the river beyond that last *prayag*. "Could I have a copy of the gradient map?" I asked. Without a moment's hesitation the engineer tore the map out of his very official-looking book, and handed it across to us.

In a more sombre mood we drove on. It was the pattern of our moods for the whole of our journey up the gorge, swinging between wild optimism after surmounting a difficult rapid, and back into pessimism at each setback.

We drove on up the gorge, gloomy now, for the sun had left us. A few miles on, the roar of rough water swelled again in our ears and we rounded the corner to see a most horrifying-looking rapid ahead. My heart sank. What a blow to our pride if we were stopped here, before

even the first of the *prayags!* After running ashore, I walked and
clambered up the bank, inspecting the rapid while Michael nosed *Kiwi*
up the other side. I have never tried driving really big water myself,
but by now I knew roughly where a boat might go. Rapids come in
all shapes and sizes, but all have basic features in common. They can
be formed by the river dropping over a ledge of hard rock and, if
more than a few feet high, they form impossible waterfalls. In Ganga
so far we were facing boulder rapids, often formed by a side-stream
carrying down boulders from the hills. Above the low dam thus
formed, the river banks up into a deep, smooth pool before pouring
over the lip. It does this in the form of a fast, smooth V, called the
tongue of the rapid, and a boat of sufficient power usually has little
difficulty in climbing the tongue, once on it, except when it is unusually
steep. The difficulty is to reach it, for the arms of the V enclosing the
tongue are formed by diagonal waves or "stoppers", that curl and crash
back on the lower edges of the smooth water. Often the worst moment
in driving a rapid is in the attempt to cut across these diagonal waves
on to the smooth fast water beyond, for the boat's bow can knife in
and be tossed violently downstream; or worse still, as the bow drops
on to the tongue, it can bite deep into the wave or tongue, and the
pressure of water on the foredeck flip the boat end-over-end. Jet boats
rarely capsize sideways, most sinkings being of the end-over-end
variety.

Below the V of the tongue, the pressure crumples the water's
surface into big standing waves across the line of flow. River waves
are quite different from ocean waves, which move onwards while the
water in them stands still; in a river the waves stand still with the water
flowing through them downstream. Usually these waves do not stretch
from side to side, and one can creep up beside them, close to one bank
or the other in slow, relatively flat water, and then it is only the leap
on to the tongue which presents difficulties. But big rivers can throw
in all sorts of obstacles to force the driver out from the shelter of the
bank into the big waves: boulders near the bank, or bends in the river
which cause the central waves to crash first against one bank then the
other—these will force the driver to cross the trough between two
waves in the hope that he will find smooth water on the far side. A
steep drop between confined banks may spread big waves from side to
side and then the driver is forced to negotiate them. The technique
here is not to attack the waves too violently, but rather to ease over
them, waiting for the best moment to move down into the trough
beyond. For although the wave is stationary, it changes all the time:
now lower, now higher, now breaking upriver, now easing to leave a

gentler slope down which the driver can attempt his move. For the danger is that, while the stern of the boat is still held high by the waves behind, the depressed bow will plunge into the wave ahead and a wall of water will swamp and sink the boat. This is exactly what happened to Jim in the Arun during our 1967 expedition in Nepal and, as this was his first time in big water since then, he was ill at ease for the first few days.

Another type of water is the unpredictable turbulence that can form where water has no room to make a regular "tongue and wave" pattern. A bluff protruding into a rapid can cause this turbulence, as can extreme pressure through a narrow gap. The water level can rise and fall abruptly, now suddenly draining away down a deep hole that seems to reach the bed of the river itself, now welling up as boils of firm water on which a boat can move easily. In foaming water, which is full of air, or when driving across a hole, the jet unit sucks as much air as water, losing power; whereas on boils of hard water with no air, the boat maintains full power, a matter of critical importance where a move is marginal.

The simplest rapids are straight ones, with an initial tongue raising waves which can be avoided by a route close to the bank; though even with such "simple" rapids, too abrupt a fall can throw up violent diagonal curlers which can prevent a boat's passage. Some rapids are far from simple, however, and ring in a combination of boulders and twisting courses and big waves which have the driver struggling desperately, even before the tongue is reached. Some rivers throw rapids so close together that there is scarcely time to pause for breath after one before entering the next. Usually, however, there is some semblance of calmer water where boats can hover or even beach after not more than a hundred yards of wild confusion.

Route-finding is just as important as on a mountain, and in a big rapid the driver will carefully plan his moves and his course from the bank. Needless to say these moves are more difficult to make, in the right order at the right time, when you are actually in the midst of great hills of heaving water and hungry holes. And indeed, when you are actually in the maelstrom it takes a cool mind to remember and follow the chosen course, no matter how exhaustively it has been researched from the stable vantage-point of the bank.

The difference between an expert and a less expert driver is partly experience, partly innate ability. Experience teaches that you can hover on difficult waves, keeping the boat stationary while looking carefully around to find the direction and timing of the next move (for the water boils up and down, changing constantly). Speed of reaction in a dangerous situation is a critical factor, and again depends partly on experience, partly on one's basic physiology. When a boat lurches suddenly, or a wave drops away beneath you, or your boat hits a fast tongue at an awkward angle and is thrown violently, or if the bow plunges beneath a wave and the boat fills and the motor cuts—in these situations the speed of your corrective movements, countering the swerve or restarting a swamped motor, makes the difference between saving the boat and sinking.

Jon was superb on all counts. His reactions were fast, and he had behind him probably more experience in big water than anyone else in the world. I particularly remember one occasion in Nepal when he hit a very steep tongue at a bad angle. The boat was swung round too far for a normal correction, and seemed doomed to crash into the monstrous waves below; but without a moment's hesitation Jon went with the deflection, swinging the boat right round 360 degrees, quickly enough to claw his way back up the tongue before he was swept into the wave.

Mike Hamilton, with nothing like the same depth of experience in big water, was none the less very much at home in his boat, and seemed to make the right moves instinctively and very quickly. It was hard to know what was going on in Mike's mind, for he seldom talked about a rapid either before or after the event. He just drove straight in and did it. As Prem wrote in his diary, "He is a young man of few words. Bragging is not in his nature."

Jim alone, with whom I mostly travelled in this white-water section, had worry writ large across his features during those first three days in the gorge, for he had less experience than the other two by a long way, and the memory of his sinking in the Arun was still strong. He was tense, as I had not seen him before, and his temper flared quickly. He was a person quite different from the easy-going Jim I was used to. But he seemed to have in good measure either a blind folly or a raw courage with which he hurled himself into desperate-looking situations, and with this he combined strong and rapid reflexes by means of which, often in nerve-rackingly dramatic fashion, he battled his way out again. And as we progressed upriver, though the rapids became rougher and rougher, his confidence grew, his mood relaxed, and he drove with a skill and mastery that matched those of the other two.

We camped on a beach of white sand at the foot of the rapid. The sand was fine and smooth, unmarked by man or beast. I thought we had achieved the impossible—a camp entirely separate from the rest of mankind—but then I saw across the river, high up on the forested slope, the winding line of the road with people crowded on it, gazing down at us. It didn't matter. We pitched our bright tents on the white sand and soon had a fire flaming and crackling in the gathering darkness. Pemma bustled about, cooking the evening meal; Mike Dillon cleaned his camera; Jim was writing; Jon and Mike were checking the boats. And then, as the night turned black, a lovely full moon sailed into the gap between the hills so high above us, casting its pale light on the sand and on the leaping waters of the rapid, which we called Moonlight.

I woke early to a fine clear morning. As we let the sun dry the dew from our tents, we discussed how best to run Moonlight, eventually agreeing to run the rough upper section of the rapid unladen. Mike Gill assured us we were worrying about nothing: he'd just checked the Wilson-Jones Recce Report, which described the section of river between Rishikesh and Deoprayag in the following words: "We had a good view of the river all the way, and though we saw this stretch only once, we are both sure there is no difficulty—a broad flow in confining, but not sheer, banks."

Amidst the derisory comments that followed, Jim leaped to his feet, seizing the Recce Report from Mike's hand. "Bastards," he said, "the lot of you. You're quoting me out of context. Why didn't you read this bit? Page 8: 'Remember we were seeing the river from a moving bus at variable heights above the river.'" Murray, too, leaped to the defence of the Report. "And how much did Ed pay for it? Fifteen hundred dollars. Fifteen hundred miserable bloody dollars! I tell you, you pays the cheap price and you gets the cheap job." I could see ahead of us, over the next few days, many hours of interesting discussion on the contents of the Recce Report.

We struck camp and loaded up the boats. The first part of our plan went easily enough. We raced up in foaming waters under cliffs on our right to a beach about one-third of the way up the rapid. While the rest of the party set off up the boulders along the bank of the river, six of us prepared the jet boats for the upriver run: Jon with Mohan Kohli in *Air India*: Mike and B.B. in *Kiwi*; and Jim with me in *Ganga*.

We fitted the white nylon spray-covers protecting the rear half of the boat so that, even if a wave washed over us, most of the water would be shed. Jon led off up the right bank, only to find the way forward blocked by choppy cross-waves and rocks, and a very nasty cut-over on to the tongue. Returning to where we were milling around, he shot off across-river in the trough between two giant waves. It looked easy.

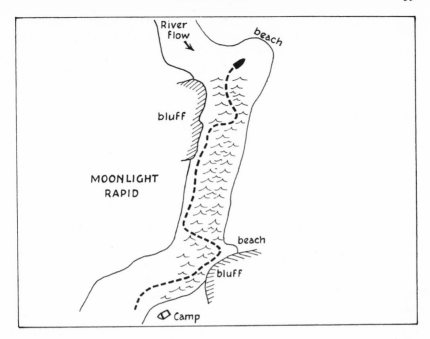

Jim and I followed, sidling across gently. Halfway over, Jim eased his foot off the throttle, and to our horror the motor cut. Immediately the boat settled off the plane, and the current seized us. At a crazy angle, side on, the boat swept down-stream up the face of the wave below, throwing Jim heavily on top of me (like fools we were both standing). For an awful moment we teetered on the crest of the wave, then down we crashed, dropping a good six feet into the hollow below, with a swish of water washing across the newly buttoned-down spray-covers. Jim scrambled for the starter button. The motor roared into life on the instant and we scuttled ahead into calm water under the left bank. A bad start, I felt.

Jon led ahead up a narrow foaming alley between huge pressure waves on our right and a cliff forming the bank on our left. A rock forced him briefly out into the waves, but then he was back again on to the steep, fast-moving slope of water. The bow rose sharply as the boat jumped up a fall between two rocks, and then Jon was cutting across on to the tongue in the centre of the river with Mohan's red turban showing only intermittently above the crests of the waves.

Then it was our turn. Jim handled it magnificently—the only thing that stopped me slapping him hard on the back in congratulation was the thought that he might slip off the throttle again and cut the motor.

Michael followed with the sort of firm decisive run we were coming to expect from him. It was all much easier than I had dared to hope.

Although we still had a couple of hundred yards of rapid to run, it was easy now, and we loaded up with the gear and the other nine men standing on the bank, the film crew delighted with the footage they had just shot. Jim had his engine cut once more, fortunately not in a bad place; after Michael had adjusted the idling, the problem occurred no more.

For half an hour we had an excellent run, with only minor riffles to contend with. White wakes creaming, we drove on up the deep V of the gorge with soaring sides heavily bush-clad, and here and there the houses of hill people tucked on to a terrace. At one point we passed a lovely well-kept temple, with a crowd in front waving cheerfully as we swept past.

Suddenly, ahead of us on a bend, we saw a figure waving wildly at us. At first I thought it was a *sadhu* performing some extraordinary austerity, but it turned out to be Max Pearl waving us ashore to warn of a substantial rapid ahead. Max had been travelling by road on this stretch, for our numbers had to be kept to five per boat. With him was Jon's wife, Joyce, who had joined the road party the day before.

"It's a bad one, Jon," she said, advice not to be treated too casually,

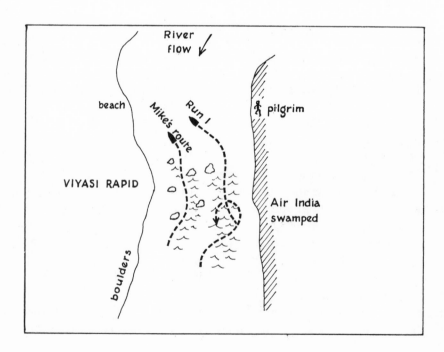

raycovers firmly fastened, we face the rapids above Rishikesh.

Going up The Chute, the sternest test of boats and drivers.

for she had been with Jon on many of his river trips and understood white water. There was a crowd waiting beside the rapid, for the road and a small village were nearby. We called the rapid Viyasi, the name of the village.

While the film crew got themselves set up on the bank, always a lengthy procedure, Jon drove into the rapid for a closer look. A big fan of boulders came in from the left, forcing the river round a wide arc, with the main flow of current on our right, but still with water dropping down through boulders on the left. With a full load of five people and gear, Jon worked his way up the main flow alongside the line of waves.

The jump across to the tongue was a nasty one, but in his usual masterly fashion Jon timed his move perfectly, across a ramp of smooth boils with holes on either side, and on to the tongue. To watch the movement of the boat one would have thought he was on calm water. In the pool above, he unloaded people and gear before returning to where Jim and Michael were hovering below. No need to unload boats, we decided, though in order to even weights Murray and Waka moved into Jon's empty front seat.

When he moved into the rapid the second time he seemed slightly right of his original line. He approached the jump across to the tongue. But this time the water was different. We saw the bow drop and bury itself in the wave ahead. The boat seemed to skid sideways into a hole. And then it disappeared from view entirely, with nothing to mark the spot but foaming white water spraying into the air from the jet unit still driving on under water. We stared, numbed and unbelieving, certain that the boat had gone, but incredulous that this could happen to the master. A long, long, couple of seconds later *Air India* lurched to the surface, now facing down-stream, having turned through 180 degrees while under water. The boat wallowed heavily through the waves with Waka and Murray floating around the cockpit, Jon still sitting down looking completely in control, or as much as anyone could in a semi-submerged boat with water up to his waist. Amazingly, the motor started again and *Air India* limped out of the tail-race of the rapid across to a sandy landing-spot. "Oh dear," said Jon. "I really should have waited."

We unloaded and pumped the boat out. There was damage high on the front left side where the deck had separated from the hull — there must have been a terrific crushing effect from the water. Jon found the engine-oil level above normal, and brown; so he and Michael set to work changing the oil. Max and Joyce and a few hundred awed bystanders came over to watch the emptying-out process.

"I'm glad that happened," said Joyce quietly. "Jon was getting too cocky."

We were a bit demoralised at first, as we didn't expect things like this to happen to Jon. Moreover, this was our fifth major rapid since Rishikesh, whereas the Recce Report had mentioned none. ". . . We are both sure there is no difficulty—a broad flow in confining, but not sheer, banks . . ." Quotations from the Report were a source of merriment to all except Murray and Jim, who suddenly didn't seem anxious to share their copy of the Report any more.

By the time *Air India* was O.K. again we had packed all the gear to the top of the rapid. With light boats and only the drivers on board the latter had very little difficulty coming through a route on the left which I had noticed earlier on—slower water between boulders, with an exit by way of a small green tongue.

We reloaded the boats. And then, in that mysterious and comforting way to which we were now accustomed, one of B.B.'s relations appeared with hot *puris* and bean curry. We were happily munching these when someone drew our attention to a small bundle of rags lying on a ledge jutting out from the steep wall forming the far bank of the river. Jim and B.B. drove across in *Ganga*. As they approached, the rags moved, and with difficulty sat up, being inhabited by a very old pilgrim in the last stages of starvation. He had fallen from a track high above and, being unable to climb back up, had made his way down to the river. Trapped, he had remained there without food (though certainly with plenty of water) for two weeks. He was very weak, and B.B. had to carry him to the boat and up the far bank, where we left him in the care of the villagers. A moving though minor incident for us, but to him it must have been a miracle beyond his wildest imaginings to be thus rescued, having abandoned hope, by strange men driving an even stranger craft. Truly, Mother Ganga looks after her devotees in strange ways.

We drove on at good speed, still in the beautiful gorge, in water fast and deep but with little turbulence. The miles dropped behind as we admired the tall forests and the road high above, carved from the living rock and crowded with people at vantage points; spidery wire bridges hung from side to side and twice we saw packs of monkeys swarming across them and gibbering at us as we drove beneath. Here and there, pockets of houses and fields appeared with people watching, wondering no doubt what all the noise was about.

Suddenly, I caught a glimpse ahead of an ancient temple surmounted by a golden spire shining in the sun. As we rounded the corner I saw, below the temple, whitewashed houses clustered together, piled one on top of the other on the steep sides of a prow of rock jutting towards us. Two rivers mingled at the confluence, their troubled waters gleaming like gun-metal. They formed the arms of a Y-shaped junction: on our left was Bhagirathi, whilst the larger Alaknanda emerged from a sunless gorge on our right. We had reached Deoprayag.

My brief moment of elation was tempered by the realities of the situation. The two Mikes insisted on being put ashore a quarter of a mile short of the town in order to film our arrival from a distance. Cameras and tripods were passed up the steep rock of the bank, while the boats hovered in fast water. As we waited for them to get set up I was able to see that Deoprayag was covered with people as well as houses, and my heart sank. My mind was totally occupied with forebodings about rapids ahead: a big welcome was the last thing I wanted. A shout came through to me, above the noise of the water and the roar of the boat engines, and looking up I saw Mike Dillon waving us forward. Moving together, we skimmed up the last quarter mile of Ganga, for it is here at the confluence that the river first takes its name.

We moored at the foot of the steps leading up the steep prow of rock—though I was aghast at the huge crowd piling up on the steps. A cheer went up as I stepped ashore, assisted by a dozen clutching hands. Before I knew what was happening, garlands were around my neck, a *tilak* was on my brow and I was into a *puja* with the local priest. After Prayag at Allahabad there is no holier place than this confluence, at which a pilgrim should bathe and do *puja*, but all I felt, distracted as I was by the boats banging and thumping in the turbulence below, was an overwhelming desire to escape. It was late, I was tired, and for the last few miles there had been nothing remotely resembling a camp-site.

The moment the priest had finished, I scrambled back into *Ganga*. Quickly I despatched Mingma and Pemma to find the truck and get food for our evening camp.

"Come on, Jim," I said. "We're going. Let's find ourselves a camp." And we shot off without bothering to tell the others what we were doing. *Kiwi* hovered uncertainly for a few minutes, wondering what was happening, while Jon went back to pick up the two Mikes. Finally *Kiwi* took off up the gorge, following *Ganga*, now well out of sight. Jon arrived back to find not a sign of anybody, and he too set off up the Alaknanda.

Jim and I drove on up in the gloom, with the gorge closing around us. Black walls of rock fell sheer into the water. I never saw a less hospitable place. The first miles fell away behind us as we kept going on, climbing small rapids and always hoping there'd be a good spot around the next corner. Suddenly we came to a big rapid in a narrow section, short but steep.

"I don't want to try that on my own," said Jim; so we waited for the others to catch up—*Kiwi* first, then *Air India*.

"Where are Mingma and Pemma?" I asked.

"I thought you had them," said Jon. Now in a thoroughly bad temper with myself and everyone else, I unloaded gear from *Ganga* before sending Jim back to Deoprayag on his own. Jon and Michael, lightly laden, successfully negotiated the rapid and, after loading up, carried on to find a camp-site.

Jim eventually returned but without Mingma and Pemma, who, thinking we had forgotten them, had hitched a ride with the truck. Joginder Singh and I were waiting for Jim on the left bank by the rapid, and explained the route to him. I already had a name for the rapid— Discord—a good description of the present mood of the party.

Discord was formed by the constriction of a bluff jutting into the river from our right, deflecting the current diagonally across to the left bank. It fell in a steep green tongue, crossed by strange flattish swells, before breaking into the usual lines of pressure waves.

"Be careful as you cross the waves," I said. "Jon shipped a bit of water on the way through. Ease up the far bank under the bluff and jump across on to the tongue. They came up very slowly and easily," I added encouragingly. "Jon said not the sort of place to make a bad mistake—but no trouble."

"Thanks," said Jim grimly. "That's just what I want to hear. It looks like the sort of place where I habitually make bad mistakes."

He crossed the waves very neatly and moved up in the lee of the bluff, eyeing the tongue sweeping past on his left. For a long time, looking worried, he watched and waited. Perhaps he was nervous from the wait, for when he moved he was travelling too fast and, after crossing the diagonal wave, knifed into the tongue at a bad angle. The bow spun left downstream and, though he was on the tongue, he was drifting under the first big curler. On full throttle he turned sharply back upstream, but counteracted too far, spinning right this time. Again he recovered, this time perfectly and with jet plume flying, he climbed the tongue to the pool above. I felt as relieved as if I'd driven it myself. Jim was not entirely unhappy with the experience, despite his spiral course, for no damage had been done. The power of the unladen boat and its ability to climb out of a bad place reassured him, and he had the confidence to tackle such rapids more slowly next time.

We hurried on to the camp which the others had already set up on a high dramatic terrace of white sand. Jim and I stepped ashore to a very cool reception. Even mild Max, who had come down a long steep slope from the road carrying food with Mingma and Pemma, was angry with us for shooting off and leaving the Sherpas behind. The other two boats, and especially the film crew, were dissatisfied with the gaps in communication which had been highlighted by Jim's and my misdemeanour. Mike Gill gave Jim a solid lecture and Ding gave me a firm discourse, too. Jim and I are not the world's best at meekly receiving such a telling off, though I was prepared to concede that we were partly to blame on this occasion. The incident and the anger were an accumulation of the difficulties and tensions that had developed over communication within our large group, plus the hassling circumstances of the crowds that pressed in on us at every major stopping-place. Jim and I went off and sulked a little together, in a tiny stream between huge sand-banks, and by the time we drifted back for Pemma's lemon tea our sins seemed to have been forgiven. It was difficult to remain ill-humoured in so beautiful a camp, and we talked over ways of improving our co-ordination.

We decided also to transfer Mingma and Pemma to the truck at our refuelling stop next day at Srinagar. Mingma's prayers, evening and morning, had, since the rapids began, increased markedly in length and intensity. Since the day of our sinking in the Arun, ten years earlier, jet boats had acquired in the Sherpa community a reputation for danger not exceeded even by the worst mountain faces of the Himalayas. At the time Jim's boat went down, one Sherpa, Ang Pasang, had been aboard. He couldn't swim—I have never met a Sherpa who can. His instructions were to stick with the boat at all costs, and so when it flipped upside down, Pasang, wedged behind the front seat, simply hung on tight. He admitted later that he decided, on the moment, that if this was jet boating he wanted no more of it, but meanwhile he was following instructions, sticking to the boat at all costs, even if it was upside down and under water. He was saved by Jim who dived down, dislodging him with one powerful heave and staying with him till Jon came to the rescue in the remaining boat. I decided that the Alaknanda was no place for two non-swimming Sherpas, despite the fact that their loyalty inhibited them from asking to be transferred to the truck. Max, travelling by road at present, had already said he would be delighted to join us, even though he too had been a passenger in the Arun sinking. At least he could swim.

I woke next morning to hear Mingma bargaining furiously for something which turned out to be a three-pound river trout caught beside our camp by one of the local hill people. Small though it was when divided between fifteen people, it was a welcome change from curried vegetables and *chapati*, particularly for Murray who, without protein, could feel strength ebbing from him day by day.

I expected the day's run to take us at least to Rudraprayag, a distance of about thirty miles. Not far ahead we would be refuelling near Srinagar, situated in the only flat valley of any size in the whole mountain region of Garwhal, and even that was only half a mile wide. Jon and Michael had repaired *Air India*, fibre-glassing the scratches and tears and returning it to almost its former glory.

Mike Gill gave us the daily reading from the Recce Report. "On the stretch from Deoprayag to Srinagar we are both sure there is no great difficulty. An even flow in a wide V 100 feet or so below the general level of the valley, then opening out into a broad shingle bed. From Srinagar to Rudraprayag is still quite O.K. Getting livelier, quite a few rapids, but none right across. Interesting but not difficult."

As a preview for the morrow he threw in a few snippets on the section above Rudraprayag. "Three miles above Rudraprayag there is a short gorge . . . at the upper end of the gorge there is a chute which I think is fairly tricky . . . this is a real problem, the first . . ."

We moved off upriver towards Srinagar over fast water in a steep-walled gorge, keeping in tight, disciplined formation for once. After a short while the valley opened out, as expected, and we drove up channels between coarse white shingle beaches. The water remained easy, the scenery superb, with green high hills set back from the river. Crowds of people waved from a bridge where the road crossed the river. It was a peaceful interlude under a hot sun, and we relaxed as we drove up safe and predictable shingle river-beds of the sort we knew so well.

Soon we were at the refuelling place where the truck was waiting for us, with Max and a thumping great crowd. Misinformation about our schedule was as rife as ever, and at this refuelling spot a *cha walla* (tea fellow) had been keeping his tea hot for two days, only to give up in disgust two hours before we arrived. The Bharat Petroleum people, who had taken over from Indian Oil in this mountain section, had waited faithfully on, but we put in little fuel, knowing we had only about twenty miles to go to Rudraprayag.

Max and Joyce had been watching a roadside acrobatic show while waiting for us. A tall pole had been hoisted and held upright, more or less, by tattered guy ropes tied to pegs driven insecurely into the dust. Two girls moved out, hitching the ends of their saris between their legs. After a few preliminary contortions, one girl took a gold ring from her finger. Building a small mound of dust on the ground she placed the ring on its edge, and then bent over backwards, her head between her ankles to pick up the ring, not in her teeth, but in her eye, held between her eyelids. Borrowing a second ring from a spectator, she stood it on a second heap of dust close to the first and repeated her act, this time picking up a ring in each eye. There followed acrobatics on the ropes, and the show was reaching its climax when suddenly shouts came up from the riverbank—"The boats have arrived! Sir Hillary is here!" The crowd vanished on the instant, rushing down to the riverbanks, leaving one girl still gyrating like a helicopter blade on top of the pole.

Max now joined us as planned, leaving Mingma and Pemma with the truck. We soon ran through the rest of the Srinagar plain, up straight stretches of fast, chuckling water between green banks. The sun was striking a sparkle off the tossing water as we ran on past goats and cows grazing, with young girls and boys herding them. It was an idyllic interlude in the increasingly tense battle with rapids.

We drove through a big S-bend with the current swirling under magnificent arching cliffs, and we entered once more a confined gorge. A number of minor rapids gave us no trouble. Jon was our detailed chronicler of rapids, and to those that stood out from the innumerable minor skiffs and raffles he gave the dignity of a number or, better, a name.

The eighth major rapid was called Kaliasaur. It looked tricky, a long tumbled affair, very fast and with a considerable total drop-off. We unloaded the gear and passengers, our plan being to film the lower third of the rapid, which looked the most difficult section, and reload for the other two-thirds. But again our co-ordination fell to pieces. Jon misinterpreted some hand gesture as a wave to start, and to the despair of our camera-men all three drivers cut quickly through the lower difficult part, and instead of stopping they raced up the easy central section, to disappear over the lip at the top. For a while we sat in the sun waiting, but no one came; so we picked up the loads and set off over a tricky bluff, clutching the rocks and grasping for holds as we traversed the more difficult parts. We reached more open water in the middle section, where again we waited for the jet boats, but still nothing happened. After a while we started clambering along the shoreline again—it was a long, long way under a hot sun. Peter, in front, nearly fell off his holds into the river when he heard a scuttling noise, like the sound of a snake, but it was only a two-foot long lizard.

Just before we reached the top of the rapid I was met by Jim Wilson, coming back to give a hand. I asked him in somewhat undiplomatic fashion why the boats hadn't come down for us. He sparked up and said the top rapid wasn't easy, and they didn't want to put the boats at risk.

"The exercise will do you good, anyway," he said, which was like pouring petrol on a fire.

As I laboured around the last steep corner in the stinking heat, Jon came dancing down the rapid in his boat with the greatest of ease, to pick up Mike Dillon with the big camera. In gloomy silence we watched him return just as easily.

We jolted on to rapid after rapid, with the gorge getting more spectacular. And then down a long narrow defile, far in the distance, we saw a small town, which could only be Rudraprayag, sitting on the steep point of junction between two rivers, the Mandakini on our left and the continuation of Alaknanda on our right. We raced up to the foot of the township, a spidery staircase climbing a steep rock blade and capped with a small temple. And I was horrified to see on our right the Alaknanda plunging down the most appalling rapid—certainly the worst section of river we had yet seen, and easily identifiable as the one in the nightmare picture on the bungalow wall at Rishikesh.

II

"You can go no further"

WE NOSED INTO THE RIGHT BANK OF THE POOL BELOW THE rapid, and securely tied our lines to the rocks. The leaping white water and the continual roar of the rapid combined to make an impressive and terrifying scene. There was no chance of crossing the river to the steps of Rudraprayag where people were gathered, for the rapid thundered past the sheer rock of the left bank, below the town, surging against its walls in white foam. Below, huge waves swept in a curve past the quiet green Mandakini slipping in from the left, crashed into a cliff and raced down the way we had come. I walked across for a close look and it didn't seem to get any easier. I thought I could see a possible line through, but it was a pretty fine one.

People were streaming down around me in their hundreds, and there were lots of Press people with clicking cameras and incessant questions. "Can you give me the precise moment and place you will camp tonight?" one of them asked.

I looked at him in amazement and anger and snapped out, "Until we get up that rapid I'm not sure we'll have boats and people to camp with." But he was a lot more confident than I was. "You will overcome it," he said, "even if your boats have to fly through."

We unloaded the three boats and securely lashed down their spray-covers. Jon, Michael and Jim spent a long time examining the rapid from the bank and I thought they were pretty quiet and subdued. Jim looked closely at the waves down-stream as well, trying to work out breathing-places, he said, for when he was swept down through the waves past the Mandakini corner—an outcome he regarded as nearly inevitable.

The right bank on which we stood was formed of boulders shelving into the rapid and, though the boats could go part way in the slower water between these boulders, there was a step which must, they thought, force the boats into the terrible turbulence of the main rapid. From there they planned to move back right, above the step, to a flatter but very fast and foaming section, and to creep under a huge

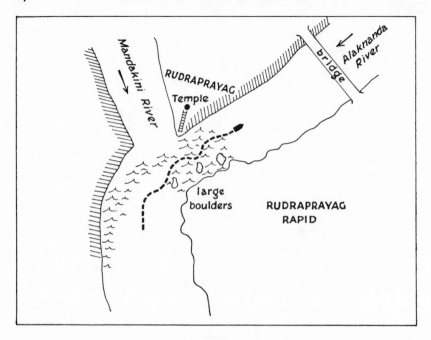

green diagonal curler with a crest that broke and re-formed continuously. Then they would have to cross the stopper to get on to the incredible tongue, which was short and steep, and crossed with large moving swells.

The camera crew seemed to take an age to get into position. The three drivers skulked around in the boats, waiting. I was still being harassed by the Press and giving them a pretty energetic brush-off. I felt quite claustrophobic in the depths of this thundering gorge, with people pushing in all around, and I had that old familiar gripping feeling in the pit of my stomach. This was a place where we could lose a boat—or a man—and the tension was building up inside me.

Finally the camera crew gave their wave, and Jon headed into the rapid. He paused carefully at the foot of the step, and here luck was with us, for a curious narrow bridge of water, boiling but solid, led across the hole below the step and up on to the foaming plateau above. He eased across this and under the diagonal curler, its green overhanging crest seeming almost to touch his left shoulder. For a long time the boat hovered on the hurtling water while Jon looked carefully ahead at the big stopper guarding the tongue. And then, with a look of utter commitment, he sank into his seat and the engine note rose higher as he moved forward. Across to the stopper he went, and there he seemed to hover at full power, with the bow pointing heavenward as if in supplication. For a moment I thought he was slipping back into the trough below, but then he stood up to give weight forward, and the bow dipped over into the hollow and on to the tongue. The boat hesitated a moment with engine screaming, then climbed triumphantly into the pool above. It was a masterly run. A roar of applause went up from the crowd and Jon raised one arm in acknowledgment.

Jim circled around below, waiting for his wave from the cameramen and obviously very tense. "At moments like that my gut knows I am terrified," records his diary, "but my mind thrusts the gut-knowledge under and concentrates on selling my life dearly." Finally he got his wave. He eased across the slanting bridge and on to the fast, flat section. Now came the tricky piece. Hardly daring to look at the diagonal green curler over his left shoulder, he inched across under it. Then he was hanging on the stopper as Jon had done, bow lifted high on full power, desperately trying to ease over the crest. He hung there for half a lifetime, it seemed, and then he stood and leaned forward as Jon had done, and again the boat eased over. But the descent into the trough beyond was too violent and the bow struck at an angle. The boat slewed heavily right, throwing Jim against the windscreen. The noise of the engine stopped and I knew his foot had been thrown from the accelerator. Without power *Ganga* drifted down towards the gaping hole at the foot of the tongue. Jim seemed headed for certain disaster. But I had reckoned without his reflexes, for in a flash he was back on the accelerator, the floorboards bending as he jammed his foot hard down. The boat responded just in time, swinging upstream with the curl of a wave poised over its stern as Jim clawed his way out of the hole. And then the angle eased and in a surge of power he shot into the pool where Jon was waiting.

Another roar went up from the crowd, and for a moment I felt relief as the tension eased. But then it was *Kiwi*'s turn. Michael didn't hesitate. He plunged in, handled the stopper without a hitch or hesitation and surged over the top in a magnificent run.

"He's a real cool kid!" said Murray, his features lit up with pleasure and relief.

I climbed wearily to my feet, for it had been hard on me as well as on the drivers. They were all safely through and I felt surprise as well as relief—I'd really expected trouble here.

Still harassed by an excited Press and a stimulated mob of onlookers, we lugged hefty loads up the bank and down some tricky rocks to the refuelling spot in a lovely little natural harbour with a narrow entrance guarded by rocks. But a huge group was gathered round it. My only wish was to get away from the Press and the crowd, and so Jim, Joginder and I went upriver to find a camp-site while the other two boats refuelled. Good sites weren't easy to come by, but in the end we found a small flat spot on the precipitous side of the gorge. We took some firewood from a woodman's pile across the river, leaving ten rupees in payment. Jim went back to refuel *Ganga*. Left there with my gear and tent, I felt subdued and deflated, with a feeling of anticlimax.

Jim arrived back at the refuelling spot and to the others issued the instructions to "proceed for three to four kilometres upstream; to observe one only *Bara Sahib* sitting on the banks of the Alaknanda, all alone, with one only Sears tent pitched beside him". The boats duly arrived, and we set up the rest of the tents. We were all over-stimulated or exhausted, and so we broke out a bottle of gin to go with an excellent stew of curried mutton. Mohan and Joginder, amidst the lively clinking of mugs and bottles, proved themselves the story-tellers of the trip, and much loud and raucous laughter rose from the camp up the steep faces of the gorge to the starry sky and near-full moon.

We slept well and rose late. Jon and Michael drained some water from one of the sealed buoyancy chambers of *Air India*. Mingma, Jim and I went across the river to check that the woodman was happy with our deal in his absence the previous evening. Yes, he had found the money, he told us, and was very happy, but we would have been welcome to the wood anyway; we needn't have paid.

After a relaxed breakfast we packed the boats and made preparations for departure. No one seemed anxious to move, for we knew we had a hard day ahead. Mike refrained from reading the Recce Report, for its description of the piece of river above was known to us all. It was the first patch of rough water that looked bad enough to make Murray and Jim, travelling by bus, get out and inspect it on foot. The river suddenly narrowed, to pour in a fall of white water through a gap only twenty feet wide. For half a mile it flowed calmly in the same narrow slit between sheer cliffs two hundred feet high, before emerging down a similar but easier fall into the wider river-bed below. It was, they said, "a real problem, the first" — words to strike terror into the hearts of those of us who by now had broken the code and could translate the language in which the Report had been written. The upper fall had always been referred to as The Chute. The lower one had a local name, Kakar Bhali, meaning Deer's Leap. As always there were several explanations for the name. Some said that barking deer could be seen leaping the gap from time to time, but a *sadhu* living in a cave nearby had said that the deer was none other than Lord Shiva in disguise, and his leap was described in the *Mahabharat*.

Although we had accurate descriptions from Jim and Murray of both The Chute and Deer's Leap, we were still uncertain how they might look in the high water of September, for the Recce had been in May at the end of the dry season. The night before, local advice had ranged from "No trouble at all" to "The worst spot on the river". One man solemnly assured us that Deer's Leap was only six feet wide and was quite impossible (except for barking deer) – he'd been there that day and had come straight to tell us.

We set off upriver in choppy water with short violent rapids for a couple of kilometres. Very shortly we swung round the corner and there, unmistakably, was the entrance slit to the gorge. I was pleased to see that portaging would be no problem, for the gorge opened into a small pool, and it was the narrow exit below this which formed the rapid. It was more like twenty feet than six, but was impressive none the less, with the full river foaming through it. It didn't look easy, but not bad enough to stop us, either.

We off-loaded all the gear and carried it over some high broken rocks to the edge of the pool above the rapid. Little steps led up from the water's edge to a small Shiva shrine in a cave where the old *sadhu* lived, and a short way beyond we could see the walls and roof of an *ashram* half hidden by trees. The sun beat down into the gorge; turquoise butterflies were massing on the steps and fluttering about. An idyllic scene. It was a pity about The Chute.

Joyce was watching our progress from the road, a thousand feet above us and about half a mile distant. There were thousands of people watching and waiting: pilgrims and *sadhus*, peasants and businessmen, women with babies on their backs and children at their heels. They hung around patiently with that curious capacity Indian people have to stand or squat for hours, untroubled by the passage of time, waiting for something to happen, if only for night to fall. At last, on the river one thousand feet below, the boats appeared and pulled in behind a low ridge of rock below Deer's Leap. As the crew leaped ashore and tied up the boats, the crowd, which had watched their approach with bated breath, relaxed again. They waited. The tiny figures below crawled about over the rocks. What were they doing? Why did it take so long? The children grew restless. The women scolded.

Then a boat edged out of the pool and nosed up into the boiling white water below the rapid. Silence descended over the watchers. A second boat moved out, downstream from the first, and stood poised, waiting. And then the first moved forward cautiously, and hovered,

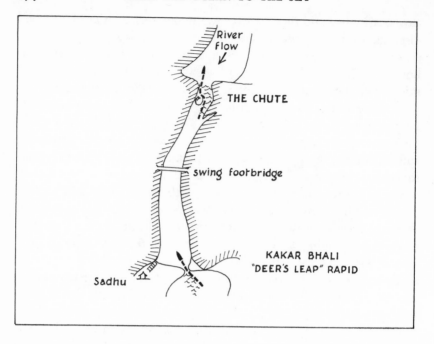

swinging gently like a kite in the fierce current. For a long minute it paused. Then suddenly it darted forward into the full force of the descending water, faltered briefly, then leaped forward over the crest into the blue water above. *Air India* was up.

The cheering and clapping of the watchers died to silence as the second boat, *Ganga*, launched herself at the rapid and it too roared up and over the top. By the time *Kiwi* entered the fray, a large section of the crowd was chanting wildly, a rhythmic repetitive stirring chant which broke up into cheers and shouts of triumph as *Kiwi* joined the other two boats above the rapid. The chant was no less than the Garhwali battle-cry—*Jai Badri Vishalji!*—Victory God Supreme!

When the boats left Deer's Leap and vanished into the gorge above, the crowd took off. They scrambled on to the road and ran. They went three on one bicycle. The bus staggered off, bulging with passengers. A river of people flowed up the valley, spilling down the hillside half a mile on, where a track led to The Chute.

Down on the river, the three boats moved together up the sunless chasm of the gorge, its walls sheer and polished smooth by floods. The sky was a slit of blue above. The thunder of falling water ahead grew louder, and there was spray in the air. We came around a corner and there was The Chute—a plunging white torrent, short but steep, forcing its way through the gap between two cliffs. The rock formation was like the diversion canal of a dam, for the river above The Chute widened abruptly and its level was six feet higher than ours. Between us and that haven of flat water beyond, the whole flow and force of the river funnelled down at an angle, to rebound off the left-hand rock wall and corkscrew down a series of violently-changing waves, holes and cross-currents.

It was the impermanence of the water pattern that impressed me above all else—and it was this that made the passage of the rapid possible. For at one moment the central turbulence would empty down a great hole as if a plug had been pulled out, and at this time the rapid was not only impossible but exceedingly dangerous. Seconds later the water would well up in hard boils, providing an almost easy ramp to the pool above. It certainly looked possible, though I knew I would have no hope of driving in such a place myself.

Fifty feet below the rapid, we found a slanting crack in the wall of the gorge and up this we hauled our loads. The three drivers went to have a look at The Chute from the bank, at close range, and Peter, Ding and I took over the boats, for there was no place where they could be moored. It was an impressive experience, just holding the boats in the fast-flowing stream, with the foaming Chute above. Peter and I did a run down the gorge and back again, and we could feel the power of the water sucking and surging in the restricted space. When the drivers returned we disembarked and fervently wished them good luck.

Jon went first. He paused on the last stable boil before the worst of the rapid started, huge waves to his right; then like lightning he saw his chance, dashed out centre, and was up relatively easily. The crowd cheered and shouted; the boats were performing miracles, just as they had hoped. Waka and Murray, who were perhaps disappointed at not getting something more spectacular for their cameras, used their rock-climbing ability to climb down to the water's edge on either side of the gap at the lip of the rapid.

Now it was Jim's turn. The whole place was so small and confined that none of us was more than thirty feet from him as he took his place on the boils, and we could see his brow creased with anxiety. The crowd fell silent as he waited, minute by minute watching the movements of the water as it swelled or drained away. There was no regular rhythm to the pattern that I could see, for it seemed to fill and drain by some capricious whim all its own. Sometimes the ramp of easy boils was well sustained; sometimes it seemed to fall away almost immediately.

Suddenly Jim sat down. The engine roared and he made his break. He was a fraction late, and the water was subsiding beneath him as he hit the hard green lip of the fall. He was thrown hard left, but at least he was on the tongue and not in the holes below. He gunned the engine hard as he steered right to correct, and a plume of water blasted out of the jet unit straight into Waka who was filming on the right bank. As the bow turned upstream, the stern swung round hard and fast. The boat was right against the rocks of the left bank and I flinched as the stern spun across, for it seemed certain it would smash into the cliff and wipe off the jet unit. It missed by inches, but the jet plume lined up perfectly on Murray, who received a 240-horse-power column of water at a distance of three feet, spinning him sideways and bringing laughter into the sounds of cheering and applause as Jim cruised off into the wide open water above The Chute.

"Oh! Yes!" said Prem standing on the bank. "Jim is quite an actor. He has put in those sweeps for the newspapers and cameras!"

"This rapid is too desperate for play-acting," said Mohan softly. Never a truer word did he say.

Michael followed, in the dangerous position of last boat up. To sink in The Chute would be worse than in any other rapid so far, for to descend it in a jet boat in order to rescue someone would be very difficult indeed, and the tumbling reversed flow below the main drop could recycle a man in a life-jacket down and back again, revolving him until he drowned. Unlike Jim's, Michael's face was quite expressionless as he moved on to the take-off boils to time his run. But when he went, he followed Jim's pattern, knifing and losing the throttle as he did so, but recovering to swing his stern close past the same cliffs.

The crowd went wild, and I must have looked pleased myself, for Ding wrote in his diary, "Ed was almost ecstatic. Oblivious to the crowd for the first time, he let out a loud yippee! His face was lit up with a grin of relief and triumph." I felt relief as much as anything else, for The Chute had been in my mind all the way; and as for Jim, he had lived with the thought of it for two years and four months, ever since he first saw it during the Recce of 1975. Even if we were brought to a halt no more than a mile further on, I felt we could retreat with honour, for the rapids of Rudraprayag had tested the boats and our three drivers as close to their limits as I wished to see them.

We reloaded the boats and headed on through really big water — one rapid running into another, but we were handling them with increasing skill and confidence, drifting across the face of big waves to find easier

Filming at the rapids above The Chute.

Turban ceremony at Nandaprayag. In moments of stress Mohan tied his on with a bit of string.

Mingma pays off the porters at Base Camp.

water on the other side, or hovering carefully on the diagonals below tongues until the hole filled a little or the angle eased. It was fine jet boating, full of challenge. In three hours we did only ten miles, battling every inch of the way.

Then we came to another monstrous rapid. I knew we were all too tired to tackle this, and so I called a halt. Mingma and Pemma climbed down to us from the truck on the road some hundreds of feet above, and with them we drove back a mile to a beautiful camp-site—a gentle sandy beach with grass and trees behind.

We pitched our tents and made ourselves comfortable, as Pemma and Mingma got to work producing an excellent meal. I was very tired and so were most of the others. As Jim and I were dragging ourselves slowly across the sand for dinner, we came up with Jon shuffling in the same direction, knees sagging with tiredness. I think he'd emerged from his tent in that bent position and just didn't have the energy to bother to straighten up.

I was worried about our progress and the difficulties ahead. The river seemed never to let up and the pressure on drivers and passengers alike was constant. To make matters worse, we'd just had an unwelcome reminder of the killer reputation of the Alaknanda—while ashore at the big rapid just above, we had found part of a battered orange crash helmet, presumably from one of the two Czech canoeists drowned a month earlier. I was becoming more and more sure that the only way we could keep going safely in this big water was to reduce the loading on the boats. I worked out a changed plan before darkness set in. Just then Peter came over to see me.

"What's the score? When can Murray and I head off up-valley to do a recce on the mountains around Badrinath?" I was pleased to be able to tell him they could leave the following night—pleased for my sake, too, for Peter and Murray were quite unable to understand that they might well be doing useful jobs even if they weren't the ones who were performing heroic deeds. It would be peaceful not to have them around for a while.

Jim wrote his weariness and anxiety into his diary: "I was glad we turned back from that rapid today, for I felt demoralised looking at it. I think I would have asked Jon or Michael to drive *Ganga* through for me if Ed had really wanted to go on. Maybe it's the hat of the drowned Czech canoeist. I don't normally think of drowning—and I still can't imagine how the Czechs drowned, both of them, if they were wearing life-jackets and could swim—yet in my weary state today beside the rapid, especially as I looked at the rocks just below the surface, I kept having morbid visions of the others pulling my drowned body ashore and wondering how to tell Ann. Aghast, they were. It's the thought of Ann and Steve and Guy and Mac that dominates my whole being at pessimistic moments like that, deepening the pessimism frighteningly.

"Already, thank goodness, I've recovered and believe again I'm undrownable—my belief confirmed by the many times I've failed to drown despite promising situations."

On Wednesday, September 28th, over an early breakfast, I discussed the change in plans, and everyone seemed to think it was the only course of action. Max, Peter and Murray would go on the truck with all our gear, thus lightening the loads considerably.

We set off up the river with Jon, Mohan and Mike Gill in *Air India*; Michael Hamilton, Waka, Joginder and Mike Dillon in *Kiwi*; and Jim, Ding and me in *Ganga*. Our only freight was the camera gear.

We drove up to what we called Czech Hat Rapid where we had stopped the night before and off-loaded passengers and cameras. It was a spectacular run. This time Michael took the lead. He came in tight on the right side, up roughish water on the very edge of big waves. A jump near the bottom, which had looked the worst of the rapid, went surprisingly easily under carefully controlled power, and then he was through on to a flattish boiling section. From this to a fast narrow central tongue where he hovered for a while, and then, with a swish, left, then right, to avoid boulders, he was through. It had been a great run. Jon, in calm control, made it look easy in slow motion.

Jim appeared at the foot of the rapid wearing Ding's orange climbing helmet, not for comic effect but because his nightmare visions of yesterday were still with him. But he did a near-perfect run and indeed from that time on he never faltered. The rapids of Rudraprayag marked the end of Jim's apprenticeship in big water, and for the rest of the river he drove like a veteran—a change lamented only by Mike Gill, who said sorrowfully that the film had been relying on Jim for spectacle, with the sinking of *Ganga* somewhere, he hoped, as a climax.

We reloaded the boats and as we carried on I could sense a feeling of confidence in the party. The ten miles to Karnaprayag was some of the most glorious jet boating I've ever done—huge rapids, but everyone in great form. With the lightened boats we surged through and around them in complete control, doing things we wouldn't ordinarily do. Though the rapids were big, we were going so well that we didn't off-load gear or passengers at any of them. Ding wrote in his diary: "Jesus, what a day! Ed came up with Plan 64b at breakfast, which was devised to lighten the boats. We carried the absolute minimum.

Chunderous rapid followed chunderous rapid in a blur, and slowly the rapids got steeper and more bony as the river cut deep into the beautiful granite hills—but there was scarcely time to notice the beauty. I soon had that constricting feeling in my gut, that grips and leaves one completely exhilarated and feeling brave when it's all over. Jim was driving masterfully, hovering on the brink of stoppers and slipping with minute precision between rocks and big breakers, applying the throttle exactly when needed. He sang the praises of the boats continually and, with each rapid overcome, Ed and I would cry out 'Incredible, Jim!' or 'Masterly!' and pound him on the back."

We covered the ten miles in only two hours and when we came round the corner and saw Karnaprayag we all cheered. It was the third of the five confluences and another exciting step forward.

Karnaprayag was typical of all the *prayags* in its steps, peepul trees, temples, steep hills and two rivers meeting below; but there were no tall prows of rock as at Rudra- and Deoprayag, for the valley was less austere here than lower down, with shingle banks replacing the high walls of the lower gorge. There was a very large and excited crowd, and a big burly Bharat Petroleum man was so carried away by the excitement that he made the error of misjudging my weight, and tried to lift me down from the deck of the boat. His knees buckled and he went down in a heap beneath me. But he struggled manfully up again and he and the drivers refuelled the boats while the rest of the group signed autographs—thickets of waving arms thrusting forward books, scraps of paper, rupee notes or even bits of driftwood—anything that could take the imprint of a signature. With the passage of Rudraprayag our star was in the ascendant, and there was nothing the people would not do to get close to us. Even the journalist from Calcutta who had been so scathing about the early part of our journey—describing it as an easy river cruise from which I would make money to retire on—was effusive in his praise. "Such bravery! Such skill!"

One old man approached Ding and, after placing a garland around his neck, said in halting English, "*Sahib*, you are a big man. These people are waiting two days. What is the difference between you and God?"

One Pressman sadly complained, "It is impossible to do anything. I cannot buy food. I cannot get my washing done. I cannot despatch my articles."

"Why?" said I, naïvely. And he looked at me in astonishment.

"Because of the jet boats, of course. All Garwhal is on holiday for a whole week. They have all been waiting for 'Ocean to Sky'."

Max and Joyce were there, scarcely able to believe the speed of our progress since Czech Hat Rapid, for the river had looked difficult even from the road. Wild rumours were circulating amongst the locals; they said that our boats could perform prodigious feats: they could jump twenty—no, thirty feet. More than that, said others, "They can fly!" As they drove into Karnaprayag just ahead of the boats, everyone was running down to the riverbank. Shops were left deserted. Food was thrown aside half-cooked. The post office was left empty, with the cash-box lying open on the counter. "No worry," they were saying. "Even the thieves have gone down to watch 'Ocean to Sky'!"

After a while the crush became so great that we took to the water and went a mile upstream to a pleasant shady spot where we had lunch. Rested, and refuelled, we set off on the twelve-mile journey to Nandaprayag. As a big river, the Pindar, had come in at Karnaprayag, it meant that the Alaknanda was now appreciably smaller in volume. We drove up through shingle river-bed at first, then increasingly through large boulders; shallows and rocks were our problem now, not huge waves. Jon was in his element, for he had cut his teeth on this sort of driving on the rivers beside his father's back-country sheep station in New Zealand. We raced on and on, constantly twisting and ducking amongst the boulders on some beautiful tight courses. And as we drove on, our spirits rose higher.

It was a fine afternoon with a bright sun. We were in pine forest now, with a tang of resin in the air. Kites and eagles wheeled and hovered in the intense blue sky. It seemed then that our dream was close to realisation; we had only to sweep on, up and up these rapids with their easy falls, and tomorrow we would reach the fifth con-fluence at Vishnuprayag.

But then gradually things got tougher again. Mike led a rough rapid, passengers still aboard, and for the first time he seemed tense. He went up into really big waves and was tossed around, to land clawing on the tongue. He poised there for a long time, on full power, wavering on very narrow fast water with big holes each side. Finally and slowly he crept up and over. We looked at each other, then landed and went up for a look on foot. Jon went off with an empty boat to try an alter-native route which tossed him on to the tongue of "Mike's Hover" from the opposite side, higher up. Jim followed Michael's route but, like Jon, with an empty boat, and though he was apprehensive, he made it up all right.

On we went, but the waves seemed to be getting bigger again. The river was narrowing between shingle banks, with tall pines crowding down the walls of the valley. The confined water was fast all the time;

the gradient on this last stretch to Nandprayag was now fifty feet per mile. Jon was leading in *Air India*, driving steadily without pulling ashore to look ahead, for no single rapid looked bad enough for that. Then a stretch of tall white water appeared, with big boulders forcing the boats away from the banks.

We watched Jon drive up the right bank. He moved slowly towards the main flow, looking for a route through the big standing wave we could see blocking his way forward on to the tongue. Suddenly the three of them, Jon, Mohan and Mike Gill, sat down as if seeing something they didn't like the look of. The boat turned across the line of the current into the centre of the river at the lower end of the tongue. We saw the bow swing upstream, but with the stern rising now, up the wave behind. And as *Air India* went forward, the bow bit deep into the tongue, and a wall of hard green water poured across the foredeck, breaking into a great flurry of white water over the windscreen as the boat disappeared from view.

We stared in blank disbelief. *Air India* had gone down. But then through the white water appeared a red turban, still tied to its owner, closely followed by the heads of Jon and Mike and the foredeck, heavily awash. They wallowed agonisingly through huge waves, with water washing into the cockpit as they rolled over each crest. It was only a matter of time before they sank. *Kiwi* and *Ganga* circled helplessly in calmer water, like mother whales watching the death-struggles of a wounded calf.

And then Jon did one of his miraculous saves. Somehow he got the motor started, and the boat limped out of the line of waves, gunwales awash. Then Mike Gill was over the side into knee-deep water, stumbling over the smooth boulders and pulling desperately at the bow-rope. In a moment we were beside him, heaving the boat ashore, just as the hull was settling on to the bottom of the river but with its nose on dry land.

Jon was his usual imperturbable self.

"Gill," he said, "did you think that wave was going to do that?"

"No," replied Mike, "I didn't."

"It was a great experience," said Mohan beaming. "I will never forget it."

"I feel you let me down there, Mohan. You can't have been saying your prayers properly," said Jon to Mohan, who each morning had stood in prayer on *Air India* before starting.

"That is absolutely not true, Jon," replied Mohan. "Only my prayers kept us afloat!"

We did some vigorous baling and checked the oil, and in fifteen minutes *Air India*, which was a remarkable boat, was ready to go again. We could see the houses of Nandaprayag ahead on our right, but our optimism had gone since the swamping—though I attributed that to over-tiredness more than anything else. A short distance back was a good camp-site amongst pine trees, and we drove down to it. It was a fine moonlit night as we sat around, with shadows cast by the fire dancing against the trunks of tall pines. Our euphoria of earlier in the day had evaporated and there were rumours of a bad rapid just around the corner. We'd heard such stories before, often enough to discount them, but it might be true. We consulted the Recce Report— "Just below Nandaprayag there is quite a rough-looking rapid."

"Is that the one we had trouble with today?" I asked.

Jim thought for a while. "I doubt whether it is. Murray and I saw that from at least a mile upstream, and the road was near the river-bed then—a hopeless angle to see it properly. I seem to remember it was wide and bouldery, with quite a drop, but we couldn't see the details at all. It could be anything."

It gave us something to think about as we retired to our sleeping-bags.

In the morning we ran Swamp Two, the rapid which had nearly finished *Air India*. Mike led, a fine crashing run through the really big waves with their treacherous breaking crests, some stretching almost right across the river. The boat was leaping violently and disappearing into troughs, but always it appeared again, eventually to sweep up the final tongue and to weave through the upper rocks.

Jim watched, horrified, as he waited his turn. "I hate those waves. I really hate them," he said. He climbed around the edges of the bottom big waves on the extreme right, almost ashore, to where a gentle flow came down a gap between two rocks. He stared long and hard, as if his yogic powers might cause the gap to widen. And then he moved through it with an inch to spare on either side. Thereafter, as Jon put it, he followed the damp smear on the bank left by Mike's wake. In fact this was a thin but adequate route, gently touching one underwater rock only, but to those watching from a distance, it looked as though Jim had abandoned the river and was driving the boat on dry land. Jon followed, glad to use what he called "the Old Man's route".

We drove on a quarter of a mile, uneasy at the swelling roar of white water ahead. On around a corner beneath a wooden footbridge where we were stopped in our tracks by what we saw. Right across the river was a vertical waterfall some ten feet high. It was completely impossible.

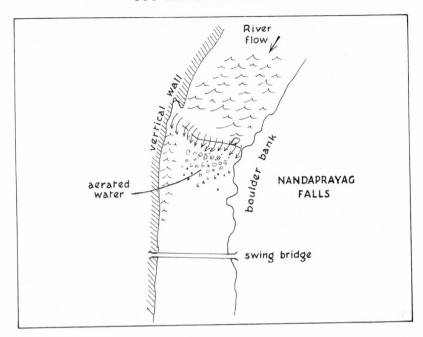

I felt as though I'd had a kick in the stomach. We had winching gear
with us and could no doubt have hauled the jet boats up one end of
the waterfall. But I couldn't really see the point. I remembered the
engineer's figures for the stretch ahead, which showed the river's
gradient twice as steep as that we'd just come through. I recalled the
words of the Recce Report which said, for the first time, that the river
above Nandaprayag was "rough" all the way. To drag the boats
overland around the hard bits would not be in the spirit of our journey.

We drove up to the face of the waterfall. What a place it was! The
whole river poured over some huge obstructing boulders, a vertical
wall of water. The area below was boiling and tossing, and even fifty
feet from the fall the boats had lost all grip in the white foam. It was an
awe-inspiring position, and in a way I was pleased at the absolute
finality with which the river had brought us to a halt.

But to some of our faithful friends on the bank it was not nearly so
obvious that the boats could not go on. Stories of our feats down-
river had grown with the telling, and many believed that nothing was
impossible for these wonder boats. We had to get used to being asked
"When will you attempt this rapid?" then, impatiently, "Why are
you not going on?" Even as we were nosing round below the fall,

Mike Gill was losing an argument about our boats with a riverside expert.

"When will your boats go up?" he enquired.

"They can't climb waterfalls," said Mike, mildly exasperated.

"Of course they can. Your boats can jump twenty feet."

"I assure you they can't," said Mike tersely.

"You are wrong," he said, almost pleading now. "I have seen them jump. With my own eyes I have seen them climb a rock wall." And there were almost tears in his eyes as he realised that we had no under-standing of the magic powers of our own boats.

That afternoon we drove the boats ten miles down-river to where three army trucks stood ready to take them back to Delhi. Mike led down in fine style. On the worst tongues, he faced upstream, backing down to ease slowly between awkward gaps. But for the most part they thundered through the big stuff, a wet and wild switchback ride. Jim clunked a rock in one rough rapid, but it took only a minor chip out of *Ganga*'s hull. It was a sad moment when the boats gave a couple of farewell sweeps across the river, then beached onshore, their journey over.

"Dear old *Ganga*!" said Jim. "The best boat I'll ever drive."

As I drove back to Nandaprayag I thought of what we'd done. We'd travelled 1,500 miles from Ganga Sagar, every inch of it on the water, and had reached to within forty miles of Vishnuprayag. In a way Ganga had said, "You can go no further!" And I had come to accept this decision. But it was difficult not to feel a sense of sadness. For six weeks we'd been living and adventuring with *Ganga*, *Air India* and *Kiwi*, and now those good days were behind us. Our jet-boat journey was finished. From here we would continue on foot into the mountains.

12

Advance on Foot

He who thinks of Himachal, though he may not behold it, is greater than he who performs all worship in Kashi. In a hundred ages of the gods, I could not tell thee of the glories of Himachal. As the dew is dried up by the morning sun, so are the sins of mankind by the sight of Himavat.

Skanda Purana

SO WE SET OFF WALKING. WE WERE A DIMINISHED PARTY, SIX of us, consisting of Jim, Ding, Mike Dillon and Mike Gill, Waka and me. B.B. drove ahead in the jeep to help Murray and Peter, who were being held up in Badrinath for lack of a permit to enter the mountains. I could picture their frustration, and what they were doing we feared to imagine. Max was flying to Nepal to visit our hospital- and school-aid projects there, leaving Mike Gill as medical officer. The Hamiltons were supervising the return of our boats to Delhi; and Jogi was returning in connection with the impending visit of the Governor of Hong Kong. Mingma had a nasty infection on his ankle and so was travelling by truck for the next few days, and Pemma with him. Mohan had also run out of time and was worried about his family, for there had been threats and actual violence against Indians in Australia from an extremist group there. Before leaving, he arranged a turban ceremony.

"For us Sikhs," he said, "it is a custom to tie a turban on a visitor we love, and symbolically make him our brother."

I looked at myself in a mirror, black turban tied neatly in place.

"Now you can get a job as a general in the Indian Army," said Mohan.

"Or as a steward on Air India," suggested Ding.

"Or as a taxi-driver in Calcutta," I added.

We were sorry to see Mohan go, particularly as he would have so much liked to join us on the journey to the Sikh shrine of Hem Kund.

Our two faithful Indian camera-men, Prem and B.G., were returning to Rishikesh where they would join Harish Sarin and his wife on their trek to Gangotri and Gomukh, at the head of the Bhagirathi tributary of Ganga. We were told later that they had not gone far when they heard rumours of jet boats flying up the rapids ahead, weaving their way between saffron-robed saints on the banks of the holy river. After five days' travel they reached the cave of ice called Gomukh, the Cow's Mouth, which is the place where Shiva receives the celestial flow of Ganga into his matted locks. They did *puja* there. "It was," wrote Prem, "a joyful experience for us, with a sense of fulfilment. My heart was throbbing with delight—we had made it from Ganga Sagar in Bengal to the source of mighty Ganga, the only three expedition members to do so. I asked Harish what he prayed for in our *puja*.

" 'Success of the expedition and safe return of all members,' was his reply."

The walking, though on a road, soon eased the tension built up on the river. It was the relief, partly, that we were all still alive and without further opportunity to drown ourselves. The road ran up an easy valley, under a hot sun with the river in full view. A mile above Nandaprayag we saw on the river bank a gold and crimson banner saying "Welcome Ocean to Sky". It was the last refuelling depot, the one we never reached, and it looked sad there, and lonely, on the rocks and shingle beside the fast-flowing river. Occasionally a car drove past, or a battered red pilgrim bus, but the road was nearly empty, and even the buses were only half full. It was the end of the season.

The decision to walk to Badrinath, a climb from 3,000 up to 10,000 feet above sea level and a distance of sixty miles, was not part of our early plans, but it seemed now the right thing to do. When I came this way in 1951, on my first Himalayan expedition, there was no road, just the ancient pilgrim trail winding through the hills. I wondered why they built the road at all, for the merit of a pilgrimage is in proportion to its difficulties—though Jim hastened to assure us there was nothing safe or comfortable about the local buses used by pilgrims. Apart from the rightness of it, the walk would help to get us fit, and start the process of acclimatisation as we climbed higher. The sixty miles would take us five days, and to this I planned to add three more for a side trip off the road to the Valley of Flowers at 12,000 feet and the Lake of Hem Kund at 15,000.

We walked on in good spirits in the midday heat. We were soon thirsty, and before long stopped at our first tea-shop, a rickety thatched affair of rough-hewn planks tacked together somehow, with low seats beside a charcoal fire. A small Garhwali squatted cross-legged, polishing chipped cups with a dirty rag. It was three cents for a cup of thick sweet tea and we drank four each, along with a pile of roasted nuts, sweets for Mike Dillon, and *pakora*—fragments of chilli and other vegetables fried in spiced batter. It was the first of innumerable stops on our way to Badrinath, for the road and foot tracks are lined with tea-shops, and our thirsts were unquenchable—our total for the journey would be beyond computation.

At the six-mile mark we entered the small town of Chamoli, to be conducted down its main street by the Mayor and a few hundred people gathered from the surrounding hills. We were given tea, fruit and sweets. Then from behind us came the unmistakable sound of jazz from a pair of hi-fi stereo speakers, a saxophone wailing out in the noonday heat in a very Indian tea-shop surrounded by a thousand onlookers. I think we all felt nostalgic, and realised, perhaps for the first time, that the end of the expedition was near: a walk through the hills, a quick climb on an easy peak—within a month we'd be home.

We walked on to Birehi, where the two Czechs were drowned, and before them the two Indian youths on their home-made raft. We knew more about the Czechs and "Ganga '77" by now. They were no beginners. The rafting group had made the first descent of the great white-water gorge of the Indus not long previously, and they had rafted many big rivers in East Europe. Of their canoeists, one had been world champion in 1969. The tragedy occurred before they'd even started properly. The two canoeists were practising together on a clear patch of water above a long bouldery section; one was wearing a life-jacket, one was not; suddenly and inexplicably the canoe capsized and they were swept down through boulders and drowned. The more we saw of the river above Nandaprayag, the more glad we were that we had been stopped by the waterfall; too much of the river here was marginal, with sustained rapids full of boulders, and we had looked closely at one rapid that would almost certainly have sunk the boats if we'd been tempted to try it.

As we walked on through afternoon into evening, the road zig-zagged to a height of a thousand feet or more above the river, to enter a gorge, tall and narrow, with the road chiselled into its wall like a tunnel. The river below was narrow, and so calm that it must have been of great depth. On the far side we saw the ancient pilgrim trail, no longer used except by hill people with their flocks. Old stone bridges arched across torrents entering the gorge, and in places the trail was supported round cliffs by great walls of moss-covered rocks.

A few miles on, we turned a corner to see our first snow mountain, immensely high above the shadows of the gorge; the light still shone on its summit, capped with ice, and, as the sun set, the sky was filled with purple light, darkening as the night closed in and the waning moon rose behind the hills.

We called a halt after fourteen miles, quite enough for a first day on a hot road, and I had some good blisters to show for it. We had barely arrived at this stopping-place when a private truck pulled up and out got Raj Narayan from the New Zealand High Commission with some mail. Ding, Waka and Jim, who received nothing, looked despondent — the eternal drama of expedition mail, when the absence of a letter gives more scope for imagination than its arrival. There were Indian newspapers, too, and we seemed to have caught the headlines again:

HILLARY CALLS OFF EXPEDITION

The Ocean to Sky expedition has been called off at Nandaprayag. Yesterday, the expedition came face to face with a "stopper", one kilometer outside Nandaprayag. The crew led by Sir Edmund Hillary, made a minute inspection of the spot.

Afterwards, the ace driver of the team, Jon Hamilton, said, "There is absolutely no chance. No, we cannot be the Ganga's driver." Dr. Jim Wilson added "How can we? This is what is called a stopper." Jon's son, Michael, the third driver said, "We might not make it here."

"What do they mean?" said Mike Gill. "Expedition called off! Were they expecting us to drive jet boats up the snout of the glacier? Or on to the névés? Or off into outer-space? What do the rest of the papers say?"

GANGA BEATS HILLARY, they said. EXPEDITION ABANDONED.

I realised then that our honeymoon with the Press and the people of India was over. To us, the source of Ganga was the southern side of the Garhwal Himalaya with its snowfields and glaciers and forests, and from them, trickling and tumbling, swelling streams and torrents of water, flowing together to form the river known as Ganga. But to most of the people we met, whether in India or outside it, for that matter, the source was a place: a great cave in the mountainside, perhaps, or a huge glacier, from which the river ran, a great flow even at its source, and one which might be reached by boat. Only magic boats with wings could climb the rocky beds of those high mountain torrents. And now that we had proved we were mortal men and not magicians or gods, we walked on almost in solitude.

After three miles across a terraced hillside we reached Pipalkoti for a substantial breakfast of omelette and potato curry. As if to emphasise to me my mortality, the blisters on the soles of my feet had blossomed to an astonishing size, as I had known they would. After opening them with a razor blade, Mike padded my soles with cotton wool held on by double-sided sticking plaster – double-sided because the heat of the plains had run the stickiness into goo spread equally on either side. "I'll put some toilet paper around the outside to stop it sticking to your socks," added Mike. I liked neither the razor blade nor the double-sided sticking plaster – it seemed to me that Mike had no understanding of the finer points of blisters, and after that I referred my medical needs to Dr Wilson, who at least had some single-sided sticking plaster.

We sent back some mail with Raj through the New Zealand High Commission, and as we passed through a tiny village, Jim dashed off another letter to his wife, Ann, this time through the local postal facility, which took the form of a rusty red letter-box, the size of a treacle tin, hanging by a wire from the eaves of the most humble-looking post office I have seen anywhere. Posting a letter in India often seems an act of faith, but this was asking for a miracle. The miracle happened: the second letter reached New Zealand ahead of the one taken by Raj.

The road climbed on into the mountains, round terraced hillsides like those of Nepal. At times foot tracks left the road, and disputes arose as to which were genuine short cuts and which were not. Jim and Mike recklessly plunged down the hillside to the tattered remnants of an old sealed road far below at river level, while the rest of us made a long detour inland around the head of a side valley. Two hours later, our road, called the Belakuchi Realignment, returned to the main valley where we saw below us the fate of the old road and of Jim and Mike, who could be seen climbing overhanging grass cliffs in an attempt to escape from it. Two huge iron bridges that once had spanned the Alaknanda rose from the river, fantastically contorted as if cast there by the hand of a giant, with white water pouring between their girders. Downstream from these, the old road, nearly defeated by nature's luxuriance, ran on through grass and trees, and then it vanished beneath an immense landslide, overgrown with vegetation. It was up this that the two had climbed, and from it they were trying to escape. At length they rejoined us, sweating, hair matted, socks and tatty clothes beaded with bidi-bids and grass seeds.

"Nice little short cut," said Jim nonchalantly. "A couple of pitches of Grade 6 climbing up that grass towards the end – probably would have been easier if I hadn't been wearing jandals. We'll let you know next time we see a good short cut."

Later, we heard the story of the old road and the two twisted bridges which once had been part of it. In July 1970, after days of heavy rain, a landslide dammed the river upstream from the two bridges. When the dam burst, a tidal wave seventy feet high thundered down the valley, sweeping all before it, including thirty busloads of pilgrims and the two bridges, and adding to its devastation by bringing down the landslide which had engulfed the road and the village of Belakuchi.

All the while as we walked, we watched the rapids in the river and made comments on the Recce Report. We came to a place where the river could be seen as a ribbon of white, two thousand feet below, plunging in cataracts through boulders. Jim defended his Report to the bitter end.

"I've described that," he said, rummaging in his pack for the Report. Here! 'We both saw one point seemingly choked with boulders.' Well, that's it. There's only one inaccuracy. I shouldn't have written 'seemingly'."

Jim wrote in his diary that evening: "As we walked this upper section we were seeing with our eyes and hearing with our ears how fearsome a stretch of river the Alaknanda is. Why the Recce Report thought it possible to reach Vishnuprayag remains a mystery even to me—perhaps most of all to me—and occasioned much abuse from the others. Murray was lucky to be at Badrinath, avoiding it. I can only put it down to the very difficult viewing conditions from a moving bus (tiny windows, crowded, sitting on wrong side) at varying heights above the river (as the Report cunningly words its escape phrase), plus the lower water making it look less rough from a height."

As we walked along we passed large flocks of sheep and goats having a rest—and some curious in-betweens—geep perhaps, or shoats—their little saddle packs stacked by the edge of the road and their herders cooking a meal on the grassy verge. The flocks arranged themselves up and down the steep grassy slopes above and below the road, all munching steadily. Despite the fact that my feet were giving rather a lot of trouble, B.B. and I were still able to win a short cut against the rest on one of the great zigzags cut by the engineers into the hillside.

On October 2nd, we entered the hill town of Joshimath some 6,000 feet above sea level, and the military and administrative headquarters of these hills. It sprawls across a sunny hillside facing north—some old temples, an old bazaar, scattered houses painted white with timber facings, surrounded by flowers and apple trees, and above and below the old town some new military barracks.

As we approached, I was met by a large crowd plus a guard of honour of military cadets. Blisters and all, I was forced to march down the road to an official welcome where I was presented with many garlands of flowers and taken to a tea-shop for refreshment. Jim had a sore, skinned toe; my blisters were troublesome, and it looked an interesting town—so we decided to stay the night in the Nanda Devi Hotel. While I rested my blisters, the others went shopping for fresh apples and tomatoes, sunglasses and sandshoes; Mike even bought a heap of old hemp rope and some iron pegs which he said would be good for fixed ropes on the mountain. Ding and Waka, after failing to get a seat in the local movie house, introduced the sport of rock climbing to the children of Joshimath; and the big boulders with which the slopes of the town were littered were soon swarming with excited children. Late in the afternoon Ding found a beautiful temple and in the gathering dusk Jim and Mike, while trying to re-find it, stumbled instead into a brightly lit cave with two white statues and a translucent stone *lingam*. A *pandit* was chanting evening prayers, his voice ringing off the stone walls. It was the cave used by the great Hindu reformer of the tenth century, Shankaracharya, when he meditated here before passing on to Badrinath and Kedarnath, where he died at the age of thirty-two.

That evening B.B. took us to an officers' mess where we met the successful Indian women's expedition, just returned from the 22,000-foot peak Rataban in the Valley of Flowers. It was sobering to realise that they had completed their climb before we had even begun to acclimatise for ours. We congratulated them warmly on what had obviously been a fine climb.

Indian Army hospitality is generous and, on stomachs accustomed to endless tea, a few assiduously applied beers had a dramatic effect. I was thankful that the party remained well behaved in the Mess, but on leaving, handstands on walls were the order of the day. Ding describes what followed: "Back on the porch of the Nanda Devi, tension was running high and a fight broke out between Wilson, an innocent table, and me. Just then an enemy convoy roared into the main street and we knew we had a duty to the women and children and mastiffs that cringed in doorways. It wasn't a large convoy—one army truck to be exact—but it looked dangerous. In several complex moves, Wilson and I disentangled ourselves from each other and from the legs of the table before leaping with a spine-jarring bound from the porch to the street below. A pregnant hush fell over the crowd of watchers, particularly from Sir Hillary who was doing mental arithmetic to calculate the amount of damage Wilson and Dingle could do in five minutes before exhaustion overtook them.

"A drunken surge of speed, and we leaped on the canvas top of the truck. I crawled forward to the hatch in the driver's compartment that they throw grenades down in the war comics. It wouldn't open. It had either seized up, or was never intended to open, or was painted on, or the cunning sods had designed it so that it could be opened only from the inside. The truck stopped—this was dangerous—we leaped wildly across to the roof of a passing officer's jeep. It stopped immediately and a man with stripes and an important uniform leaped on to the road— 'Get down from there!' Wilson showed his true colours, and fled, snarling at a passing mastiff to restore his pride, then traversing a pilgrim bus—up the back, over the top, and down the bonnet. We returned to the Nanda Devi, to the relief of Sir Hillary and the sorrow of the proprietor."

We continued the next day on the road to Badrinath which dropped 1,500 feet to Vishnuprayag, the highest point we hoped we might have reached in the boats—"Getting pretty marginal," said the Recce Report in yet another of its laconic understatements. Ding's fantasy life continued unabated in his diary: "We descend from Joshimath, fight our way through an enormous breakfast, shake 150 military hands and then continue our hazardous journey. After 1,500 feet of descent we cross the chunderous Alaknanda, curse the Wilson/Jones Report a couple of times, pass a very slow pilgrim with multiple sclerosis and reach Vishnuprayag. As the merciless sky blazes down from a cloudless sun we cross the river on a bridge displaying the familiar 'no photography' sign, so I take a photo with a soldier shouting at me, and another with a soldier hanging from one arm—we photographers are a ruthless and dedicated group. This journey must go on. The Ganga can be conquered only by sheer guts."

It was hot as we made our way slowly up the spectacular Alaknanda gorge, a narrow cleft between towering cliffs and soaring hillsides of trees and grass. The road clung now to one side, now to the other of the white torrent crashing down over and under huge boulders.

We stopped that night at Govindghat, a village of stone walls and paved tracks, with a large *gurudwara*, the name given to Sikh resthouses supplying free food and lodging. Fresh snow lay on the rock peaks a few thousand feet higher, and in the village light rain was falling, our first for two weeks.

I received here a letter from Peter who was in Badrinath with Murray, making a reconnaissance of Narayan Parbat, the mountain which we hoped to climb, and which could be reached quite easily from Badrinath in four to five days. Although I had no memory of seeing the peak in 1951, it had sounded ideal and I had been happy to accept the Indian Mountaineering Foundation's recommendation. We read Peter's letter with great interest.

"Dear Dad,

"When we read that you'd 'abandoned the expedition' we were quite worried as we thought we'd have to climb Narayan Parbat on our own. It really is a very big mountain and there's nothing easy about it.

"We left Joshimath on September 30—it's an unbelievable piece of road. We were packed in like sardines—if one person moves the whole bus has to. Tell Jim I now understand the problems of the Recce Report. All is forgiven! We said our prayers with the rest of the bus when we came in sight of Badrinath—they all raised their hands, including the driver.

"The hotel was ten rupees a night. Not much in the way of good food up here, as there's no meat or even eggs. Murray's getting low on protein again. Most of the time the mountains have been in cloud, the weather generally looking fairly ominous. On our second day we had a view of Narayan Parbat. It has a long jagged summit ridge running east to west and we didn't much like the look of that. The two main faces are a south face and a north face and, of these, the south is the only one we've really looked at. From Badrinath we went up the valley towards Nilkanta, a magnificent mountain, though its east face looks terrifying. We had the south face of Narayan Parbat on our right. It looked exceedingly difficult, with colossal rock buttresses stretching vertically into the cloud base at about 16,000 feet. There are a couple of routes on it, but very difficult and quite out of the question for the sort of climb we're looking for.

"Our Inner Line Permits have just arrived, which means we can go up-valley to see what the north face looks like. We start from the military camp at Mana, a very difficult place to get through to by phone, incidentally, even though it's only three miles north. We've just had breakfast with the Army—tea, toast and marmalade and fried eggs served on silver plates with delicate china cups. Ah, at last someone has recognised us!!

"When we see you in a few days' time, we'll have all the answers.
Love,
Pete."

I wasn't cheered at all by this news. Murray and Peter were not in the habit of exaggerating difficulties on a mountain, and if they said it was hard, I knew it was close to being impossible for the sort of quick dash I was hoping for. It gave me something to think about before I fell asleep that night.

Next morning we left the road for three days to follow the Sikh pilgrim trail leading to another *gurudwara* at 10,000 feet, called Ghangaria, and there we planned to spend the night. At Ghangaria, according to our map, the track forked, the main valley continuing to a high pasture known as the Valley of Flowers, the other fork of the track climbing steeply to the sacred lake of Hem Kund at 15,500 feet.

It was a lovely walk of eight miles, off the road at last and on a really beautiful forest track. Fortunately "off the road" in India does not mean out of touch with tea-shops, and our progress was, as before, a series of erratic hops between numerous cups of tea. Our fellow foot-pilgrims were now much more numerous and interesting than on the motor road – largely Sikhs wearing turbans, some in bright robes worn specially for this last stage of their pilgrimage.

We passed many coming back down and their pleasure at having made the pilgrimage was evident on their faces. One in particular impressed me, a striking old lady making her way carefully, almost laboriously, down the track, her face a picture of pleasure and serenity despite the effort she had to put into her movement. Unlike that of so many old people in our society who are just eking out their days, the end of her life was filled with purpose and satisfaction by her religious belief and her goals of pilgrimage. I felt almost envious, realising that my own shadowy religious beliefs, all long since faded, could never let me feel as she did.

It was a very beautiful valley with magnificent forest and a tumbling stream, and as we gained height there were superb views down-valley, of pine forest and pastures framed between steep rock walls that rose into the clouds. We reached Ghangaria at two p.m. The *gurudwara* and a group of buildings were buried deep inside a pine forest. We were given a large bare room to ourselves and I was glad to crawl into my sleeping-bag for a rest and a warm-up. After dark we were called to the *gurudwara* meal. First we went to the Sikh temple to hear chanting of the scriptures and then into the community eating-house. It was a large, dark barn of a place, with some fires at one end and a team of volunteers doing the cooking. Beside a huge iron sheet over one fire sat the man who cooked *chapati*, turning them, a dozen at a time, then flicking them over his shoulder to be stacked in a basket. We sat in long lines on the swept earthen floor. Large brass plates were plonked before us, and a small metal bowl and tumbler; then *chapati*, *dal*, pickle and rice plopped on from baskets and buckets, the volunteer servers moving back and forth along the line with deftness and courtesy.

Not long after seven we retired to bed. The nights were long now, twelve hours of darkness, and at a place like Ghangaria, with no amenities to speak of, the hours spent inside a sleeping-bag seemed interminable. B.B. told us how once he had made a special pilgrimage to the shrine of Vaishno Devi in Kashmir and it gave us some insight into the sort of hopes and attitudes pilgrims bring with them to any of these numerous holy places in India. The story went roughly like this:

Vaishno Devi was a very beautiful goddess and she was seen and desired by Bhairon, a great rajah of the area. She repulsed his advances, and when he tried force, ran away with her followers. He pursued her until he found her bathing in a pool in the forest—which inflamed his lust still further. "Yield to me or I will take you by force," he vowed in typically gentle male fashion, and, when she still refused, a battle ensued between her followers and his soldiers. Most of her followers were killed and she again fled, this time into a very narrow cave. Alas, the cave had no exit and Bhairon started in. He was a very fat fellow and had to enter on his hands and knees, and when he got his head into the cave she warned him, "Go away or I will have to kill you."

"I must have you!" he replied; so without further ado, she whipped out her sword, struck his head off and tossed it away. It fell a mile down the mountainside, and where it landed there is now a shrine to him. But Vaishno Devi vowed that if anyone came to her shrine after first visiting his, they would not be able to enter and have *darshan* off her; but if they came direct they could get in. She then forsook human form. But her presence remains in the cave and a rough rock projection there is believed to be the form of her head and shoulders, and is the only image in the shrine.

She is believed to be responsive to all sorts of requests and problems—sickness, career problems, childlessness—and to this day it remains an enormously popular shrine and hundreds of thousands of people visit it each year. Even now, B.B. assured us, if you come by way of Bhairon's shrine, no matter how thin you are, you cannot squeeze through the entrance: if you come direct you can get in, no matter how fat you are.

B.B.'s parents believed in Vaishno Devi. Their first son died at four months, so when B.B. was conceived his father made a pilgrimage to the shrine—and of course B.B. lived. His uncle, too, visited the shrine with a child sick with fever—103 degrees for four days, yet as soon as they entered the cave, the fever left the child. "You can say it was coincidence, if you like," said B.B., "but certainly my uncle believes it was the power of Vaishno Devi." So when B.B. was facing a crisis in his own career, not long after his marriage, his father urged him to visit the shrine. "I didn't really believe in it," said B.B. "but my father persisted; so I said to my wife, 'Why don't we go—it can do no harm?' We climbed up to 10,000 ft., entered the shrine and made our request. And ten days later I got a letter post-marked the day we made our request. While I was actually in the shrine, the decision was made which solved my problem. It may have been just coincidence, but . . ."

I had a restless night, with many bad dreams. I didn't know if it was our altitude of 10,300 feet, or what. When I woke it was a fine morning and quite cool and after an excellent breakfast at the *gurudwara* we left, up a beautiful track through forest rich with autumn colours. After a climb up a steep but short gorge, we emerged into the Valley of Flowers, a mile wide and perhaps four long. It was a superb place, even though no flowers were left, only fields of withered stalks which once had been alive with blooms. All around were fine mountain peaks and we ambled round in groups or singly, all at various times sleeping long periods in the sun, and spending other long periods gazing at the peaks and clouds. No wonder, I thought, the people of the plains have their gods live here; no wonder, too, that anyone seeking the world of the spirit should travel here to find it amidst the mysteries of snow, mountains, sky, and clouds and high pastures.

For the first time we met juniper and rhododendron and the pungent herbal smell of the dwarf azalea, so evocative to anyone who has lived in the Himalayas. We met two horses, a grey foal and a mule. A big flock of grey pigeons was feeding on seeds in the pastures, inconspicuous birds on the ground, but their wings flashed white when they rose and wheeled around or flew overhead, with a sudden rush of noise. At the far end of the valley was the toe of a glacier at 13,000 feet and there, tucked beside it, were the deserted remains of a mountain basecamp with the words "Welcome Home Summiters" painted across a boulder. We descended back to Ghangaria at good speed and in good heart—our first day in the mountains.

I had another uncomfortable night and came to the conclusion that it was the effect of altitude. It had been a wild and stormy night, with hail hammering on the roof, though we were snug enough in our room. When we emerged we could see fresh snow quite low on the peaks above; the winter seemed to be closing in on us with frightening speed. At about seven thirty we headed off for Hem Kund, making rapid pace up a well-graded track. At thirteen thousand feet we struck the fresh snow, two inches deep on the ground; it was still excellent walking, and the last haul to the lake was "The Golden Staircase" of 1,064 carefully fashioned stone steps climbing steep and straight up the mountainside. There were Sikh pilgrims of all ages—a boy of four, some young people, some young men supporting a woman who was clearly suffering quite badly from the altitude (15,000 feet is a considerable height for those not acclimatised), and an old man, making his tenth visit, carrying a tiny child in his shaky arms—he was going very slowly, but with impressive determination.

The lake was cradled in the mountainside with steep rock below and bare rock peaks towering high on three sides. A half-completed temple filled the foreground, a tangle of steel girders supporting a huge domed roof, large enough, they said, to house five thousand pilgrims. We moved past this unsightly structure to the edge of the lake, where two young Sikhs were disrobing on the stones of the foreshore before bathing. The lake itself was a quarter of a mile across, calm in the still air, and black except where the snow of peaks rising steeply around was reflected in the mirror of its waters. Jim, Ding and Mike had a bathe to complete their pilgrimage, a frantic flash in and out of the near-freezing water, while I made do with a chilling face-and-hand wash. Our guide-book said, "Hem Kund will tempt anyone to take a plunge, but one minute in its bareness will make anyone freeze and he will quickly clear out of it to be warmed by the sunshine—the frigorific stage is so intense that a longer time insphering is apt to squeeze out the soul from the body."

Hem Kund has been a place of pilgrimage for centuries. To Hindus the lake is known as Lokpal, a place on whose banks Lakshman meditated. It is known to Bhotias of nearby valleys, Tibetan Buddhists whose women visit the lake annually over high passes in the belief that this ensures the good health of their menfolk. But its recognition by Sikhs as a place of great sanctity dates only from 1932, when a religious teacher from the Golden Temple of Amritsar went searching for a glacial lake surrounded by seven peaks. Such a lake had been described in the autobiography of Guru Govind Singh, the tenth in the succession of Gurus who established the Sikh faith five hundred years ago. The first Guru sought to join Hinduism and Islam, but by the time of the tenth and last Guru it was a new religion, forswearing worship of its god as images, without caste, and with fiercely militant traditions. Its disciples were forbidden to cut their hair or smoke tobacco—the only plant a pig will not eat; they carried swords and wore turbans. Govind Singh described how he had meditated on the shores of a lake with seven peaks in a previous life and there he was commanded by God to take birth again. "There is lawlessness and you must fight against it, and you must take the side of the poor and down-trodden." For centuries the place described by Govind Singh was not identified, but when the teacher from Amritsar came to Govindghat in his search, he met an old man with grey hair and piercing eyes who pointed up into the mountains. After a difficult journey he reached the lake of Hem Kund. Even here he doubted, but just then the old man reappeared to him, pointing to a flat rock on the lake shore and he heard a voice from heaven saying, "Do not doubt. This is where I meditated and where I received the command from God." And since then its importance as a place of Sikh pilgrimage has increased year by year.

It is said that sincere devotees can hear Govind Singh coming on his horse to visit them. Pilgrims who stay the night on the shores of the lake can hear splashing in the water, but this ceases on the instant if a light is shone into the dark. If any impure object is cast into the lake a bird descends from the mountain to remove it, but so swiftly as to be invisible to unbelievers.

By the time we left Hem Kund it was snowing. We raced down the icy mountainside to Ghangaria where we gathered together our possessions. By evening we had descended to the relative warmth of Govindghat beside the road. As we swung down the last stretch of track we were met by the Director of the *gurudwara*, a great, cheerful old character with a luxuriant grey beard. He led us inside the temple and in penetrating tones delivered an address: "Every man has a mission and you have come here up our sacred river Ganga, not for money or material wealth but to inspire people with a sense of adventure. You have made your pilgrimage to Hem Kund and it is our custom, on returning from there, to pray to God that our journey has been a holy one recognised by the Almighty. We thank you for the honour you have done us and pray that God will be with you on the rest of your journey." He then presented me with an orange turban and a fine curved sword in a red velvet scabbard. By the end of the day I felt we had completed something at last—a pilgrimage to one of the ultimate shrines of India.

On the morning of October 7th we set off for Badrinath. For a while the valley had a sunny, friendly feel to it and we passed through a fine village, its gardens filled with flowers, which grew also in pots on the roofed balconies. But then the road steepened into a big zigzag, climbing beside the river which plunged down cataracts and low falls. The trees and scrub gave way to alpine grass, and much of the time we walked on tracks away from the road. We passed a group of soldiers walking down the track. We looked closely at them and they at us. Without doubt they were as tough-looking a bunch of soldiers as I've seen. They moved easily down the rough track with their loads and some well-worn automatic rifles casually slung across their shoulders; they fitted into the landscape the way the mountain sheep do, or the yaks, or the yak-herds. Ding watched the first group disappearing into the distance. "They look like a bloody good bunch of scrappers, that lot."

"You can be thankful you didn't tangle with them during your drunken effort at Joshimath," I said. When a second group went past we stopped to talk. They spoke no English but in their replies I recognised a few words of the Nepali language, identifying them as Ghurkas.

In the late afternoon we climbed the last rise, to find ourselves on the floor of a high flat valley, five miles long by half a mile wide, from which steep walls climbed upwards into cloud. Before us, on our left, a village of rusty iron roofs sprawled outwards from the banks of the river and amidst them the gilded roof and bright paint of a temple. It was Badrinath, and these steep walls hard beside it were the flank of Narayan Parbat, the mountain we had come to climb to complete our journey to the sky.

13

Hillary in Devlok

Ever since the dawn of civilisation, man has continued unravelling the mysteries of nature. But allowing all opportunities and helping periodically man to know His secrets, God keeps something to himself in every field. If there were no secrets, perhaps, man might challenge God himself for supremacy and ultimately conquer death.

Sir Edmund Hillary's expedition "ocean to sky" is one such attempt to unravel the secrets of the Ganga and its source in the valley of Gods ... Sir Hillary succeeded in boating through the Ganga right into the heart of the Devlok.

It was only near Nandaprayag that Ganga defeated him and he had to abandon his expedition without completing it. But he continued the trekking part of the expedition's journey to the valley of Gods ... As their reconnaissance parties went round the northern face of Narayan Parbat, they were baffled by difficult ascent, which they had earlier thought to be very easy.

According to reports reaching here, the Hillary team is now trying to scale the Nar Parbat. The gods who have their permanent abode on both the Narayan and the Nar Parbats might not be happy. Even in normal routine, they do not like any visitors to this area after the Vijyadashmi day, but atop the mountains, they might not like it even in early October. The wintery weather conditions are created at the sweet will of the gods who preside in this land.

The progress of the expedition will be watched with interest. The ocean was co-operative and pleasant. So was the Ganga after absorbing all the sins of the land. But the gods may not; it is their playtime in the Devlok. They might like the mortals to keep their hands off their territory in the limited period of their absolute possession. Man has already challenged them everywhere. They might not relish too much intrusion into their privacy.

Daily Himachal Times, October 12th, 1977

IT WAS COLD AS WE WALKED THE LAST MILE INTO BADRINATH
and we put on down-jackets or wind-proofs. On the outskirts we walked
past ugly new rest-houses made of concrete, and painted pink or prim-
rose or pastel greens and blues. There was an autumnal air to the valley;
an icy wind whistled down the half-deserted streets, raising whirlwinds
of dust, and the few pilgrims left were wrapped miserably in woollen
shawls and balaclavas, their arms wrapped around themselves as if to
keep the wind out. For a moment the clouds overhead parted and we
saw the cold summit of a mountain, a sharp spire of ice so close and yet
so high it seemed unreal, more like a dream than something solid
made of rock and ice. The peak was Nilkanta, sometimes called the
Queen of Garhwal. The name means Blue-throated One. Once there
was a battle in the ocean between gods and demons and the snake
secretly mixed venom in the churning waters. But Shiva, the all-seeing
one, saw this with his third eye and, realising that the gods might be in
danger, he drank the venom, which collected in his throat and turned
it blue. Thus he was called *nil-kantha*, the blue-throated one. From
Badrinath it is one of the supreme peaks – not high, but steep and sharp,
and guarded by cliffs of ice. George Lowe and I had climbed round the
back of it in 1951 looking for an easy route – but there was none.

We made our way to where we were staying, an army bungalow
made of concrete, cold and bare. For the first time some of the expedition stomachs began to rebel against curries. Although we had more
palatable fare for the mountain, in Badrinath our food was of the
plainest sort — boiled rice, curried potatoes and *dal*, and *chapati*. Nor
was there anything more appetising in the bazaar, which was almost
empty: meat and eggs were forbidden by both law and religion.

We were joined here by Murray and Peter, just down from a long
climb to 17,000 feet on Narayan Parbat. Their news, most of which
was bad, spilled out of them, the words tumbling over each other. They
had obviously enjoyed themselves enormously, racing around these
high valleys on their own. For neither of them had the travelling by
jet boat been easy. Murray had always been something of a loner.
Down on the plains they had both felt they were making no positive
contribution, though none of the rest of us had felt that—I'd been
through a lot with both of them over the years, and even when there
were no mountains to climb, I just liked having them around. Murray's
devotion to the mountains was probably more single-minded than that
of any of us, and now that he had reached the peaks of Badrinath he
was intent on throwing everything into his climbing, and Peter, who
had climbed a lot with Murray, had become no less dedicated himself
over the past year.

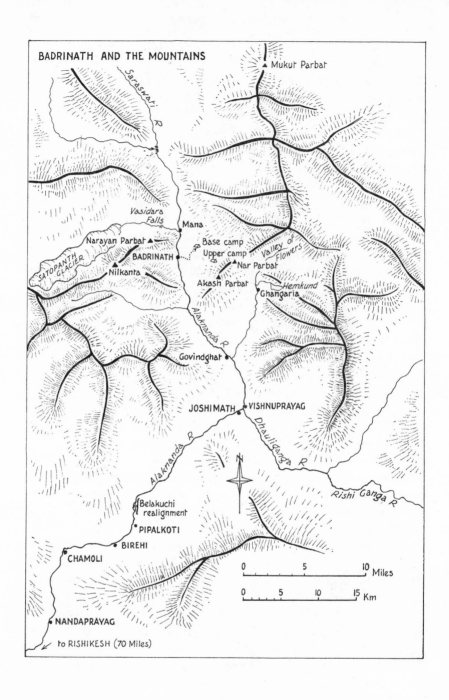

BADRINATH AND THE MOUNTAINS

▲ Mukut Parbat

Saraswati R.

Vasidara Falls

Mana

Narayan Parbat ▲

Base camp
Upper camp

Valley of Flowers

BADRINATH ●

▲ Nar Parbat

SATOPANTH GLACIER

Nilkanta ●

Akash Parbat

Hemkund

Ghangaria

Alaknanda R.

Govindghat ●

JOSHIMATH ● ● VISHNUPRAYAG

Alaknanda R.

Dhauliganga R.

N

Rishi Ganga R.

Belakuchi realignment

PIPALKOTI ●

BIREHI

CHAMOLI ●

| 0 | 5 | 10 Miles |
| 0 | 5 | 10 | 15 Km |

NANDAPRAYAG ●

to RISHIKESH (70 Miles)

On October 4th they had set out from the Bhotia village of Mana, three miles up valley, to ascend the Satopanth Glacier which runs east to west along the northern faces of Narayan Parbat and Nilkanta. It was the same route George and I had used in 1951. Mana, by the sound of it, was unchanged: stone houses and stone walls, which from a distance made it barely distinguishable from the moraine boulders amongst which it was built. They walked past terraced fields of golden wheat being harvested by local Bhotia girls who had mischievous smiles like Sherpanis. They continued up easy pastures beside the glacial stream of the Vishnu Ganga.

Beside them, on their left as they walked up-valley, was the north face of Narayan Parbat. It looked very bad indeed. Huge walls climbed steeply up, with only two routes through, along the whole length of the face. The first was a cleft in the wall leading to a narrow glacier descending from a col between the main peaks of Narayan Parbat and some steep rock pinnacles on the east side above Badrinath. But it certainly wasn't the easy route they were looking for; so they moved on up-valley to the second gap in the mountain's defences, some steep slabs split by greasy gullies. They camped on the grass of a lateral trough beside the ice and moraine of the Satopanth Glacier.

Peter wrote in his diary: "What fabulous country, soaring rock spires, shattered glaciers, ghostly clouds swirling around the summits and the mighty lammergeiers riding the mysteries in the air. Such is this splendid Himalayan panorama.

"We made dinner and reclined into our sacks; the sky clear and star-filled; Nilkanta huge and awesome above; across the valley the fabulous Balakun arching its fantastic form to the sky, displaying its bold and threatening flanks to all who should dare to scan it.

"On the morning of the 5th I woke with a resounding headache due to the altitude and one of my boots was rubbing on the bone on the inside of my ankle. So whilst I struggled with padding systems for my foot, my head like a piece of stone, Murray headed upwards alone to check the route. It took me three hours of fussing about, allowing for a one-hour snooze, to invent a system to cure my ill. It consisted of one nylon sock, stiff with dirt and sweat, twisted into a cord and shaped to a circle. This I placed around my anklebone; it seemed to do the trick. At ten a.m. I climbed the gully and steep slabs to a glacier at 15,000 feet, the same direction taken by Murray. When finally I caught sight of Narayan Parbat I was appalled. My God! We were still a valley away from the peak and the north face was steep black rock plastered with fresh snow, quite impossible for our expedition. I saw no more of Murray until we joined up again in camp that night. He had soloed down a difficult route into the valley. He agreed it was no use going further in this direction. That night, with the help of two Mogadon tablets each and some Codeine, we defeated the sleeplessness and headaches of high altitude and enjoyed the deep sleep of the exhausted."

Next day, disappointed, they walked back down-valley to Mana.

On the morning of the 7th the two of them set out to climb the second gap in the north wall, the cleft leading to the little glacier that they'd seen two days ago and rejected. This time Peter was in the lead, winding back and forth amongst the slots of the glacier, following some cat's footprints all the way to the crest of the col itself. Murray wrote: "The lack of good food and this bloody crazy vegetarian diet started to tell on me and for the first time since Peru I plugged behind. No way I could catch Peter. He climbed well, weaving his way through the intricate glacier system. Mainly it was a dry glacier covered in about six inches of fresh powder. We both felt the effects of altitude, going a hundred feet or so before resting. I was nagged by a hacking cough and wondering whether at 32 I should give over gracefully to the young blood, Hillary. Still, 7,000 feet in five hours is no mean effort at any age. The view that greeted us at the col was even worse than we'd thought from down below — definitely a no-go for the expedition, with 3,000 feet of steep slabs covered in fresh powder. So we trundled down in fast time, two and a half hours, to Mana and so back to Badrinath. Ed and the rest of the gang were there. My God, it was so great to see them."

So the reconnaissance had presented its views. Narayan Parbat, far from being too easy, was in fact too hard, and most of the time enveloped in snow and cloud. It could be climbed, they reckoned, but not with our movie-camera gear and the limited equipment and manpower we had.

But then Peter and Murray came up with an idea which sounded like a way out. East of Narayan Parbat, across the valley but equally close to Badrinath, was another peak. Its name was Nar Parbat, its height not much above 19,000 feet, and the approaches to it were infinitely easier than those to Narayan. I was reluctant at first. God knows, it had taken us long enough to get permission for Narayan Parbat — how could I possibly change to a new peak at forty-eight hours' notice? I decided to have a direct look at the east ridge of Narayan Parbat next morning, to see both mountains for myself.

On October 8th we were away promptly on a lovely clear morning. We ploughed steadily up the first steep grass, then more slowly across the gentler slopes above. To begin with we were followed doggedly by a 63-year-old pilgrim from Dehra Dun, who gained strength to stagger up by touching my feet and those of Jim and Peter—and then kept going by eating two biscuits Jim gave him in admiration for his determination. I was spurred on by his presence and managed to go fast enough to leave him behind—but he was a doughty trier.

Around 13,500 feet, the grass gave way to steep rock. I had the view I wanted; so while the rest climbed on I lay in the sun with Mingma and Pemma. On previous mornings the clouds had closed in by eleven o'clock, but today, as if the onrushing winter were in retreat, the sky was clear and there was no wind. Across the valley rose Nar Parbat, a peak I soon warmed to. From the valley floor, steep grassy bluffs led up to rock slabs 15,000 feet below an immobile-looking glacier. Easy snow slopes by-passed the slots of the glacier to an expansive snow plateau at 18,000 feet, and from the rim of this rose several peaks, the highest of them Nar Parbat. Mingma liked it. We'd get porters to a base camp on the slabs at 15,000, then carry our own high camp to 18,000 feet on the plateau. It was just the sort of peak I'd wanted, and soothed by that thought I lay back to enjoy the morning.

The view to the north was stupendous. Far ahead on the border with Tibet was the great bulk of Mukut Parbat, the peak that our four-man expedition had climbed in 1951. It seemed a very long time ago but, as I looked, the memories of the expedition came flooding back—our trek up-valley towards Mana Pass; the many virgin 20,000-foot peaks we had climbed; and the ascent of Mukut Parbat itself. In Badrinath we had received news of Eric Shipton's 1951 Everest Reconnaissance, which led ultimately to success on Everest itself in 1953. How much younger and stronger I was in those days—but I had little cause for complaint. The years between had been mighty ones and I was now happy to let the younger "hot shots" have their turn to meet the tougher challenges.

While I dreamed on, the others climbed upwards by various routes towards the rock peak above, an eastern outlyer of Narayan Parbat and separated from it by the col reached by Peter and Murray the previous day. Only Murray and Peter reached the summit (Murray's diary: "Reached the top three-quarters of an hour ahead of Pete—so I'm not finished yet, mate"), but the others weren't too far below. They all came to the same conclusion I had reluctantly reached—Narayan Parbat was difficult, while Nar Parbat across the valley was accessible and attractive.

To our delight and astonishment B.B. said he would take full responsibility for our change of objective. "Go ahead and start on the peak—if permission isn't granted I'll send a message, otherwise climb it. There'll be no problem, I'm sure." And he set off back immediately to Delhi to formalise it. What a liaison officer he had proved to be! As Ding said, "Expeditions dream about such an officer but never believe he exists."

Before turning in for the night I drew up a plan. Next day, Jim and Mike would find a route for porters up the bluffs to Base Camp while Mingma and I and the rest sorted loads and found thirty porters. The day after, we would carry up Base Camp in one lift. I fell asleep to the sound of animals stomping up and down the ceiling of the bungalow. They could only have been rats, I suppose, but they must have been immense, now marching slowly back and forth two by two, now galloping at speed or snarling and scuffling in some form of gang-warfare.

Mike and Jim had the easy job, for they had seen the route the day before. The only difficulty was finding running water, but at length they located what seemed to be the only trickle emerging from the whole glacier system, for it was all, or nearly all, frozen for the winter.

Sorting loads was no problem either. But finding porters was. With the arrival of the road, load-carrying had become a lost art. We tried the Bhotia village of Mana, which was where I had recruited porters in 1951. Our guide-book then had described the Bhotias as "few in number, powerfully built, both men and women, dirty in their habits and greatly addicted to drink". All this may have been true, but they were very hard to find and of the mischievous girls described by Murray there was not a sign. A few old men came forward, reluctantly—they looked very much like the same bunch I'd hired in 1951 and none of us had grown younger or stronger in the intervening twenty-six years.

In the end I appealed for help from the local military establishment by calling on Major Bawa, who had been seconded by B.B. to act as our liaison officer during his own absence in Delhi. Major Bawa was a fine colourful character, a Sikh who strode about, hunch-shouldered, with his hands thrust deep in the pockets of a huge army great-coat. Instead of a turban, or perhaps on top of it, he wore a balaclava with a long pointed crown which drooped forward like a court jester's. He had merry eyes, a loud laugh and a voice like a foghorn, made hoarse by perpetual shouting into the telephones of the district. We found him living halfway between Mana and Badrinath in an unpretentious little hut which, though small, was wonderfully cosy inside owing to the efforts of a flaring drip-feed oil fire.

"Don't worry!" he said with a shake of his head. "I will get you porters!" And he let out a great bellow which made us leap from our seats in surprise. He was calling his servant, we discovered, not the men from Mana, though they might well have heard him, too. On days when his voice was running low, the Major summoned his servant with a siren operated by applying two bare wire leads to a car battery in one corner of the hut. The food he served was excellent; somewhere he had a case of rum, and at one elbow stood a telephone. It was a very functional headquarters.

With the Major's promise ringing in our ears, we drove back down the dusty road to Badrinath, for at three o'clock we were to make an official visit to the temple. As always in the afternoon, the cloud was down low, with snow falling not far above and the wind ruffling the snow tussock of the bare valley. Holy it might be, but Badrinath looked strangely out of place in the desolate beauty of this Tibetan landscape. We walked into the town where the temple and bazaar and old houses crouched on the banks of the Alaknanda, which here ran through a small gorge, its waters green and opalescent with silt brought down from glaciers, whose melting fed the river.

The temple had a brightly painted façade with steep steps leading from a lane up to the entrance, whilst on the river side, steps dropped to hot pools which steamed in the cold air, spilling into the gorge and spawning as they did so a curtain of multi-coloured algae fed by the warm water. Mythology aside, one suspects that at least part of the reason for the original selection of Badrinath as a sacred site was these dramatic hot springs so high in the mountains and beside so cold a mountain river. In the river at this point there are also the Panch Shila, fantastically carved boulders, eroded by the river and perhaps also by the hot springs.

Badrinath has been sacred for as long as anyone knows, its origin being, according to mythology, in the first and perfect age of the Hindu cyclic timetable. It is a shrine sacred to Vishnu, of whom Narayan is an incarnation. *Badris* are pear trees which once grew there in profusion, providing food for those who meditated in their shade, including Narayan who thus became known as Badri Nath, Lord of the Pear Trees. Another story has it that while Narayan was meditating, the sun beat down on him and Lakshmi his wife took on the form of a pear tree to give her lord shade.

Badrinath is described in the *Mahabharat*, the great epic poem whose historical basis is a war between two families of brothers living in northern India around the tenth century B.C. The Pandavas were one family, five brothers who wandered in exile for twelve years before regaining their inheritance in a great battle in which they were assisted by Krishna who, like Narayan, was an incarnation of Vishnu. Of the five Pandavas, the greatest warrior was Arjuna and he was no less than an incarnation of Nar. Hence the names of the twin peaks standing on either side of Badrinath, Nar and Narayan Parbat—for Parbat simply means mountain.

There was a fascination about these tales as they were told to us, for they slowly came together like the pieces of a jigsaw puzzle. The *Mahabharat* was said to have been written at the confluence of the Saraswati and Vishnu Ganga, where the village of Mana now stands. And the Pandavas at the end of their lives climbed to heaven past Badrinath, up the valley to Mana. Here their way was blocked by the Saraswati River until one of the brothers threw a huge rock to span it — a natural rock bridge is there to this day. They turned west towards the Satopanth glacier and the 400-foot high Vasodara Falls, where they bathed. The water splashes over a wide area but no drops fall on a man of impure thoughts—even the sight of an impure person is said to halt the flow. Finally, after passing a glacial lake at the confluence of the Satopanth and Bhagirath glaciers, the Pandavas climbed by way of a natural ladder up to heaven.

When at length we visited the temple of Badrinath on that afternoon before we left for the very real ice-clad slopes of Nar Parbat, we were reassured by the senior temple officer of the wisdom of our choice of Nar in preference to Narayan Parbat, which was indeed, he said, the peak of God. Moreover, he believed that I was an incarnation of the warrior Arjuna and hence of Nar—what could be more appropriate?

He gave us a temple banner to take with us to the summit and then we did *puja* briefly in the temple. The ceremony was conducted by the Rawal, an ascetic-looking *brahman* so holy that he could not place garlands directly round our necks lest he pollute himself; so he threw them from a distance, fastidiously and very expertly, as if he were playing quoits. The central image of the temple, some three feet high, was carved of black stone with blurred features, the result of immersion in the Vishnu Ganga for several hundred years, for the image had been thrown there by a Buddhist fanatic before being rescued by Shankaracharya and reinstated in the temple.

Before we left I pointed out the site of our Base Camp. There was a legend about that even — Kuber the god of wealth keeps his treasure under the terminal ice of the glacier and there is a popular belief that the mountain contains precious stones like diamonds, rubies and emeralds, the most precious stone being guarded by a snake. The lines between reality and myth were blurring in my mind. I lay in my

The author contemplates mountain alternatives.

Pouring the sacred Ganga *pani* onto the snow plateau.

The unmistakable symmetry of Nilkanta.

sleeping-bag that night listening to the rats prancing and leaping on the ceiling. Perhaps they were demons. I wondered what success we'd have with our push to Base Camp next day.

We had the loads lined up ready for departure early next morning, but the porters were slow in arriving. And when they did come it was clear to me that the Major had wrought no miracles. The old men seemed to have brought their fathers to help out, rather than their sons — their average age would have been greater than mine. During our journey across the plains we had grown used to people expressing surprise at the advanced age of some of our party. Back at Joshimath, the Colonel had politely enquired Mike's age. "Thirty-nine," he replied. The Colonel's expression changed to one of concern as he looked at Mike's well-lined face. "Oh . . ." he said, sympathy in every inflection. "Is that all?" And he shook his head sorrowfully. Jim, too, was widely accepted as an ancient *sadhu*. At Rudraprayag, when Jim had started up the big rapid there, an expectant murmur had gone around the crowd, "Ah! Now the old man is going to have a go!" As for me, I might as well have stepped straight from the pages of the *Mahabarat*. Mike produced an appropriate quote from *Count Belisarius* describing the return of his soldiers to battle in old age—"Old men, with wild eyes, and white hair streaming." It wasn't a description that fitted us all that well, but it was even less appropriate for the men from Mana. They huddled together in groups, shivering in the cold, wondering what had made them agree to carry loads for us. A couple of younger ones wore flared trousers and city shoes, while another, wearing beret and jerkin, looked as if he'd just flown in on the last flight from Paris. They appeared to be discussing whether or not they should return home then and there, but we had Major Bawa with us, in truculent mood, and with a few well-timed bellows he prevented any of them scuttling back to the village.

"We have had no breakfast," said their spokesman. "First we must eat."

We had a great argument—they'd agreed the day before on extra pay to cover food and now they wanted both—but I had no alternative, really. They certainly looked as if they needed food; so I gave them two rupees each and sent them off to a nearby shop. I wasn't too surprised at this reaction by Mana men, because they'd been like that when I first dealt with them in 1951—in fact, as I said to the team, they look like the very same bunch. While they were eating, Jim and Murray went on ahead to cairn the route and make it usable if cloud and snow should come in. As the porters drifted back, I sent each group up the hill with a couple of expedition members to accompany them. It was ten-thirty before the final loads were moved and Mingma and I brought up the rear.

The first thousand feet led up a steep grass-covered fan. We crossed the tumbled rock at the foot of the slope and then zigzagged our way upward. The men were very slow, even though they were carrying only forty-four pound loads, and I kept wishing I had a bunch of Sherpa women who would have carried sixty-six pounds at twice the pace. We picked up quite a lot of height and then traversed left to a sort of saddle on a subsidiary ridge, and here I caught up with Peter, who had left with a bunch of the really old men. They were proving very slow and reluctant and as Peter was finding them rather trying, I took over the job of harassing them on.

One old man was particularly slow and kept stopping, holding up those behind. I tried persuasion, then food, but in the end I simply took his load and shoved it on top of mine. As I was now carrying more than any of them I had no qualms about forcing all the tail-enders to keep going. A good yak-trail traversed left across a flat area of well-grazed pasture, obviously in use till recently, for the animal droppings were still quite fresh, and the fireplace in the camp-site was full of ashes. We walked on easily for a while, through mountain strawberries with patches of azalea and juniper scrub. But then we were into bluffs, following grass ledges winding up between rock cliffs. There were still animal trails but much smaller—goats perhaps. An old Bhotia proverb says, "On the road to Badrinath, it takes ten men to lead nine goats." It certainly fitted this place. We went on for a couple of hours with my flock of elderly porters getting slower and slower. Where on earth was everybody else? I thought irritably. At that moment Jim arrived down out of the mist to give a hand, and I was pretty scratchy with him, too—though without much justification. He took over the job of handling the tail-enders plus my load, and I traversed across and dropped down on to the camp-site.

It was a magnificent position—we estimated about 15,000 feet—with enough ledges for tents. The ice tongue of the glacier was perched about 500 feet above us and it was hard to know if we were liable to ice avalanches or not. We completed the paying off of the porters, giving them more than they had asked. Considering their age they had done remarkably well and we'd got here in one lift. We also fed an unhappy-looking youth who had spent much time and energy during the day moving from one group to the next asking for food. We christened him Hungry Boy. They all seemed pleased as they took their thirty rupees and scuttled off back down the bluffs.

I'd brought up the canopy of one of the jet boats, and we set this up for a cook-tent between a boulder and a big rock wall we'd built—it worked well. With a fair bit of hacking with our ice-axes we made level spots for the smaller tents, and in the end we had a comfortable Base Camp. The view out towards Nilkanta was superb, and to the north were the dry barren hills of the Tibetan frontier. I had arrived up in pretty good shape despite my load-carrying, but as the evening light faded I was happy to crawl into my sleeping-bag.

My idea was for some of us—myself, the two Mikes and Jim—to spend the next day sorting out gear and just acclimatising, while Murray and Peter and the other young ones established the route higher and found a site for High Camp on the plateau if they reached that far. The day after that, we'd carry most of the gear halfway up. On the third day we'd all move into High Camp, and should be reasonably well acclimatised. However, Mike Gill was keen to be up front the next day with the lead group, to ensure that High Camp fitted the needs of the film crew as well as those of the climbers—a decision that unsettled my own plans for an easy day around camp.

Next morning was fine, and Mike, Murray, Peter, Waka and Ding headed up the hill with moderate loads. Jim, Mike Dillon, Mingma, Pemma and I had a very pleasant morning, working in a leisurely way, making up loads for the High Camp, and had a delicious lunch. With most of the work done, I suggested we carry some loads part of the way to the top of the rock and depot them there. Pemma stayed behind to prepare the evening food and we headed off upwards with modest loads.

The first section was very easy—big rounded red slabs—and the advance party had built some cairns, which gave us a good line to follow. After an hour and a half the lovely rusty red slabs gave way to grey, steeper rock, plastered with snow and rather more exposed. Here we found Ding making a good route and running out the 500 feet of fixed rope. As we grunted up after him we complimented him on his fine steps. I was finding the altitude and my load a bit of an effort here, particularly up the final narrow ice gully, before starting on the steep snow of the glacier itself. We depoted our gear there, and then the rest of the team came down to join us. Mike Gill was most enthusiastic: "It's all good news. A beautiful camp-site, on a flat plateau with fine views of the mountains all around. Nar Parbat's not too bad but there's no need even to climb that if we don't want to. There's another peak beside the camp—only 500 feet higher, with an easy lead on to a narrow summit ridge—and to make it look good there's a big fluted snow face dropping from it into the next valley." They warned us of a long tiring plug up to the camp-site, but no difficult section, we'd just come up the worst bit. They all liked the place and their enthusiasm was infectious. Why not some of the party move up tomorrow? Why not everybody, for that matter? In a moment it was all settled.

And a name for the peak? "Ganga Sagar," suggested Mike.

"Not Ganga Sagar, but surely Ganga Parbat," Jim protested.

"Or Akash Parbat—Sky Peak," Mike countered, and so the peak was named for us anyway, since this fitted with our "Ocean to Sky" theme.

We came down the rope and then the snow and rock without much difficulty but I was glad to get back to camp and have a fine cup of lemon tea from Pemma. Jim and Peter had detoured off to the right to check the ice danger to Base Camp—very little indeed, they confirmed. Earlier we'd had a scare. Jim, Mingma, Pemma and I were sitting at Base Camp drinking tea when a terrible roar had us all involuntarily making a start for the nearest protective rocks—before we realised it was a jet plane streaking over, and not an ice avalanche at all.

Nilkanta eventually appeared, a graceful spire above sunset-tinged clouds. The sun went down almost directly behind Nilkanta, with Narayan bulking angrily beside, when it wasn't sulking under heavy cloud. Narayan was nearly always cloud-covered, and when it showed itself it was a most unattractive hulk of steep snow and ice-plastered rock. It required little imagination to picture ourselves scratching desperately to cling to sloping ledges, with insufficient snow on them to plug steps but too much to get a grip on the rock.

The view up-valley was strikingly different. Almost at a line, the heavy snow and glaciation stopped, and bare dry valleys led up to scree and smoothly snow-capped peaks rising above the barren slopes of the Mana Pass area. Already it was Tibetan landscape, and over beyond, out of sight, was Tibet itself, dry high plateau and the fabled Mount Kailas, home of Lord Shiva.

"Soup ready!" Pemma's call brought everyone drifting to the cook-tent, and we joined in a very satisfying meal of soup, rice, corned beef stew and marrow, pineapple and custard, and a mug of steaming Bournvita. As darkness drew itself around us it was difficult to pretend, even yet, that we were roughing it.

The tents became little orange or blue glows in the dark, as one by one we crawled in and lit candles to read books or write diaries. Peter wrote in his diary: "Established the site of High Camp in view of a fabulous mainsail-shaped peak with an elegant summit ridge and steep fluted snow face. Once again it clouded in—without our footsteps on the plateau we would have been lost. At the top of the fixed rope we met Dad, Jim, Mingma and Mike Dillon laden with three days' food and fuel for High Camp. We talked enthusiastically about what we had seen, which was received well by Jim and Mike Dillon, but quietly by Dad. I think he is pleased all the same. It was quite a tough haul up to the base of the glacier; I was pleased to see how good he looked after carrying a load up to that 16,500-foot depot. My headache problem seems to be fading into the background, though I still need two Mogadons to put me to sleep."

The silence was broken only by some muffled coughing from Waka — a common complaint at altitude. At last, unable to stand it any longer, Waka padded over to Peter's tent two yards away.

"What did you stop your cough with last night, Murray?"

"I'm on Bactrim — Amoxil didn't seem to help. But ask Mike."

"Oh Mike, have we any cough lozenges? My cough is keeping the others awake."

"No."

"Well then, what?"

"Have you taken a Mogadon?"

"Yes."

A pause, while the good doctor ponders. "Then take another," he says. End of consultation.

Wednesday, October 12th, was the day of the big lift — and also the day on which the *Himachal Times* wrote its prophetic words. Everyone was carrying heavy loads, even me. We moved slowly up the rocky section and then up the snow gullies and the fixed rope to the top of the rock. Above us was a steep snow slope, which we knew would be hard work. Some of the party picked up extra gear from the depot and made up their loads to around seventy pounds but I stuck with my basic load of about forty-five pounds, which was proving enough for me.

We started up the steep slope and then on to a long traverse to the left, and it seemed to go on for ever. The snow was soft and the tracks were very safe, but the rise was quite considerable. I was afraid of holding up the team behind me and kept driving myself along — Jim Wilson was shouting indecipherable messages from below — I thought he was urging me on and I responded as best I could. In fact he was suggesting we take it a bit easier, for he too had a very heavy load. Finally we came over the steep crest and the tracks led out to the right up an endless slope of soft snow. We unroped here and then just plugged on and on, getting more and more tired. Murray and Ding and Peter and Waka were already relaying loads, but I was finding it a terrible struggle up the last thousand feet. It was an enormous relief to come over the crest and walk along to our camp-site at over 18,000 feet. I was really too tired to enjoy the view, but noted the beautiful snowfield and sharp attractive summits.

I concentrated on tramping out a flat spot in the snow and erecting my tent, using plastic bags filled with snow as deadmen to hold the tent down. It was slow, cold work, for powder snow lay deep every-where, fluffy and difficult to compact. Finally I got the tent up, crawled inside my sleeping-bag, and just collapsed, leaving all the other chores to the rest of the party. The tents were all up by dark, but Mingma and Pemma worked on for another hour or more, cooking in a hole in the snow in bitter cold, then stumped around all the tents in the dark bringing us a steaming meal.

I had a warm but restless night with lots of dreams. Next morning was fine and clear. Mike and Jim thought we should have an easy day, though Murray and Peter, being fitter and better acclimatised than the rest of us, were restless, and plugged steps through the soft snow towards Akash Parbat. Tomorrow we hoped to have the whole party climb it. After that, those who were keen would climb Nar Parbat—though for me Akash would be as fine an end to the expedition as I could imagine. I crawled out of my tent with the idea of joining Peter and Murray, but I felt so weak and dizzy that I realised it was a waste of time.

Meanwhile Mike Gill had decided to return to Base Camp to pick up a spare microphone for the film crew, the one at High Camp having been broken. There was also the possibility of a mail runner arriving at Base, and we could do with an extra tent and more food.

Mingma went with him. Mike's diary describes his day: "Thursday October 13th—The Camp wasn't bursting with energy this morning. Waka had a headache and had slept poorly. Jim had a bad night too, waking suddenly with a feeling of being unable to breathe and a need to sit up and go outside for fresh air. I didn't like the sound of that very much, but I could find nothing wrong with him—nothing to suggest the dreaded pulmonary oedema. Nevertheless, I've started him on Lasix and he'll be having a rest day. I'll make sure we sleep in the same tent tonight.

"Mingma and I had an easy trip down to Base Camp—you can almost feel the air thickening as you drop down those 3,000 feet. While we were loading up, one of the old men of Mana turned up with a bag full of mail from Raj, who had just arrived from the New Zealand High Commission in Delhi. Something for everybody, which should be good for morale.

"When we turned towards High Camp the good downhill feeling operated in reverse. We had about thirty pounds each — nothing to

Mingma, but a lot to me, and at the foot of the steep snow I wrote out a note, 'Have mail, but am moving *very* slowly. I may need assistance if you want to read your mail before midnight', and I gave it to Mingma, who shot off as if he was breathing pure oxygen.

"I ground on through the rest of the afternoon. And then close on dark, Ding came over the horizon to pick up my load. Wonderful it was, going up with nothing but mail. 'The camp's not a very cheerful place,' said Ding. 'Jim and Waka aren't all that well and Ed has stayed in his tent all day.' It was snowing and dark when we arrived back.

"There was a ripple of excitement as I went from tent to tent handing out mail, feeling like Father Christmas. Ed looked snug in his small blue tent. As always his pile of letters was by far the biggest. The others began shouting scraps of news from tent to tent.

"Peter: 'Sarah's baby was a ten-and-a-half pound monster.'

"Murray: 'Bloody hell! My brother's smashed up my car.'

"Ding: 'The new truck at the Centre's stuffed, because someone forgot to put anti-freeze in it.'

"Jim: 'Max says all Ed's bridges in the Dudh Kosi have been washed away by a freak wave.'

"Murray: 'Peter's girlfriend has left New Zealand.'

"I drank some tea and soup but was too tired to eat much. It's eight o'clock. I've just taken the two Mogadons I need to make me sleep up here—they give me a hangover but not nearly as bad as the hangover from not sleeping."

★   ★   ★

Later: "Woken by Murray at about ten p.m. I slowly surfaced through the Mogadon and focused on Murray, who was obviously worried. 'Ed's been calling out for Jim. He's got a bad pain in his back. I thought maybe you'd better have a look at him.'

"I put some clothes on, grabbed a stethoscope and my fairly rudimentary medical kit and swished through the new snow to Ed's tent. Murray, who had been spurred on to write a long letter by the newly arrived mail, was the only one awake, apart from Jim who had been woken along with me. I squashed into Ed's tent to squat cross-legged beside him by the light of a torch. He had a bad pain in the small of his back. It had just come on in the last hour or so. There was nothing else. I checked lungs and heart. All normal, except I could feel no pulse at his wrists. Why was that? But the pulses in his neck and groins were strong, 104 per minute, higher than a sea-level pulse but probably normal for a partially acclimatised person at 18,000 feet. He was tender when I thumped the small of his back. My first thought, when

Murray had called me, was that it might be some sort of lung or chest pain but it wasn't that at all. I was puzzled and a bit uneasy. Why should Ed suddenly develop severe pain in this place and at this time at night? Was it just due to lying flat in a sleeping-bag for twenty-eight hours? What could I do to relieve the pain and let Ed get some sleep? He'd tried Paracetamol without relief. My only other pain killer was Omnopon: I decided to give him half an ampoule, the alternatives being that or nothing. Back in my own tent I lay awake for an hour with questions turning over and over in my mind. Just before falling asleep, I heard Murray call out, 'How's it going, Ed?'

" 'O.K. The pain's going.' He sounded drowsy."

★   ★   ★

My own memories of the evening of October 13th are not happy ones. I remember Mingma zooming in and saying that Mike was bringing up mail—a cheerful uplift to most of the team, but I was past caring about mail by that stage. I remember waking Murray with a loud cry and telling him my back was very painful. Mike gave me an injection and I went heavily off to sleep. As I have little memory of the eighteen hours that followed I will quote from the others' diaries.

14

Rescue and Success

MIKE WRITES: FRIDAY OCTOBER 14TH, HIGH CAMP. WHEN I WOKE IT was bright sunlight. I called out to Pemma, who was brewing tea, "How's the *Bara Sahab*?"

I was hoping a cheerful Ed would greet me with the news that he'd slept well, the pain was gone and he felt refreshed and full of energy. But Pemma just said, "*Bara Sahib* sleeping."

I went over to have a look. Ed was sleeping all right, even though it was already nine a.m. He was breathing normally. It was hard to tell his colour, for he was in a blue tent, but there was nothing to get immediately alarmed about. I decided to leave things for half an hour before waking him. Nevertheless I was uneasy. A short while later, Mingma, who had taken Ed a cup of tea, came over to see me, looking very worried. "*Bara Sahab* some checking necessary . . .?"

Everyone was alert and on edge by now. I got dressed, picked up the stethoscope and went into Ed's tent, where I gave him a hard shake. His eyes opened slowly. "How are you, Ed?"

"I . . . A-a-a-h . . ." It was the best reply I could get. I lifted him upright and listened to his lungs, where there were unmistakable sounds of fluid that had not been there last night. Yet his breathing was not that of pulmonary oedema of any severity. It was his cerebral state that wasn't right. The effect of the Omnopon? That would have worn off six hours ago, and such a small dose couldn't possibly have an effect of this magnitude. Cerebral oedema of high altitude? Whatever it was, cerebral oedema or pulmonary oedema, or both, it was high-altitude sickness, and I felt a panicky sense of urgency. High-altitude sickness is a fast-changing condition, always in the process of getting either worse or better. To get worse is to die eventually. And the only way to get better is by taking oxygen, either from a cylinder, of which we had none, or by going to a lower altitude. Even a couple of thousand feet can make a critical difference. So we had to get lower, and quickly.

"Come on," I said. "Let's get Ed out of here." I hardly needed to say it. "Shall I go down and call a chopper?" asked Murray. We all stopped and thought about that one. If we raised the alarm, the noise would echo round the world, the last thing we wanted, or Ed would want, for that matter. If we didn't? Well, if we didn't, Ed might die halfway down the mountain. There was no option—call the chopper. And we agreed that Murray would be the fastest off the mountain. In five minutes he was off, running, and soon dropped out of sight.

The team swung into action as if the whole expedition had been a preparation for this situation. No one said much—it just happened. For two months we'd been an infuriatingly disorganised bunch of individuals doing things according to our own whims. Suddenly, now, we realised we were in a bad situation and we'd have to work hard, and work together, to get out of it. Maybe Ed's life was at stake—and we threw ourselves into the task with a rare sense of unity and purpose. There was almost a tangible bond between the five working on making a sledge, Murray racing down the mountainside, Mingma, Pemma and Mike Dillon clearing up camp—and Ed lying in his sleeping-bag with his eyes shut. The affection and loyalty we all felt for him suddenly seemed intensified a hundred times.

I gave Ed a big slug of Lasix to get the fluid out of his lungs and we collapsed the tent over him, just as he lay, with two foam mattresses beneath him. To this improvised sledge we tied ropes fore and aft. In fifteen minutes we were off. We grabbed a minimum of gear for ourselves and set off, hauling Ed, with his tent-sledge ploughing through the soft snow like a big seal. Peter had been distressed beyond words back at camp—on the verge of tears—and now he was out front pulling like a huge cart-horse. We were moving fast, everyone straining at the ropes and panting in the thin air.

We came to the top of the steep snow slope, with the rocks of our old route 500 feet below. Carrying Ed over the rocks would be a nightmare. But over on our right, the main glacier tumbled down a thousand feet lower—impossible in the slots and seracs of the ice-fall, but between it and the rocks was a steep but smooth gully, partly of snow, partly of hard ice with small crevasses. We steered towards the gully. Gradually the angle steepened and the pullers peeled off one by one to become anchors instead; it was difficult to adjust the pull and the brake, and at one stage Peter was pulling Ed and all the rest of us by mistake.

Soon we were braking in earnest on the steep slope, Jim and Ding belaying alternately from above, while Waka backed up behind them; Peter and I hauled laterally to get in line with the top of the gully. Mingma, Pemma and Mike Dillon appeared at the top of the slope, hardly able to believe the speed of our progress. None of them had crampons, but we just left them behind, praying they'd cope—a slip from one of them would be a final catastrophe we could all do without.

At the foot of the big slope, beside the entrance to the gully, we stopped. Ed had bunched up into an uncomfortable heap at the bottom end of his tent-sledge. He seemed a better colour already. We'd dropped 1,500 feet in less than an hour.

"Where are we?" he said, his speech slurred but recognisable. He was uncomfortable, pulling off his gloves and trying to straighten up. Then I remembered the Lasix making his kidneys work at ten times their normal speed. He needed to empty his bladder. All that fluid coming out of his lungs or his brain or wherever the damage was—I felt as relieved as Ed did.

We remade the sledge, with Ed supported more firmly, and stumbled across a patch of rock, carrying him between us to the top of the gully.

Everything depended on the belayers now. If one of them failed, Ed would shoot off down the steep ice, irretrievably. Ding and Jim worked off good shaft belays where there were patches of snow, or they climbed down into crevasses where they could wedge in firmly— "I could hold a jet boat from down here," called Jim from the depths of a crevasse—or they worked off fragile pick belays with Ding constructing intricate friction systems through karabiners.

The crevasses were only a foot or so in width and the sledge slid over easily with a bit of a lift. One was much wider, but across it ran a narrow bridge. We held our breath as we guided Ed delicately across it. And then on down again, rope length by rope length.

At midday we came to a final halt where the gully plunged over a cliff. We were down to 16,000 feet and Ed's complexion had a healthy pink glow that he'd not had three hours earlier. Till now we'd been in bright sun, but cloud was forming fast on the mountain tops and rolling up from the valley below. Soon mist closed around us and light snow began falling. The only route was down the rocks on our left, slabby inter-connecting ledges winding back and forth amongst bluffs—easy country for a fit climber on foot but desperate with our 250 lb. load. Ed was slowly taking more and more notice of his surroundings, asking again where we were and what was happening.

"How heavy are you, Ed?" asked Ding, more by way of making conversation than anything else.

"Twelve stone four," said Ed, an answer that must have come from his lean Everest days.

We made a rope stretcher with handles, and for a while struggled down with this. Mike Dillon had caught up now, and was ferrying packs for us. But the ground was too uneven, Ed too heavy, and we were falling over each other. We gave up in despair.

Ding made a one-man carrying harness from a coil of rope and for a while I tottered down the slabs, supported each side and behind, with Ed on my back; but he was hanging terribly awkwardly and in pain, and he called a halt even before I did. Then we tried walking him between four of us. Mingma had joined us now. When we came to a line of steep slabs we simply slid Ed down on a tight belay. It was painfully slow and for Ed, who was now aware of what was happening, it was a nightmare. But by sliding the steep bits, walking the flat sections between, and resting frequently, we made 500 exhausting feet down the rock to within a few hundred feet of Base Camp.

Ding suddenly stood up, listening intently. "I can hear a chopper warming up!" he said. No one else could hear it, but we all stopped what we were doing and listened. Nothing but the silence of mist and falling snow. But then suddenly we all heard the unmistakable chop, chop, chop, of a helicopter. For a moment a gap opened in the cloud for us to catch a glimpse of the far side of the valley – but no helicopter; and then the mist poured in again. There was not a chance of anyone finding us in this, but for an hour we heard intermittently the helicopter rising into the air, as holes appeared in the cloud cover.

"You know, I reckon we ought to camp here," said Ding.

Ed looked up. "I was thinking the same thing myself."

We were happy that Ed was on the mend, and there seemed little to be gained by pushing on under these difficult conditions. We made him comfortable on a rock ledge. Peter set off for Base Camp to collect a tent and food, while the rest of us stamped our feet and slapped ourselves to keep warm in the gloom of approaching nightfall.

About half past five we saw a figure moving quickly up through the mist below.

"There's Peter," I said.

Mingma shook his head.

"He's not carrying anything," said Jim. "Maybe it's Murray." But it was neither; it was Hungry Boy, sent up by Major Bawa from Mana with a small cylinder of oxygen.

While Mingma, Ding, Waka and Mike Dillon headed off for Base Camp, Jim climbed down the bluffs to collect the oxygen from Hungry Boy. Jim was appalled at how weak Ed was as he climbed back up again, but soon we had the mask on him. Not long afterwards Peter arrived carrying a huge load, including a can of peaches, Ed's favourite food in the mountains.

And what a difference the tent made! Into a small comfortable world of our own we crawled, out of the vast inhospitable darkness outside. With Ed now talking and responding intelligibly though weakly, we fed him a few peaches, and ate cheese and ham and biscuits ourselves. The oxygen had made no apparent difference, but when it finally ran out after two hours, he was sleeping easily. The wind picked fretfully at the hurriedly and loosely pitched tent and snow piled on the roof. Peter, Jim and I talked for a couple of hours whilst Ed slept. It had been an amazing day; no arguments, just action and people working together, not saying much — and here we were warm in our sleeping-bags and content. The crisis was over.

★   ★   ★

As we slept comfortably in our tent high on the mountainside, Murray was crouched under a rock on the bluffs 3,000 feet below. He had reached Badrinath from High Camp in one and three-quarter hours, incredibly fast time. He must have skimmed down the snow and slabs and grass bluffs like a snow leopard in full flight. Almost immediately he found the two people he most wanted, Major Bawa and Raja Narayan from the New Zealand High Commission.

Murray writes: They took one look at me and knew something bad was happening. As soon as I'd told them all about it we raced off to the telephone exchange and jammed all connections. First the Major tried going through military channels — he put on a fantastic performance, but the connection was bad. "Stuff this!" I said to Raja. "Let's try and get the High Commissioner in Delhi." I don't know how Raja did it, but somehow he got through on a very bad line. He had to shout — a few panicky words. "Sir Edmund Hillary is dying. Send helicopter immediately."

Poor Raja! He was overcome that he'd shouted at his boss. I reassured him, nothing to worry about — he wouldn't lose his job.

Well, in this country where all foreigners claim that nothing works, the chopper arrived in two hours. Unfortunately the weather had crapped out and there was little they could do except fly around making enough noise to reassure them on the hill that help was on its way.

I began having problems with the Lieutenant-Colonel, who wanted me to lead a company of army scouts up to evacuate Ed in the middle of the night. I could just see all the flak I'd get from Dingle and Hillary if I turned up in charge of a company of Indian soldiers. General Jones! But it would have been a disaster, all those people floundering about in the dark, and so I declined as politely as I could. The General was rung, and informed that I was an obstinate and stubborn man because I would not agree to their offer of help. Feeling bad, I compromised, saying that I'd set off now with a thirty pound bottle of oxygen, and they could follow in the morning. They reluctantly agreed. There was just no point in a company of soldiers up there in the middle of the night, so at five o'clock, in the pouring rain, stubborn old Jones took off. If Ed was no better, then he'd definitely need the oxygen.

So began the worst trip of my life. Rain turned to snow. There was hardly any track, and what there was soon became obscured. In the snow it became impossible to find the route between the cairns which Jim and I had put up just a few days before. My instinct in orientation was tested to the limit, not to mention my instinct for surviving as I traversed and climbed over snow-covered juniper and slippery snow grass.

Around seven o'clock, at about 13,500 feet, I was well and truly lost; so I pulled out my sleeping-bag and crawled under a rock to wait for the snow to stop and the sky to clear. This it did around midnight. So I packed up and turned back to the last cairn I'd seen. It was still no good—just big white bluffs everywhere. All I could do was to start going upwards. God, I was tired! Twenty steps at a time, then a breather. On the steep stuff, I was climbing with both hands and holding the torch in my mouth. I'd only been to Base Camp once before and, in this weird light, easy slabs became hanging bluffs. Lost and confused, I yelled my head off. Then I heard Ding answering. I've never been so happy to hear his voice before. He dressed and came to guide me to camp—I was several hundred feet above it. Ed was much better—thank God for that.

Ding writes: About three a.m. I woke with a start. Waka woke simultaneously. We both sat bolt upright and listened. Someone was shouting from up the mountainside.

"Must be Jim," I said, pulling on my boots. I staggered out into a very snowy world.

"Ya-a-a-a Ho-o-o-o ..." There was a light gleaming through the mist. Hello—Christ! It was Murray. He'd come up during the night, carrying a large cylinder of oxygen. We crowded into the flimsy shelter called the cook tent, where Pemma soon had a brew under way. In one corner, like a nest of vipers, were curled the six unhappy porters from Mana sent up by Major Bawa. Not one head was showing and I swear all six bodies covered no more than two square metres. We just sat and talked and drank endless brews—a really close and intimate group, all happy, knowing that Ed was well.

Then at dawn, with a very white world underfoot and a few pale stars above, we began upwards with Murray's oxygen and the stretcher brought up by the Mana men. At the temporary camp everyone was in good spirits. Ed was vastly improved. We crowded into the small tent —Ed, Mike, Jim, Mingma, Peter, Waka, Murray and me—our arms and legs around each other, and we joked and laughed until the sun hit the tent.

Jim writes: Saturday, October 15th. A much happier camp this morning. Ed was just fantastically better; he could laugh again, and soon we were all crowded into the tent with a positively convivial atmosphere. Ding launched into tales of disastrous helicopter rescues, and soon we weren't sure we wanted the chopper. Ed was so clearly better—it would be great if he got off just with us.

But at nine a.m. we heard the helicopter. It lifted steadily out of the valley, up past us, to circle round and round over High Camp, a little speck against the blue sky. I could imagine what they were reporting back: "We have looked for a long time and there is no movement—they are all dead."

And the newspaper headlines—"Deserted Camp all that Remains of Hillary and Party." But at length the pilot saw us and approached. We collapsed the tent and, with Ed walking unassisted, retreated from the flat area. Round and round went the helicopter, looking carefully. Then, with the co-pilot waving us back, it edged in, blasting us with a gale of powder snow. The noise was terrifying—I hoped we wouldn't get our heads chopped off. The pilot touched his skids down briefly, but almost immediately shook his head and pulled off again—secretly I was relieved.

We packed up, realising we should move to Base Camp, or at least to a better landing spot. Ed walked easily with support. Not much of the invalid about him this morning. A few khaki-clad figures appeared on the rocks below, and before long the slopes were swarming with soldiers. They had radios, and said the helicopter would try again from a flat spot not far down.

It came past, circling, hovering, eyeing the terrain. And then, more purposefully it came in straight towards us, shuffling forwards on the rocky ground to a firm stance and blowing snow into our faces like an arctic blizzard. There were men running. Mike Gill, crouched low, ran forward first; then Ed, staggering between Murray and Peter. In a moment Ed and Mike were inside the cabin. The engine roared louder and the big chopper lifted off, lurching sideways down into the valley.

I stood there with tears streaming down my cheeks; Peter too, Murray, Ding and Mike Dillon, though we tried to hide them. The soldiers shouted with delight. We slapped their shoulders and Murray embraced the Captain. Now they set up a great series of chanting cheers—*Jai! Jai!*—and set off down in high good spirits.

Peter writes: October 15th. As the chopper disappeared from view, sending snow everywhere, I could feel tears—and then relief as the emotion and tension of the past twenty-four hours dissipated. This morning in camp—it was so good seeing Dad laughing, though weakly; he was still with us; still the very same.

The noise of the chopper faded into the distance and very slowly we walked to Base Camp. The soldiers moved off; then the six porters, still cold from their terrible night. Jim said he'd go down to Badrinath —Dad and Mike should be comfortably settled there by now and he'd return next day with Mike to go to High Camp the day after.

Murray and Ding and I will go to High Camp tomorrow. We have to climb that mountain.

*   *   *

Ed writes: I have no recollection of the morning of October 14th when I was being lowered down the snowy face of the mountain. I only became dully aware of things as I was bumped slowly down the rock. But as I reached about 16,000 feet, I started to recover rapidly. I heard the helicopter vainly searching for us in the clouds, but realised from my companions' comments that it wouldn't be able to land. When Peter brought up the tent I crawled inside and was reasonably comfortable.

The night passed quite placidly and I was warm and slept well. It blew and snowed energetically, but the morning was clear and I certainly felt stronger. I even enjoyed some canned peaches, which encouraged everyone. Then the rest of the party came up from Base Camp and we were really very cheerful.

I watched the chopper climb upwards, but it didn't seem able to find us against the dark rock, and circled round our High Camp at over 18,000 feet. Finally it returned down (following our tracks, they told us later) and tried to touch in to our camp-site, but it was too cramped and close to bluffs. I walked down, supported by Jim and Mike, and I even gave a bit of cheek when they slipped. Then a group of soldiers appeared with radio walkie-talkies and they picked out a much broader ledge lower down for the helicopter.

hind the cairn with the Ganga *pani* bottle is Akash Parbat.

ossing the plateau to Nar Parbat.

Climbing to the summit ridge of Akash Parbat.

Finally it came in again and with considerable skill teetered on to the ledge. Mike jumped in first and I was thrown in afterwards. Next moment we were out in space, leaving the snowy world and my friends behind.

We dropped down in slow circles into Mana and landed where a line of chairs had been drawn up. The local army, including our good friend Major Bawa, gave a very warm welcome and I was handed a cup of tea. I discovered that the Press was present in force—there was a second helicopter full of them—and they started asking questions which I answered as best I could, though I was still pretty fuzzy.

"Well," said the pilot, "let's go."

"I'm staying in Badrinath," I said. "I must keep contact with the expedition." They were very polite but very insistent. Just to Joshimath, they said. There was a doctor who pointed out that Joshimath at 6,000 feet was a much better altitude than Badrinath at 10,000 feet, with which Mike could only agree. And it was only two hours away by road. I agreed—I liked Joshimath, and it was indeed very close.

So it was on again and down to Joshimath for another informal and friendly gathering and another cup of tea and Press conference. But at length we'd said all we had to say. The pilot, a tall and dashing-looking young Sikh, rubbed his hands.

"Let's go," he said cheerfully.

I tried to dig my toes in, but this time I was up against the full military hierarchy of Joshimath. "It is an absolute rule that any person evacuated by helicopter must fly down to Bareilly for full medical check." Again, very polite but firmly insistent. It would have been uncivil of me to refuse, for they had, after all, mounted a swift and effective rescue operation.

"When can we come back?" I asked.

"Once you have clearance you can come back straight away."

"Today?" asked Mike.

"Yes. If you have clearance you can fly back today."

So Mike and I climbed aboard. It was a longer flight this time, close on two hours, and at first we followed the course of the Alaknanda, the expedition in reverse. We saw the place where the river was seemingly choked with boulders; the twisted iron bridges of the Belakuchi Realignment; the Pipalkoti Gorge; Birehi, where the Czechs met disaster; Chamoli of the saxophone. And then Nandaprayag, a white line across the river marking the falls that stopped our jet boat.

At Karnaprayag we left the river to fly straight south over the foot-hills of Garhwal.

"Ranikhet," said the pilot, pointing to a town clustered across a hilltop. That was where we'd started from in 1951, for Ranikhet, in those days, was as far as the road went.

The hills ended abruptly and, before us, stretching towards the horizon, were the plains of the Ganga. On and on we went, mile after mile the same, a pattern of fields of different colours with villages scattered amongst them and little men like ants walking on paths or labouring in the fields.

We landed at the big air-force base at Bareilly and stepped out into air so warm and thick it was almost stifling. Again we were warmly welcomed; all the top military brass were there. A familiar figure in a black beret pushed forward eagerly—it was B.B., his eyes shining with emotion, and it was good to see him again. Beside us on the tarmac stood a big turbo-jet with no military markings on it.

"What's that?" I asked.

"That is the President's plane. It is here to take you to Delhi."

I really was getting the red carpet treatment. This time I politely but firmly declined, and they were happy to agree that I stay in Bareilly. I couldn't face the publicity and the hullabaloo and television cameras of Delhi. I just wanted to get back to the mountains.

We drove to the officers' wing of the military hospital where I filled out the papers for admission. So did Mike, for the only way he could stay with me was by being admitted to hospital. We had adjacent rooms. It was an old hospital made of concrete, and the rooms were tall and bare and painted green. I lay in a bed with a single window behind me and a big expanse of green wall to look at. Even at midday it was quite dark. A doctor asked me questions and examined me and took a cardiogram, which showed strain on the right side of my heart, he said. Everything else was normal.

I started to feel a deep sense of claustrophobia—everyone was very kind, but how would I get out of this place quickly? When would Mike get back to Badrinath? What was happening on the mountain? All my money and documents were in Badrinath, even my glasses—I couldn't even read or write. We seemed to have lost contact with everybody except the doctors, who were now in full control. "You have had pulmonary oedema and it is essential that you take complete rest here for several days at least," they said. "Under no circumstances can you return now to Joshimath." Mike argued my case for a while. If I'd been improving at 16,000 feet, then surely I'd continue to improve at 6,000 feet? But the doctors, understandably, were playing it safe.

Mike drove off to see the Group Captain in charge of the helicopter squadron. He was a Sikh, highly decorated in the 1970 war. He sympathised entirely with our predicament. If we could get authorisation from Defence Department in Delhi he would have a helicopter and crew ready within the hour. But as it was Saturday, Defence Department would be hard to contact. We decided to ring Colin Aickman, the New Zealand High Commissioner who had already helped so much with all phases of the expedition.

Mike writes: Bareilly, October 15th. Spent the afternoon trying to contact Colin Aickman. I can't even find his telephone number. Nowhere in Bareilly can I find a Delhi directory, nor can I make the Delhi Exchange understand what I want. All afternoon hanging on the end of the phone here, screeching hallo-o-o-o-o to voices heard momentarily on the other end before they get cut off or vanish.

I'd given up hope when at nine o'clock I was called to the phone. "Someone to speak to you." There was a faint voice at the far end. "Who is speaking?" For minutes we shouted, trying to identify each other. Then I caught it—Jogi!

"Jogi!" I shouted, joyfully. A friend at last! Someone who would understand! "Yes! Ed's fine. Get Colin Aickman to ring him."

I retired to my room. For a long time I lay there thinking about High Camp. What had gone wrong? It was so easy to be wise after the event. We'd camped too high too early. We'd exhausted ourselves, carrying big loads. We'd been too eager, and I had been more at fault than anyone. It was an easy mountain. Just race up it and be off— that's what we'd hoped. I thought back to 1960 when I'd gone down myself with altitude sickness at 13,000 feet. I'd just arrived from 10,000 feet, racing all the way. All next day I'd felt wretched and next morning I didn't wake up. Someone found me blue and stuporose, and my next memory is of sitting in a strange tent breathing oxygen from a mask. By midday I could think straight but couldn't stand up without assistance. It took me two weeks to get my strength back.

So what should we have done? Spent more time at Base, of course. Carried loads high but slept low. And that weird consultation on the night of the 13th. What was the pain in Ed's back? What about the 10 mg. of Omnopon—it should help pulmonary oedema, but what of cerebral oedema? Had that injection depressed Ed's respiration enough to swing him from a state of mild altitude sickness to one of frank cerebral oedema? It was a question I couldn't answer—but I would not do it again. And here we were, plunged from that high clear mountain to these steaming plains, with no way of escape. I tossed and turned. It was a wretched night.

*   *   *

Jim writes: Sunday 16th, Base Camp. Yesterday I ambled contentedly down the bluffs to Badrinath, expecting to find Ed and Mike there. To my dismay I learnt they'd gone to Joshimath, leaving no good reason for my not returning to Base Camp. But the marvellous Major Bawa was advised of my arrival by his network, and soon turned up with a most pressing invitation to dinner that evening.

It was an amazing evening with the Major. I walked through black- ness to a small hut, seemingly in the middle of nowhere on a hillside. No lights anywhere close around; just pitch blackness. Inside warm and cosy, a neon light tube and a flickering diesel stove. As his servant appeared through the door from a black nowhere bearing hot snacks, we drank rum and water and discussed life, hospitality and religion. But it was the radio news and the telephone that made the evening. Shouting down the lines to Joshimath, the Major discovered that Ed and Mike, despite their protests, had been taken to Bareilly and possibly on to Delhi. My heart sank, for I knew that was the last thing they would want.

We turned off the light, for it interfered with the radio, and sat in flickering firelight to listen to the B.B.C. news, and then to All India Radio news, first in Hindi and then in English. Yesterday the B.B.C. had told the world that Ed was very seriously ill on a mountain, but today they told of his evacuation and satisfactory medical condition.

Then a fabulous Indian meal. I tried to thank the Major.

"We have a Punjabi saying," he replied. "It is God who feeds us. The food is not mine but yours, though you are eating it at my table. I thank God and I thank my guests." Indian hospitality is truly in- exhaustible.

Today I waited a while lest Ed and Mike should turn up. A beautiful sunny morning but high cloud proclaimed wind, and by midday it was cold and blustery. The weather worsened as afternoon came. Down- valley, near Joshimath, it was black as night, with snow pouring from the skies. And in Badrinath the sun had gone, and angry clouds raced across on a cold, cold wind. I was packed and gloomily contemplating a wet and stormy ascent to Base Camp. I was very cold already. Major Bawa came in just after two o'clock—no news of Ed and Mike, or of oxygen for me to take up in case of altitude sickness. No chance of a helicopter arriving from Bareilly in this weather; so I set off. The Major thinks we're mad but tough. He is astonished that we should operate without radios or oxygen, not recce the river in detail, and so on. As I stepped moodily out into the oncoming storm, the little man who runs the rest-house said in some dismay.

"Is he going up in this weather?"

"Oh, they don't care about it," replied the Major. "They're all mad"

Sitting around, cold, I had chill forebodings of a miserable ascent. But once moving, and therefore warm for the first time that day, I found myself enjoying the climb, wandering in my own thoughts again. And the storm came to little: light snow, gentle wind, even snatches of sun. A fine Tibet and a stormy India seemed to meet in an in-between lull over Badrinath. Below me lay the town, and I wondered again at the contrast between the straggle of rusty corrugated iron and new pink concrete, and the inconspicuous grey stone houses and walls of the Bhotia village of Mana.

I reached Base Camp at about five p.m. to be greeted by Mingma, Pemma, Waka and Mike Dillon. Mingma had been up to High Camp with Peter, Murray and Ding, and back down with Ed's gear—what a fantastically fit man he is. Mingma is keen to be off this mountain, a mood I echo, and he has ordered the top three not to be slackers but to be off before sunrise to climb Nar Parbat in the morning. "Next day climb Akash, then clear the mountain," he said firmly.

My only worry is Mike Gill, who may want to climb the mountain. I've written a note to Ed explaining our unseemly haste and, heart in hand, have offered to go back up Nar Parbat with Mike if he insists. Meanwhile I'm praying earnestly he won't accept the offer. There's snow falling outside, but nothing desperate.

*   *   *

Murray writes: Sunday 16th—High Camp. Oh, the luxury of it all—three men in a nine-man camp! A tent to myself with two foam mats to lie on and snow slithering down the tent walls. Somewhere, I'm not sure where, avalanches are continually peeling off. They sound short; so I imagine there is a huge ice-fall nearby. Here in the middle of the Névé under the shadow of Nar Parbat rising 1,500 feet above, we feel relatively secure.

Mingma came up with us this morning and returned midday with the rest of Ed's gear. It was good, plugging up with an old close friend. He was a porter on Everest way back in '53, and so it was experience of the grand old tradition of Himalayan mountaineering. Mingma is still a bloody good mountaineer and, if he had so desired, he could quite easily have outwalked me, but we stuck together, plugging away. Something rare these days—the close relationship between Sherpa and *Sahib*.

Peter and Ding have been endeavouring to coax the old primus to boil a stew to last the next three days. After an hour there was an eruption of terrible cursing from Peter, announcing that the primus had toppled over, leaving two gallons of stew in pools on the tent floor. Ding was attempting to ladle it back into the pot.

"Christ," said Peter, "this tent's been used all the way from Calcutta. We'll all get cholera."

"We'll have time to climb Nar Parbat first," said Ding. "And if we do get sick, Murray can go and get a chopper."

It didn't sound all that funny. Outside, the weather has been packing in all afternoon, much more than the usual light fall of afternoon snow. I don't like our chances for the climb tomorrow.

★　　★　　★

Ed writes: Sunday 16th, Bareilly. A most uneasy sleep last night, my first in Bareilly. More tests this morning and my desperation increased. Mike is working his own form of shuttle diplomacy between the Air Force, the Army, the doctors, and Colin Aickman in Delhi. Eventually Colin rang to say that the Air Force Commander-in-Chief had agreed to a helicopter flight next morning, but final confirmation had to come through. The Group Captain in Bareilly could do nothing until official permission reached him. I found it a period of great tension.

In the afternoon Mike and I set off for a walk though the streets of Bareilly, but almost immediately we were surrounded by a flock of distressed nurses and orderlies. I had to rest. Those were their instructions. The Sister rushed off to ring the doctor, who gave permission and we set off with three army guards and a medical orderly following discreetly behind. We walked down peaceful streets lined with old trees. It must have been the best part of town, with park-like grounds surrounding grand old houses occupied by generals and colonels and other distinguished members of the Establishment.

Then I discovered a remarkable coincidence—Harish Sarin would be arriving that evening for a conference on high-altitude nutrition. Mike and I had arranged to go to a film that evening—we would meet Sarin there. The film was a love story, but as it was in Hindi I understood very little of it. The girl was young and of dazzling beauty; her boyfriend somewhat older; mid-thirties, I thought. My neighbour explained the story. "She is the daughter of wealthy parents but he is a poor boy though he is a very clever student. They get married against her mother's wishes and she keeps meddling and interfering all the time, and this makes their marriage very unhappy. That is why she is always singing such sad songs."

"How old is the boy?" I asked.

"Oh, he is not really a boy. He is a very, very famous Indian actor. He is fifty-five. He also writes the story and directs the film."

Harish arrived in excellent vein.

"Our medical people are not entirely happy, but if you feel you must go, then you may leave in the morning."

I felt a great sense of relief. Harish spoke to the Group Captain. My neighbour assured me the film would have a happy ending. At nine o'clock I returned to my room for a much easier night's sleep.

Monday 17th, Bareilly: The barber came to shave me at six a.m., and some breakfast arrived shortly afterwards. Sarin, looking as fresh as a daisy, called in to say goodbye. Mike and I travelled out by car through the awakening suburbs. We left the town behind and drove on down a straight road with fields of crops on either side. The car was a taxi, and an old one. We had not gone far when the motor began cutting out intermittently, and for a while we jerked ahead spasmodically with the engine sounding like bursts of machine-gun fire interspersed with periods of quiet. Eventually all was silent and we rolled to a halt. The road was as empty as the sky above. Without a word the driver got out and began walking back to Bareilly. It was hard to know whether he was going for help or running away.

Mike and I got out, picked up our gear, which was almost nothing anyway, and set off towards the air-force base which showed as some low buildings in the distance. After about two miles we found a pair of rickshaw-wallahs sleeping under a tree beside their vehicles. Mike asked how much they'd charge to take us to the Base, a futile exercise as we were unlikely to refuse whatever they asked and they couldn't understand what he was saying anyway. We climbed into separate rickshaws, pointed down the road and set off.

At the entrance to the Base we were detained by the guard. Mike went inside the guardhouse briefly.

"They don't want to let us through. Extra security this morning — Sir Edmund Hillary is departing for Joshimath."

I identified myself. On we went, past bungalows and hangers. Panting, the rickshaw-wallahs ran up to the big black Alouette helicopter with its drooping blades standing on the tarmac. A crowd of officers was there to say farewell. I shook hands with the Group Captain and thanked him warmly for all his help. He and his men had done a magnificent job.

My spirits rose as the helicopter lifted off and we turned north across the plains. The pilot this time was a stocky little Nepali. Where the hills began, he pointed out a dark lake, improbably high on a steep hillside. There were lots of old houses round it and a big quadrangle on a spur, surrounded by the red buildings of what looked like some sort of college.

"Naini Tal," said the pilot and I remembered the name, one of the famous old hill stations of India. Over Ranikhet we flew, Karnaprayag, Nandaprayag—and finally Joshimath. It was only two full days I'd been away, but it seemed like a lifetime.

At Joshimath it was sunny and warm and peaceful, though snow was deep on the mountains around. Mike departed in a jeep to Badrinath and I was given a pleasant room in the officers' quarters. Avalanches were booming down from the peaks around and I worried about the team on the mountain—what conditions would they be meeting? Six feet of new snow on the steep slope below High Camp would turn it into a death trap.

Using a pair of cheap glasses Mike had bought me in the Bareilly bazaar, I sat in the sun reading what the newspapers had been saying about us. The *Himachal Times* of October 16th wrote another editorial, sad that we had not heeded their warnings of October 12th.

GODS WHO FAILED THE EXPEDITION

"Badrikashram is presided over by God throughout the year but in the winter months, they rule it exclusively. No mortals are allowed to enter it. Stories have been told for a long time that lone *sadhus* who attempted to defy the ban never survived . . . and what is being noticed in connection with the 'Ocean to Sky' expedition by Sir Edmund Hillary proves the ancient beliefs . . .

"The peaks of Narayan and Nar Parbat are highly sanctified by the gods and goddesses who are supposed to be living there throughout the year. The courageous adventurer in Sir Hillary decided to ascend the Nar Parbat, but God failed him: he was taken seriously ill . . .

"We wish Hillary speedy recovery. But he has to seek the blessings of God. Everest has no such sanctity attached. There is no legend about the presence of Gods there. Hillary is super mountaineer. But he has to live with the traditions and beliefs of every area. It is for this reason that the goddess in Ganga stopped him, but protected him also. The Narayan Parbat refused him entry very politely. The gods of Nar got a little angry because Hillary did not understand their polite warning in refusing an entry to Narayan Parbat. We hope Hillary will be happy with the achievements made by his expedition without expecting to do any better. Whenever he plans his next visit, he must follow the rules of Devlok."

The jeep returned from Badrinath with my gear, messages from Peter and Jim who sounded in good form, and a note from Mike saying there was little fresh snow in Badrinath, no avalanches, and that all was going ahead.

Murray writes: Monday 17th, High Camp: I woke at daybreak and yelled to Pete sleeping in the cook-tent, "Get the primus going – I'll be with you in a couple of minutes and we'll get breakfast." But it took half an hour just to get dressed and put boots on. It was bitterly cold and the effort to do anything amazed me. Eventually Ding and I joined Peter in his tent for the remains of last night's stew and a billyful of Bournvita.

It was a grey dawn but maybe getting fine. We left as the sun hit the tent, straight into knee-deep powder snow. How I hate the stuff, and we had miles of it across the plateau till my feet were hard and numb like lumps of wood. Ding was quiet, Pete cursing, like me, but we all felt committed: winter was here, and it was now or never for Nar Parbat.

Three hours to plug across the plateau – it seemed hard to believe it could take so long. Ahead of us rose the mountain, a broad face of snow, steep below but easing off to a long summit ridge above. The lower face was guarded by an ice cliff on our left and rock bluffs to our right. But ahead, in the middle, was a gap filled with steep, smooth snow. I started up, but it was terribly unstable; any moment now the whole lot was going to peel off and bury us. Way to our right was a rock ridge, and I went for that, deep snow still, and getting deeper till we were up to our waists. Keep on and we'd be in to our necks; it was worse than the other place.

So we stopped, all despondent, on the verge of giving up; a lot of cloud was building up, promising more fresh snow. We just sat down, saying little, eating a bit of food and sucking at a bottle of cold Bournvita. I looked up at the bluff above us, rock poking through snow, and the others looked too.

"Stuff it," I said. "Let's have a go. It can't be worse than plugging round the bottom of this face."

So we set off, straight up. It was soft at first but better and better as we gained height. We roped up, on the front points of our crampons now, climbing crisp snow, the new powder having blown or slipped off. I'd been expecting rock higher up, but a snow ramp led left and upwards through the bluff; it was front-pointing all the way.

On the upper half of the mountain the angle eased and again the fresh snow was building up. Soft avalanches peeled off around us – nothing big, but it gave us something to think about as we plugged upward.

Peter stopped to change a film but found it snapped in two and was brittle in the cold. Suddenly the snow ahead flattened and stopped on a line. We'd reached the summit ridge and to mark the occasion it began snowing. Conditions were terrible—a cornice on our left and soft powder on our right ready to slide at the first kick.

"Stuff it," I says again, looking through the mist at a distant summit not much higher. "We've got to climb it." So I says a prayer to Lord Shiva and starts off, axe-shaft in to the hilt at every step. Complete white-out now, snowing gently, very quiet and still, the only sound the swish of avalanches, and no wind at all—an eerie place it was until I saw, quite close, two pinnacles of granite, the summit of Nar Parbat. Safe at last, I think, and just then the biggest avalanche of all cuts out from under Ding's feet.

Then we were on the summit, with Pete and I unfurling the red and white temple flag from Badrinath. The clouds cleared in patches to show glimpses of the great mountains of the north, Mukut Parbat and Kamet and others we couldn't name. Far below was a huge glacier stretching to the west and flanked by a series of tall and rocky peaks.

"Well," says Pete, "we've reached the sky. Let's go." And we turned for home.

The descent was easy, pigeon-holing down the face and stumbling exhausted back to camp. We came in like three ancient antarctic explorers returning to camp after six years in the field.

We were greeted by Jim, Mingma and Pemma, Mike Dillon and Waka. Mingma was grinning from ear to ear. He gave us cups of lemon tea laced with brandy, saying as he did so, "You no summit getting, I no brandy giving."

"We no summit getting, Mingma next day going."

He bloody well would have too.

Jim writes: Monday 17th, High Camp. It was really very cold indeed that evening. There was a beautiful sunset, peaks appearing and disappearing through ragged gaps in red-tinged clouds, and the red and blue of the tents striking but lonely in the vast white expanse of the snowfield. But then it sank into a freezing night. I spent half a night of pure misery. I kept feeling yet again that I was desperately short of air—dozing, then sitting bolt upright gasping urgently. And it was so cold our breath froze into thick frost on the inside of the tent roof, rubbing off on us every time we moved. My beard was a stiff mass of rime and my nose-drip frozen solid. Why do we get into these miserable situations? I took no Mogadon, for I was suspicious of the stuff—I felt sure it had accentuated my misery the first night at High Camp and certainly it hadn't got me to sleep then. So though Mike Dillon took some, I held out. Then, bliss, about midnight I dropped off at long last and woke moderately refreshed.

Ding writes: Tuesday 18th, High Camp. A fairly leisurely breakfast as we prepared to climb Akash Parbat—certainly less hectic, with Pemma and Mingma doing the cooking. Murray appeared dejected, but we had no idea of the reason—that he had a frost-bitten big toe. No, he wouldn't come up Akash, he was going down to Badrinath.

It was cold outside in the blue light of early morning, but once the sun had lit and warmed the camp we were up and off. Akash looked easy though spectacular; Mingma isn't saying his usual prayers. Mike Dillon stayed in camp to film the climb on long shots.

It was a short plod to the foot of Akash where an amazing panorama opened before us of the high peaks around Nanda Devi. Waka, going strongly, plugged a line of steps up to the low peak. Mingma wasn't happy, so turned back. Peter said, "I reckon Mingma's wife must have given him a good talking to before he left."

From the low peak we looked along a sharp unstable summit ridge, bright sunlight on our left, deep shadow on the right. At the first step there was a low "whoosh" and the slope on the right broke off and slid down to an impressive ice-fall. The left side was nicely compacted.

We had planned to climb on one rope but, with Waka filming, this became impracticable. Jim produced ten feet of nylon tape. "Come on, Waka—we'll tie ourselves together with this and Pete and Ding can use the rope."

Debate raged on a call system if someone fell, to indicate which side his companions should jump.

Jim said, "If I fall right, I'll shout 'left' and you jump left." Peter said, "If I fall right, I'll shout 'right' so you know which side I'm falling."

"The second man can climb the ridge backwards. Then we'll have the best of both systems."

I was tempted to suddenly shout "RIGHT!" with all the force I'd got, to see what would happen—four climbers springing in unison off the mountainside.

We climbed on, with mist thickening, to the summit. Through gaps in the cloud we saw the roofs of Badrinath, 10,000 feet below. Where was Ed? Down there perhaps? We turned our backs on the summit of Akash Parbat, intent on clearing the mountain with all speed and rejoining Ed. But momentarily, at the camp, we stayed our headlong flight. Here, highest point for the expedition as a whole, we thawed over a primus the small copper *lota* of water given us so long before by the wispy *pujari* of Ganga Sagar. Then we poured it out on a heaped-up mount of snow. It was, of course, still fresh. Earnestly we wished the water well as it began its long return journey from the sky to the ocean.

Ed writes: Wednesday 19th, Badrinath. Yesterday I awoke in Joshimath after a peaceful night. I had a very relaxed and sunny morning, reading mail, sorting gear and writing my diary. After lunch I travelled by jeep to Badrinath up the winding mountain road. It was like a ghost town now, and colder than before. Mike Gill was still there with a poisoned finger.

At midday I saw a figure moving quickly down the big grass fan below Nar Parbat. It was Murray. They'd climbed Nar Parbat. The rest were even now on Akash and could be back tomorrow. He was worried about his toe . . . we helped him get his boot off. No wonder he was worried – the big toe of his right foot was swollen, blue and numb, the whole of it frost-bitten. It was the end of Murray's climbing for two months at least.

At five o'clock, as Murray, Mike and I crouched inside around a stove, we heard heavy footsteps outside, and the thud and clatter of a big load being thrown down. It was Peter, down from a long, hard day. After climbing Akash they'd sledged the whole camp down to 16,000 feet, and from there carried loads, a hundred pounds each. The rest were at Base Camp but Peter had come down to see how I was. I felt a big load of worry coming off my back. Peter was lean, all spare weight gone. His face was burned, lips raw and peeling from the sun and snow. We went to sleep to the familiar sound of the big rats of Badrinath racing round the ceiling.

This morning we idly sorted gear, but without much enthusiasm. I wouldn't feel happy till everyone was down. At three o'clock we saw them, five figures picking their way down the bluffs. A cheerless wind, straight from Tibet, blew down the wintry valley and the clouds swirled about the peaks. Nilkanta, visible at times, rose into the sky like a flame of white ice. Nar Parbat and its twin Narayan stayed hidden. They straggled in, Ding, Waka and Mike Dillon, looking very weary. Then Jim, half hidden behind his beard and Mingma, his brown face creased with smiles. An incarnation of Arjuna, they'd said. So much for all that. We'd really taken quite a beating.

My thoughts turned to the expedition and the amazing experience it had been – the white sand and breaking waves at Ganga Sagar; the superb tiger in the Sundarbans; the vast cheering crowds in Calcutta; the chaotic welcome at Nabadwip. I could see the sparkling eyes of the high-school children at Farakka; the great *dhow* beating up against the current with their sails billowing in the breeze; the peaceful camp-sites of the plains; the fort at Chunar; the incomparable waterfront of Varanasi. There was the wild water above Rishikesh, the terrifying rapids at Rudraprayag and in The Chute, and the great mountains above Badrinath.

Ganga had been very beautiful, but perhaps my main memory was of people—lots of people ... sometimes over-eager and demanding, but kind, generous and enthusiastic, too. Our journey from the Ocean to the Sky had taught us much—that India was not only temples and ancient buildings, but adventure and variety and action as well. There had been challenges to meet and problems to overcome, and we had made a multitude of good friends. It had been a unique experience for all of us—we would never be quite the same again.

Appendix One

Expedition Diary

by MIKE GILL

August

15th Expedition leaves New Zealand.

17th Arrive Delhi.

19th Fly to Calcutta.

22nd Drive to port of Haldia eighty miles south of Calcutta.

23rd Unload jet boats and test.

24th Drive in boats to temple on Ganga Sagar Island for *puja* marking commencement of journey up-river.

25th Enter Sundarbans mangrove swamps.

26th Explore Sundarbans.

27th Two tigers.

28th Return to Namkhana.

29th Back to Haldia.

30th Travel up Hugli to Calcutta.

31st Reception by Governor of West Bengal in Calcutta.

September

1st 180 miles from Calcutta to Behrampur via Nabadwip — incredible welcome.

2nd Visit Palace of Murshidabad. Enter main Ganga. Drive through Farakka Barrage and stop for night at Farakka Township where the local school entertains the expedition with singing and dancers.

3rd Visit the Islands of Colgong. Camp in mango grove.

4th The Island Jahngir opposite Sultanganj. Camp on banks ten miles on.

5th Arrive at Patna, capital of Bihar.

6th Leave Patna and camp two hours on.

7th Refuel at Buxar and camp in village beyond.

8th Arrive Varanasi.

9th–11th Stay in Varanasi.

September

12th   Breakfast with the Maharajah. Visit the fort at Chunar. Stop at Mirzapur.

13th & 14th   Allahabad and Prayag.

15th   Camp above Fatehgarh.

16th   Camp beside small inlet after passing through Kanpur.

17th   Refuel at Farrukhabad and later at Soron. Camp at village of Mahmudpur collapsing into river.

18th   Drive through Narwa Barrage and stop at Garhmuktesar.

19th–21st   Delhi.

22nd   Lunch at Bijnor. Arrive Hardwar.

23rd   Move on to Rishikesh.

24th   Depart Rishikesh and encounter first big rapids. Camp on sandbank between Rishikesh and Deoprayag.

25th   Drive Moonlight Rapid. *Air India* swamps in Viyasi Rapid. Arrive Deoprayag, but drive on to camp a few miles above.

26th   Through Srinagar Valley. Arrive at Rudraprayag and drive the big rapid there. Camp just above.

27th   Drive Deer's Leap and The Chute. Camp below Czech Hat Rapid.

28th   Big welcome at Karnaprayag. Second swamping near Nandaprayag.

29th   End of river journey at the waterfall at Nandaprayag.

30th   Diminished expedition walks on through Chamoli and Birehi almost to Pipalkoti. Peter and Murray arrive in Badrinath to commence reconnaissance of Narayan Parbat.

October

1st   Walk past Belakuchi Realignment to Helong.

2nd   Arrive Joshimath.

3rd   Walk on to Govindghat.

4th   Leave road and climb track to Ghangaria. Peter and Murray camp beside Satopanth Glacier on recce of Narayan Parbat's north face.

5th   Enter Valley of Flowers and return to Ghangaria.

6th   Ascend to Hem Kund and walk back to Govindghat.

7th   Main expedition walks into Badrinath to join up with Peter and Murray.

8th   Climb slopes of Narayan Parbat and agree to switch to Nar Parbat.

October

9th   Prepare for climb to Base Camp.

10th   Ascend bluffs and establish Base.

11th   Reconnaissance of route to High Camp.

12th   Whole group carries up to High Camp and stays there.

13th   Rest day.

14th   Disaster day. Ed carried down to intermediary camp at 16,000 feet.

15th   Indian Air Force helicopter takes Ed and Mike Gill to Bareilly. Jim descends to Badrinath. Others stay at Base.

16th   Ed still at Bareilly. Ding, Murray and Peter return to High Camp. Jim ascends to Base to join Mingma, Pemma, Waka and Mike Dillon.

17th   Murray, Peter and Ding climb Nar Parbat. Ed and Mike fly from Bareilly to Joshimath. Base Camp group up to High Camp.

18th   Ed to Badrinath from Joshimath. Murray descends to Badrinath with frost-bite. Peter, Jim, Ding and Waka climb Akash Parbat. Peter returns to Badrinath same day. Others descend to Base.

19th   Whole expedition reunited in Badrinath.

Appendix Two

Ganga and Hinduism

by JIM WILSON

WHILE READING ROUND ABOUT GANGA IN PREPARATION FOR the journey, I came across this passage in Heinrich Zimmer's *Philosophies of India*:

"Better is one's own *dharma*, though imperfectly performed, than the *dharma* of another well performed. Better is death in the performance of one's own *dharma*: the *dharma* of another is fraught with peril."[1]

There exists in India an ancient belief that the one who has enacted his own *dharma* without a single fault throughout the whole of his life can work magic by the simple act of calling that fact to witness. This is known as making an Act of Truth. The *dharma* need not be that of the highest Brahman caste or even of the decent and respectable classes of the human community. In every *dharma*, Brahman, the Holy Power, is present.

The story is told, for example, of a time when the righteous King Asoka, greatest of the great Northern Indian dynasty of the Mauryas, "stood in the city of Pataliputra, surrounded by city folk and country folk, by his ministers and his army and his councillors, with the Ganges flowing by, filled up by freshets, level with the banks, full to the brim, five hundred leagues in length, a league in breadth. Beholding the river, he said to his ministers, 'Is there anyone who can make this mighty Ganges flow back upstream?' To which the ministers replied, 'That is a hard matter, your Majesty.'

"Now there stood on that very river bank an old courtesan named Bindumati, and when she heard the king's question she said, 'As for me, I am a courtesan in the city of Pataliputra. I live by my beauty; my means of subsistence is the lowest. Let the king but behold my Act of Truth.' And she performed an Act of Truth. The instant she performed her Act of Truth that mighty Ganges flowed back upstream with a roar, in the sight of all that mighty throng.

"When the king heard the roar caused by the movement of the

[1] *Bhagaradgita* 3.35.

whirlpools and the waves of the mighty Ganges, he was astonished, and filled with wonder and amazement. Said he to his ministers, 'How comes it that this mighty Ganges is flowing back upstream?' 'Your Majesty, the courtesan Bindumati heard your words, and performed an Act of Truth. It is because of her Act of Truth that the mighty Ganges is flowing backwards.'

"His heart palpitating with excitement, the king himself went post-haste and asked the courtesan, 'Is it true, as they say, that you, by an Act of Truth, have made this river Ganges flow back upstream?' 'Yes, your Majesty.' Said the king, 'You have power to do such a thing as this! Who, indeed, unless he were stark mad, would pay any attention to what you say? By what power have you caused this mighty Ganges to flow back upstream?' Said the courtesan, 'By the Power of Truth, your Majesty, have I caused this mighty Ganges to flow back upstream.'

"Said the king, 'You possess the Power of Truth! You, a thief, a cheat, corrupt, cleft in twain, vicious, a wicked old sinner who have broken the bounds of morality and live on the plunder of fools!' 'It is true, your Majesty; I am what you say. But even I, wicked woman that I am, possess an Act of Truth by means of which, should I so desire, I could turn the world of men and the worlds of the gods upside down.' Said the king, 'But what is this Act of Truth? Pray, enlighten me.'

" 'Your Majesty, whosoever gives me money, be he a Ksatriya or a Brahman or a Vaisya or a Sudra or of any other caste soever, I treat them all exactly alike. If he be a Ksatriya, I make no distinction in his favour. If he be a Sudra, I despise him not. Free alike from fawning and contempt, I serve the owner of the money. This, your Majesty, is the Act of Truth by which I caused the mighty Ganges to flow back upstream.' "[1]

As religious adviser to the expedition, my first task obviously was to hasten round all the members in the hope of finding one who had enacted his own *dharma* without a single fault throughout the whole of his life. What an impact on India and what a spectacle on film if we could go from Ocean to Sky in rubber dinghies on a reversed flow of sacred Ganges! Alas! Despite earnest efforts none of us could pass the initial test on a tiny trickle from a garden hose, though Murray Jones insisted that he had once stopped a leaking tap by swearing at it. This is why we had to resort to mechanical aids, and to roar noisily up the river in jet boats, and the Ganga was indeed "flowing by, filled up by

[1] *Milindapanha* 119–23. (Cited and translated by Eugene Watson Burlingame, "The Act of Truth (Saccakiriya): A Hindu Spell and its Employment as a Psychic Motif in Hindu Fiction," *Journal of the Royal Asiatic Society of Great Britain and Ireland*, 1917, pp. 439–41.)

freshets, level with the banks, full to the brim, five hundred leagues in length, a league in breadth".

But the story retained a fascination for me, not only because it was about Ganga, but also because it encapsulates, typically in delightful story form, a great deal of Hinduism.

Running through most of the diverse beliefs and practices of Hinduism is belief in Brahman, the One Holy Power. This power manifests itself in an immense variety of ways: in the cycling of the stars and galaxies and in the microscopic vibrating urgency of an atom; in the germination and growth of a grain of rice or a mighty banyan tree; in the complexities and bewilderments and excitements of conscious human activity or the intricacies of an anthill; in the fiery death of a star or the dreadful dissolution of the universe at the end of each cycle; in the death by drought of a tender rice shoot or by hunger or drowning of a tiny child.

In Hindu mythology, living beings on this earth are but a tiny part, and normally understand only a tiny part, of this great flow of energy and life. The flow also ceaselessly cycles through countless other world systems, each, like ours, with its earth and its heavens and its hells, with its gods, its earthly life-forms and its demons. And while our final goal is to understand and get in tune with as much of this diverse manifestation as possible, yet our tiny human minds can be boggled by its immensity.

So we need symbols—smaller, more concrete, more familiar things within our experience that can "stand for" Brahman the immense, and can teach us gently a little more about the great power, preparing us for greater knowledge in future days or future lives.

This is why Ganga is so superb a symbol for Hindus. Like Brahman through the universe, it runs its silver thread through northern India, from a human standpoint seemingly infinite in form and mood, yet one river, ever the same. There are many beautiful tales of people learning wisdom by watching and thinking about the river. For Ganga, like Brahman, is life as well as death. With her monsoon flow she brings water, and thus life and cleanliness, to the plains dried to dust by the summer heat. Almost overnight northern India turns green; almost you can hear new life thrusting up from the soil. With her monsoon floods, over untold centuries, she built up the fertile plains in which she annually renews life. And in the hottest, driest summer she remains; though in diminished flow, then more than ever quite literally the essential support of life, water for irrigation and for drinking, and a pathway for the transport of people and goods. But what Ganga gives she also takes away. The same monsoon floods that built the land often eat it away, undermining houses and removing fields; or they overflow the banks and inundate crops and drown croppers.

As we moved up the monsoon flow and saw both the life it gave and the destruction it wreaked, we became increasingly convinced that the villagers to whom it was happening understood this: that if they accepted and lived on the blessings of the river they must accept also the river's blows. To learn this from the river, then to apply the lesson to life as a whole—this is one way of expressing the key aim of Hinduism. Like the river, life gives and takes in a way indifferent to individual human desires. Wisdom consists in realising that it cannot be otherwise; enjoying when it gives and enduring when it takes. It seemed to us that many of the people we met by the river—most strikingly in the two villages where half the houses had been washed away—did have this wisdom, and not in a dour but in a dignified and still smiling way. Beside their wisdom, our restless attempts to force life always to give and never to take provided a bravely interesting but ultimately doomed alternative.

But the great river herself is too much for many minds to grasp. Though we travelled her length and were moved deeply by her rhythm and diversity, we acquired only an imperfect piecemeal image of Ganga in our minds. So Hinduism goes further still in breaking down the great into the smaller images, easier to comprehend. Ganga is personified, and thought of and modelled as a very beautiful woman, a goddess. We did *puja* before one such lovely image in the Ganga *mandir* (temple) at Dasashwamedh Ghat in Varanasi, before moving to the river's side to continue the *puja* to the actual river herself.

It is at this point, often, that the mind of the outsider begins to get confused. For the beautiful Ganga is just one amongst a number of striking images or manifestations of the active feminine aspect of the energy of the universe. There are also Kali and Durga, often depicted as fierce and horrifying as well as warm mother figures, to emphasise the destructive as well as the creative side of life. There is the exquisitely formed Parvati, daughter of Himalaya and wife of Lord Shiva. There is Sita, chaste wife of Ram; Radha, Krishna's favourite *gopi* (cow-girl); Lakshmi, the goddess of wealth and good fortune, and Saraswati, goddess of wisdom and learning. Images and colourful pictures of these goddesses abound in most Hindu temples and homes. On this trip I also came across some more local goddesses, new to me— Banadevi, to whom the Sundarbans villagers pray for protection from tigers; Vindhyachel-Devi, whose temple near Mirzapur we visited; and

Vashno Devi, whose cave-shrine B.B. visited when he was anxious about a crucial stage in his career.

And these are just the feminine personifications or manifestations of Brahman. Amongst the male manifestations, Shiva, who catches Ganga in his hair and lets her gently to earth, and Vishnu, from whose toe the celestial river first flows, are pre-eminent, each having a wealth of images and myths of his own. Shiva, especially as Nataraj (Lord of the Dance) strikingly portrays the ideal of poise and balance in the midst of the wild unrestrained energy of the universe. Vishnu is above all the preserver and re-creator, and is often depicted lying on the coiled serpent, Shesha, the last traces of form in the ocean of the dissolution of the universe between each cycle; in his dreams on this sinuous bed Vishnu gathers up and pieces together again the scattered elements of the formed world. But there are many other male forms. Ganesh, the elephant-headed son of Shiva and Parvati, is prayed to for success in hard tasks (we needed his help especially when trying to heave our heavy boats off sandbanks). Ram is the ideal of righteousness and fidelity, and Hanuman, his monkey helper, of loyalty and courage. Krishna, like Ram, is one of the most important avatars (descendants) of Vishnu, and from his mischievous childhood, through his loving youth to his lofty teaching in the *Bhagavadgita*, he presents a fascinating and complex figure.

To these divine figures, through images simple or ornate, artistic or crude, along the length of Ganga and throughout the breadth of India, Hindu devotees bring their offerings of flowers and fruits and milk and rice, and their chanted Sanskrit *mantra*, or simple prayers. They come with requests as basic and varied as their lives: for health when they or their children are sick; for rain when their crops wither in a drought; for success in business deals; for a higher rebirth next time round; for a happy marriage; for success in examinations; for strength in living a morally good life. With such a profusion of goddesses and gods and such a profusion of requests confusion seems at times to reign supreme, and Hinduism is dubbed by outsiders as endlessly polytheistic and crudely superstitious.

And yet, on this journey as on many others, I have found complete unanimity amongst Hindus, whether villager or sophisticated city professional, whether ordinary devotee or learned priest or earnest *sadhu*. There is but one god—*ek bhagavan*.

At a reception in New Delhi, for example, I was talking with two charming ladies. One of them had been in a small plane to Namche Bazaar, a Nepalese village high in the Himalaya near the foot of Mount Everest—a wild flight over wild country. "The light plane was tossing in turbulent air pockets," she recalled with a shudder, "and I remembered every temple in India and prayed earnestly. I was praying for the pilot—'Oh God help him fly us safely out of this!'" "Praying to whom?" I asked. "Shiva, Ram, Ganesh?" "Our family has a family deity, Durga," she replied. "But," Mrs Jay (the other lady) added, "our Hindu religion has so many gods we just call on God, not by any specific name."

In the Sundarbans, in a strikingly different social scene, I spent a lot of time in the back of the largest launch where the boatmen prepared meals on a small coke fire. In a mangled mixture of broken Hindi and English, we discussed India and New Zealand and the world, and politics and agriculture—and of course, above all, religion. They said prayers twice a day, they told me—"In the evening and again when we get up in the morning". "To Shiva?" I asked. "Yes," replied one of the group; but another said, "No, my goddess is Kali." "Kali and Durga?" I asked, probing to see if this devotee made a distinction between these two "forms" or "names" for the great mother goddess. "Yes, yes, but they are the same," came the reply without hesitation. "What about Parvati and Saraswati?" I queried, bringing in two more forms of the goddess. "Yes, the same, all forms of Shakti [the active feminine energy of the universe]." "And Shiva too—is he also a form of Brahman?" "Yes, yes, all forms of the same power—there is only one power." I was so delighted at this impromptu piece of research into Hindu monotheism that, with the dark silence of the Sundarbans all around us I sang my friends the only Hindi *bhajan* (hymn) I knew, a song of devotion to Ram. Despite excruciating mispronunciations of the lovely Hindi syllables and some wailingly off-beat notes and rhythm, this set the seal on our religious togetherness.

I must confess that my researches into how many gods Hinduism *really* has have been the butt of much hilarity and derision from many of our mob, at least since the Nepalese jet-boat expedition of 1968. In that vintage year I managed to solicit the answer *ek bhagavan* from a fine range of Hindus, from a Bengali truck-driver's assistant in crowded Calcutta to a remote Nepali *pujari* (priest) on the bank of the Sun Kosi. There was some suspicion—base and unfounded—that I made it clear in my questions that *ek bhagavan* was the answer I desired, and that my always polite Hindu respondents kindly gave me what I wanted. So I was relieved that later, in the Sundarbans, I had Ding as witness to a completely unsolicited *ek bhagavan* response. We were ashore in one of the beautiful green villages which hid behind the high protecting banks, and in a wee temple beside a lotus pond we were shown a *murti* (image) of Gauranga. "Who?" I asked, for I had not come across this name before. After much discussion we gathered that Gauranga was a part or manifestation of Krishna. But the discussion ranged wider than that. Gauranga, Krishna, Jesu Christu—and again Allah, Bhagavan?—"*ekais, ekais*" (the same, the same) the villagers said over and again. "Ah!" Ding pipes up with the magic phrase, "*Ek Bhagavan*". "Ha! ha!" (yes, yes) they said, heads wagging in agreement. "And Shiva, Vishnu, Ram, Shakti—*ekais?*" I asked. "Yes, yes," they replied enthusiastically.

Sophisticated Delhi ladies and remote Sundarbans villagers and an ebullient down-to-earth army officer, too—all give the same answer. Throughout the trip, B.B. was superb in relating to us stories about Ganga and about the gods, and on occasions also about his own religious activities and beliefs. He and Neelam, his wife, were both "sort of" religious, he said; and in chapter 12 is related the moving story he told us about how he felt he was helped at a crucial stage of his career by making a pilgrimage to the remote cave-shrine of Vaishno Devi. But the thing he didn't like about religion was the way people tried to push one god over another. He told of a Sikh friend who wouldn't go to Hindu *puja* with his Hindu wife, but would sit outside waiting for her, for hours, if necessary, rather than go inside the *mandir* (temple); and of a Christian who wouldn't go to Hindu *mandir*. "I'll go to any ceremony, any time," B.B. said, "for under any form I just pray to the one God—whether one form or three forms or whatever, there is just one God."

This ability to make offerings and requests to various gods as if they were separate beings, and then to turn and insist so decisively that there is only one God is readily understandable once Hindu belief in Brahman is understood. It is of the nature of this One Holy Power to manifest itself in a great variety of ways. Amongst these manifestations are those we call gods; and in one sense they are as separate from each other and from us as we are from each other and from mountains and rivers and trees. But they are, none the less, just manifestations of the one power; so from the point of view of deepest religious belief they are not separate beings.

Hindu theism, the strand of Hindu belief which regards Brahman as a personal supreme god, sees this varied manifestation in the form of divine beings as part of the grace of god to limited human minds. We all have different tastes. One symbol, one shape, appeals to one of us, another to another. No symbol our minds can grasp can contain the whole truth about the energy of the universe; but gradually we may be moved by this one and then by that, building up from a simple to a more complex understanding. Ramakrishna, a great Bengali saint of last century, whose temple just above Calcutta we visited, put it this way: "If God has a form, why does He have so many forms? These things do not become clear until one has realised God. He assumes different forms and reveals Himself in different ways for the sake of His devotees." Ramakrishna uses the image of a mass of water, which is of uniform composition throughout, and formless in its liquid state, but which can in cold temperatures take on separate forms as blocks of ice. So too, he suggests, God, who is everywhere and is everything, under the cooling influence of His devotees takes on separate forms.

But even the personal imagery of one supreme god is just one way in Hindu thought of viewing Brahman. Equally it may be thought of as impersonal, not a person or a being from whom we are at all separate, but the power or energy of thought, of consciousness, which is our own innermost nature.

The ultimate goal in Hinduism is fully to understand this power, and thus to enter fully into relationship with it or simply to realise that we are one with it, not separate particles battling forlornly against the flow. And those further along the path can dispense with all these partial forms and images. M. K. Gandhi expresses this point in a typically tolerant way: "I do not forbid the use of images in prayer. I only prefer the worship of the Formless. This preference is perhaps improper. One thing suits one man; another thing will suit another man, and no comparison can fairly be made between the two." A hymn by a South Indian devotee of Shiva makes the point more forcibly—a hymn I had to keep carefully hidden from my fellow travellers as it pulls the carpet out from under much of what we were doing on our pilgrimage:

> Why bathe in Ganga's stream, or Kaviri?
> Why go to Comorin in Kongu's land?
> Why seek the waters of the sounding sea?
> Release is theirs, and theirs alone, who call
> In every place upon the Lord of all.

> Why roam the jungle, wander cities through?
> Why plague life with unstinting penance hard?
> Why eat no flesh, and gaze into the blue?
> Release is theirs, and theirs alone, who cry
> Unceasing to the Lord of Wisdom high.

> Why fast and starve, why suffer pains austere?
> Why climb the mountains doing penance harsh?

Why go to bathe in waters far and near?
Release is theirs, and theirs alone, who call
At every time upon the Lord of all.

We were a long way from such a lofty stage of freedom from the props and crutches of partial symbols and ritual acts. Here we were, laboriously making our pilgrimage up Ganga, dependent on Indian Oil barrels and Hamilton jets. So too were a great many of the Hindus we met along the river, whether villagers at a simple shrine, or *sadhus* making a thirty-five-year pilgrimage up the length of Ganga. What hope, for them or for us, of attaining the goal of direct full understanding of the Holy Power in the ten or twenty or thirty years of limited groping left to us?

It is here that Hindu beliefs about time and about rebirth are crucial; the doctrines of *samsara* and *karma*. According to these beliefs I have all the time in the world, literally, to grope my way from one limited understanding of life to another, perhaps higher, understanding, an endless series of lives. For Brahman manifests itself in cyclic, not linear, time. The universe itself repeats a cyclic pattern over and again, evolving from Brahman into its concrete diversity of form, then dissolving in fire and flood back into Brahman at the end of each age. As if the time scale of the universal cycle were not enough on its own to make the mind boggle – 311,040,000,000,000 human years for one cycle, according to one computation – Hindu mythology adds infinite space to its sketch of the universe, and quietly speaks of countless world systems existing side by side during each cycle. "But the universes side by side at any given moment, each harbouring a Brahma and an Indra: who will estimate the number of these? Beyond the farthest vision, crowding outer space, the universes come and go, an unnumerable host. Like delicate boats they float on the fathomless, pure waters that form the body of Vishnu. Out of every hair-pore of that body a universe bubbles and breaks. Will you presume to count them? Will you number the gods in all those worlds – the worlds present and the worlds past?"[1]

Not just the universe as a whole, but all things within it, animate and inanimate, revolve through their own cycles within cycles, according to their diverse natures and to diverse laws. Many of these cycles are simple mindless repetitions. But for living creatures purposeful spirals are possible, up or down a scale of spiritual ability. And the law which determines patterns of rebirths for us living beings is the law of *karma*. As we go through any one life we act in certain ways, consciously or

[1] Zimmer, H., *Myths and Symbols in Indian Art and Civilization*, p. 6.

unconsciously, and thus build up certain habits of behaviour and of thought. These habits form and express our basic character, and they have a momentum, an influence, long after their initial formation and far beyond their original sphere. One writer gives the example of a businessman who, through long immersion in his job, builds up certain habits of seeing and dealing with every situation in economic terms. Such habits are beneficial, even, one might argue, essential to the success of his business. But though he formed them, they take control of him and go with him out of office hours and into his relations with friends and family. There, of course, where less tangible, more complex techniques and measures of success are needed, these narrow habits are a disaster; and even when the sorry state of his human relationships finally convinces him that this is so, the force of habit is such that it will take him a long time and much effort to break these habits and forge a new character and a new life.

The Hindu belief is that such habits and character traits have an influence over the barrier of death, and cause and determine the status of your next life. It follows that your present status and nature are the result of your past deeds, over a beginningless series of casually connected previous lives. This can give you a peace of mind and a calm acceptance of the limitations of your present lot. It should not make you resigned to whatever the future may bring, however; for it follows also that your future is, within the limits of your past habits, very much in your own hands. As you act now, so you will be in your next life. The dominant note in beliefs about *karma* is one of over-optimism rather than of fatalism and resignation, as is often supposed by outsiders.

It can still seem a very daunting prospect: your future in your own hands, but with limited room for manoeuvre in any one life; countless lives to come; and an infinite cycling universe surrounding you. But again Hinduism gently breaks down the immense and incomprehensible into smaller manageable chunks. It provides three basic frameworks to help us cope with and plan our slow progress towards full understanding.

For society as a whole there is the framework of the four classes, made incredibly complex through the centuries by the development within it of a tremendous number of castes. The class and caste structure of Hindu society, with its associated ideas of superiority and purity of some groups and inferiority and impurity of others, has undoubtedly given rise to, or been used to justify, some sad aspects of Hindu history. The "higher" classes have used religion to bolster their privileged position in society, the "lower" classes have been confirmed in poverty and social inferiority. Many Hindus in many ages have protested about this aspect of the social framework, culminating in our time with the scandalised protest by Gandhi against the "blot" of untouchability.

But the framework of classes and castes has also a beneficial side. In a large and complex society an individual can feel very lost and lonely. The caste groups, based originally on a variety of cultural or linguistic or occupational differences, gave each individual a smaller, more manageable slice of society within which they belonged: something of a mutual aid society, indeed, for a caste member, so long as he had not conspicuously transgressed against the rules of the caste, could be sure of support from the group, either by way of provision of the necessities of life or, if necessary, against a threat from other individuals or groups in society. In a way it is the social application of a central Hindu theme: break down the big and incomprehensible into smaller more manageable bits. In your "bit", your caste, you are "at home", because from birth onwards you have imbibed the customs and obligations of your group. And in Hindu belief, of course, you are also "at home" at and *by* birth. In your previous lives you have built up habits and personality characteristics (*karma*) which fit you for this particular niche and occupation and status in society, and indeed cause your conception in the womb of a member of this particular caste.

This same theme applies even more to the four great classes of traditional Hindu society, into which the castes are slotted, not always neatly. The servant class, the trading and agricultural class, the ruling and military class, and the Brahman or priestly class, it is believed, divide society into groups of ascending order of spiritual merit and ability. Each has its own *dharma*, or role, to play in society, essential to society and consonant with the characteristics of each group built up over previous lives. It was by perfectly living by the *dharma* of her group—no matter that the group was considered lowly by "respectable" groups of society—that Bindumati gained the ability to reverse the flow of mighty Ganga. And so, surrounded by the vastness of the universe and the infinite duration of its cycles and hence of our own, we are each provided by Hinduism with a finite and manageable span of space and time, in accordance with our abilities and merit passed on from previous lives to live out our allotted role in this group of this society in this period of this age, in the confident belief that if we do so the law of *karma* will ensure we get the due benefit of a higher birth, of more spiritual capacity, in our next life. In this way progress towards the remote ideal of full understanding of the energy of the universe is broken down into small steps which we are, in theory at least, well fitted to take.

The second basic framework is that of the four aims of life. This scheme performs a similar service for us in relation to the welter of human aims and desires which crowd in upon us in any of our lives. First there are the two "lower" aims of material success (*artha* — wealth and/or social or political position) and sensual pleasure (*kama* — aesthetic and physical, including sexual enjoyment). Far from condemning these aims and urging us to forgo them, Hinduism recognises them as legitimate human aims, and urges us to express and fulfil our desires for them. But it insists that we should do so in accordance with the moral law, central to which is the precept to injure no other living thing. And it believes that in due course, maybe in this life, maybe many lives hence, we will learn by experience that these aims give no lasting satisfaction — that material possessions all fade and decay, and relationships ebb and flow and end. Then we shall willingly move on to the third and higher aim of social and moral and religious virtue (*dharma*), placing others before ourselves and moving away from the self-interest which underlies the lower aims and which causes our rebirth as selfish individuals again and again. As we pursue this aim, falteringly at first but with increasing conviction as we find, again by experience, that it brings far greater happiness to ourselves and to others than does pursuit of possessions or pleasure, we shall build up habits and characteristics which fit us more and more for the fourth and highest aim—*moksha*, full understanding of the universal processes, and hence freedom from rebirth into partial and selfish involvement with limited parts of these processes.

Fine, in theory! But what hope, when actually involved in a busy life, of learning about these four aims, let alone working carefully through them? Plenty of hope if we follow the third basic framework, which lays down the four stages of life. Here, for each life of an individual, Hinduism again breaks down the large into smaller portions. First comes the student stage, during which we do indeed learn of the four aims of life and as much more of the beliefs and frameworks of Hinduism as we can comprehend with our current spiritual ability. If we were brought up in a traditional Hindu home, we would learn from our grandmother, perhaps, and from our mother and father, and would learn also as we listened to readings from Hindu scriptures at various family or caste ceremonies. Of, if we were very orthodox, we might be attached to a priest or *sadhu* as his disciple, helping care for his material needs in return for his spiritual guidance and teaching. Then comes the householder stage: we would be expected to marry and raise children, earning our living in the occupations appropriate to our caste, and contributing in this way to the well-being of society. This is the busy, responsible period, and while we would be trying to keep to the rules of *dharma*, both in our moral conduct and in our offerings and devotion to the gods, yet we would of necessity be heavily involved, though for our family and caste and not selfishly for ourselves, with material matters (*artha*) and with at least some sensual pursuits (*kama*) in order to conceive a family. But we can be comforted throughout our busiest periods by the lovely notion of a third and fourth stage of life. When we see our children's children, that is when our family has grown up into independence and our responsibility to them and to society is fulfilled, then we have the right to turn to spiritual matters. We can if we wish leave home and family and wander off in search of enlightenment, first in a moderate way with still a minimum of possessions for comfort and a family home to retreat to, but in the fourth stage, if we are determined and serious enough, with no possessions and no ties at all.

There are many ways in which we can use these latter stages of life to advance our spiritual capacities and enhance our prospects for our next rebirth. Some are very lofty, and repudiate all material props and symbols, fiercely demanding of the mind direct understanding of the secret of self and the universe. But by far the most visible and popular way is to go on a pilgrimage. And by far the most popular pilgrimages are those associated in one way or another with Ganga.

Small wonder, then, that on our pilgrimage we saw so much evidence of the way in which these latter stages of life are still taken seriously by many Hindus. On the 1975 recce, for example, Murray and I chatted with a group of retired businessmen who were living in a small sacking tent on Ganga's banks at Hardwar. No ulcers and dying in harness, nor any retirement problems, for them. They had handed over their businesses to their sons, and felt themselves free to come to Hardwar and in a companionable group meditate on and discuss life's meaning and prospects. And on our way to and from Hem Kund, we passed many really elderly people, some being carried, some painfully but with moving determination struggling along on foot. Ed was moved to comment on how fortunate they were by comparison with many of our old people in New Zealand. There, many are almost rejects from society, eking out their last days as a burden on their resentful relatives. Here, their religious belief and framework were giving their last days a purpose and a joy which was shining out through exhaustion and pain.

For a pilgrimage of any sort is believed to bring great merit and hence lead to a better rebirth next time. How much more, then, some of the really arduous pilgrimages. At Hardwar, we spoke briefly to a *sadhu* who was making, as were we, the full pilgrimage up Ganga, from Ganga Sagar to the source. Unlike us, he was doing it on foot, with full attention to ritual detail at every stage of the way, and he had already been thirty-five years on the way. I felt he must either have hustled or omitted the student and the householder stages of life—as Hinduism gave him every right to do if he felt that previous lives had fitted him for such a life this time. Even his efforts pale into insignific- ance, however, beside stories that are told of performing the double pilgrimage, Ganga Sagar to Gomukh and/or Badrinath and back again, while "measuring your length"—stretching out full length, marking the ground with outstretched fingers, standing up again at that mark, then again stretching out full length . . . While personally, being of lazy temperament, I prefer the gentler means of gaining wisdom by sitting quietly contemplating the flow of the river, I have always been impressed by the fierce determination shown in such feats. And the belief underlying them—that the greater the pain and suffering endured on the pilgrimage the greater the merit acquired—was a great comfort to us on the few occasions when we felt we were suffering mentally or physically on our pilgrimage.

The all-pervasive hold a Ganga pilgrimage has on the Hindu imagination accounts, at least in part, for the incredible reception Ed got as we progressed up the river. For Hinduism is endlessly tolerant of individual variations of method in pursuit of enlightenment. And though we were by no means in an orthodox fourth stage of life— even if some of our families thought we had been permanently on expedition, if not pilgrimage, for as far back as could be remembered; though we would return to households and possessions and all sorts of lowly desires and pursuits; and though we were travelling by the most unarduous means imaginable—yet we were making the pilgrimage so many Hindus would dearly love to make. By associating with any of us, many people, particularly in the villages, believed some of our merit would be transferred to them. And if this were so for us, the ordinary members of the expedition, it was a thousand times more so for Ed himself. Ed was a text-book figure stepping out of the pages into their lives, for a commonly used school history book had a whole chapter on Tenzing's and Hillary's 1953 ascent of Everest. So he was already for many a symbol of the spirit of adventure. Now, with all the religious associations of a Ganga pilgrimage surrounding him, he was being toasted in speeches more generally as a symbol of the greatness of humanity, and, in the all-embracing Hindu sense, of the potential

divinity of humanity. For me, this came to a climax in the *puja* at the
Ganga *mandir* at Varanasi. Ed was welcomed by a Hindu priest at a
Hindu shrine, or so it seemed to me, as the latest in a long line of great
men elevated virtually to divine status in the capacious mansions of the
Hindu pantheon. If so, to my mind there is no doubt that the priest
was echoing the thoughts of thousands of those who flocked to have
darshan—to see and be in the presence of (Ed)—along the length of the
river. It was both profoundly moving and a considerable emotional
strain for Ed, but as usual he kept his sense of humour and kept it all in
perspective.

"You know," said an Indian Oil man at one of our crowded
enthusiastic receptions at a refuelling spot—"You know, they think
you're a sort of god." "But you know I'm not a god," Ed replied
confidently, for the Indian Oil man knew well by now our many
failings and moods. "Oh yes, I know you're not," he said with a grin.
Not so a devotee of Bhagavan Hillary further up the river at Karnaprayag. He mistook Ding for Ed, and after a long earnest conversation
with him asked him, "Sir, you are a very great man—what is difference
between you and God?" An awesome Hindu responsibility for a New
Zealander to live up to, and Ed much preferred the kindly cynicism of
the Indian Oil man.

The four classes of society, the four human aims, the four stages of an
individual's life—with these frameworks, as with the idea of many
manifestations of the One Power or God, Hinduism breaks down the
immensity of life and the universe into portions more easily digestible
by ordinary humans. At the same time, and by the same means, it
holds ever before us a higher goal: the heroic aim, indeed, of attempting to digest the universe itself, entire, to understand the Holy Power
as it really is, not as it is partially represented for us in image and in
myth.

Ordinary Hindus live in tension between the two ends of this scale.
Their pressing immediate problems are those of a limited life here and
now: problems of physical well-being for self and family, of personal
and community relations, and of emotional adjustment to an often
harsh life. As students and as householders, concerned with the lower
aims of life, they approach partial manifestations of Brahman through
concrete physical images, seeking help and comfort. But always there
are reminders that these lesser symbols, these lower aims, are not the
final answer to life's problems. On the one hand, the results of their
petitions to the deities can only be of limited duration. The sick family
member may be healed, but will sicken again and eventually die, as
will we all; the crop may be saved by timely rain, but the next crop

will be at risk again next year. On the other hand, there are always abroad in Hindu society symbols of a loftier search for more enduring ends—wild *sadhus* and gentle retired businessmen in the fourth stage of life, gladly supported by the community because they do hold ever before us this higher goal. And of course around the very goddesses and gods to whom they bring their petitions there is the all-pervasive sense of something greater, some One Power of which these many deities are but partial manifestations.

Above all, this is so of the goddess Ganga. Small partial manifestation of the universal energy she may be, against the backdrop of our huge universe, but in microcosm she gives a full representation of the whole —nearly endless variety within an enduring form, source of life and death, of fertility and of destruction. I cannot help thinking that those who come with specific requests to this symbol are likely to stay and meditate more deeply, and to gain from Ganga something of the wisdom we felt in the people of the destroyed villages. And then they would indeed be moving from the lower to the higher aim of Hinduism: moving from specific requests to partial symbols of life to the attempt to understand and accept life and death, pleasure and pain, as a whole, realising that we should try to alter, not life's outer circumstances, but our inner selves.

Of course Hinduism is not as simple as this—no religion is. I have painted far too unified a picture, simplifying, for brevity, what I see as the main themes and threads. And here at the heart of Hinduism there is a fundamental ambiguity. What does this "acceptance of life" amount to? Is it really just an adjustment to our attitudes, leaving life outside us unchanged and uncaring? Or are we then in a position to control life from its centre, to send its current where we will, as did Bindumati with the monsoon flow of Ganga?

There is a very ancient, persistent and pervasive human belief that knowledge is power, that understanding gives control. It was as evident in the magical rites of our ancient forbears as it is in modern scientific theories and technology, though with more justification and success in the latter than the former. This belief has always been strong in Hinduism. Yogic powers are believed to be evidence of it on a small scale. Full understanding of Brahman, it is believed, can give powers beyond the ordinary because one is in tune with the fundamental energy that activates all things. And yet, side by side with descriptions of such powers in Hindu texts, there are warnings against being ensnared and beguiled by them, for they are not the final goal. Indeed, it seems that such powers are little more than childish gimmicks, as a tale told by Ramakrishna portrays it:

Once upon a time a *sadhu* acquired great occult powers. He was vain about them. But he was a good man and had some austerities to his credit. One day the Lord, disguised as a holy man, came to him and said, "Revered sir, I have heard that you have great occult powers." The *sadhu* received the Lord cordially and offered him a seat. Just then an elephant passed by. The Lord said to the *sadhu*, "Revered sir, can you kill this elephant if you like?" The *sadhu* said, "Yes, it is possible." So saying, he took a pinch of dust, muttered some *mantras* over it, and threw it at the elephant. The beast struggled a while in pain and then dropped dead. The Lord said: "What power you have! You have killed the elephant!" The *sadhu* laughed. Again the Lord spoke: "Now, can you revive the elephant?" "That too is possible," replied the *sadhu*. He threw another pinch of charmed dust at the beast. The elephant writhed about a little and came back to life. Then the Lord said: "Wonderful is your power. But may I ask you one thing? You have killed the elephant and you have revived it. But what has that done for you? Do you feel uplifted by it? Has it enabled you to realise God?" Saying this the Lord vanished.

Childish pranks — or dangerous interference with the balanced forces of nature, as another story of Ramakrishna makes clear:

Once a great *Siddha* (possessor of extraordinary powers) was sitting on the sea-shore when there came a great storm. The *Siddha*, being greatly distressed by it, exclaimed, "Let the storm cease!" and his words were fulfilled. Just then a ship was going at a distance with all sails set, and as the wind suddenly died away, it capsized, drowning all who were on board the ship.

Now the sin of causing the death of so many persons accrued to the *Siddha*, and for this reason he lost all his occult powers and had to suffer in purgatory.

Consider again, in this light, Bindumati's feat. It was a bit like the dilemma which we imagined (wrongly) faced engineers as our boats approached their barrages. Should they let us through and impress us, but flood a hundred villages, or make us drag our boats around? Each action has its chain of reactions. Bindumati surely impressed the King — and centuries later may have helped us to understand a little about Hinduism. But equally surely she must have inconvenienced a thousand boatmen and maybe even drowned a pilgrim bather or two. It is to be hoped that she rapidly called off her Act of Truth and allowed Ganga to flow downwards to the sea again.

Hinduism does dabble with and delight in the thought that full understanding of the energy of life might give spectacular control over life. But she is too deeply imbued in every part with the idea of the orderliness and inevitability of the flow of life and the universal processes to do more than dabble and delight. I think that fundamentally she inculcates, as does that part of her we call Ganga, the feeling that the energy of life is incomprehensibly greater than any individual manifestation of it. True understanding does not bring control of it by any individual—and in any case, so unified, so interconnected are all its manifestations that any such control would be at the expense of other individuals. What true understanding can bring instead, more marvellously, is an ability to accept and delight in life: no longer is an individual isolated fighting against, or at the mercy of, the current, but flowing harmoniously with it, an integral part of the whole.

We didn't learn this properly on our pilgrimage, I'm afraid, let alone experience it fully. Many of us are rather unbelieving materialistic beings, immersed in possessions and pleasures (artha and kama). We were not really on a pilgrimage to enhance our spiritual capacity in a future life; many of us don't believe in a future life. We just wanted to travel up Ganga from ocean to sky, against the current, in response to strong but not fully analysed desires for adventure and excitement and variety. If we had found Bindumati—and I searched eagerly for her in all the crowds—we would probably have asked her to reverse Ganga's flow, after we had got to Nandaprayag, so that we could be the first to traverse the river from sky to ocean upstream! And yet—even on our restless minds Ganga-mata worked her magic. As her flow and the life of her people mingled with our lives, though so briefly, almost imperceptibly she imparted to us something of the gentle wisdom of Hinduism, leaving us a memory of a moving alternative to our excited search for adventure, should we ever need one.

Appendix Three

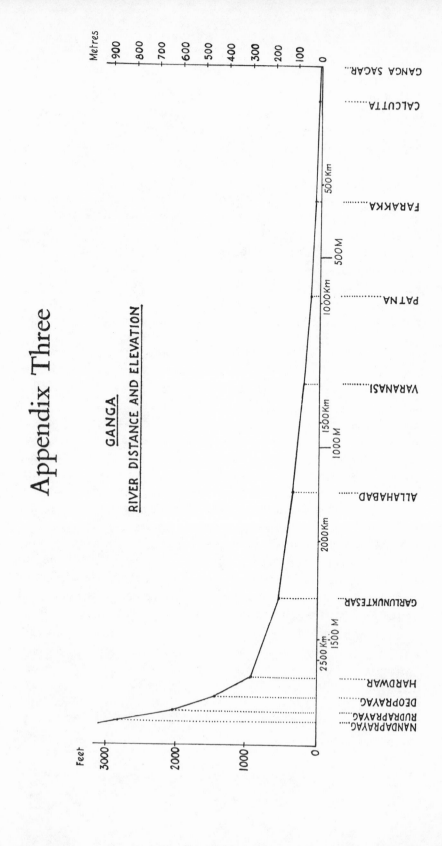

GANGA

RIVER DISTANCE AND ELEVATION

Appendix Four

Jet Boats

by Jon Hamilton

THE JET BOAT IN ITS PRESENT FORM, A LIGHT PLANING CRAFT cabable of navigating shallow and turbulent rivers, was the invention and development of Bill Hamilton, high-country sheep farmer and equipment manufacturer. Bill was used to thinking up novel machines, building and developing them and then manufacturing them for sale in New Zealand, but the river boat was just a private hobby, with no commercial end in view. All he wanted to do was to navigate the beautiful snow-fed streams around his home.

The first attempts in 1953 were far from satisfactory: a tunnel boat which wouldn't "prime"; an air-screw-driven boat which could be heard five miles away; a boat with a retractable propeller; and finally a boat with a water pump discharging from a swivel nozzle below the bottom. Only the last showed any promise for further development, and when the nozzle was shifted to discharge its jet clean into the air through the transom, success was a modest reality.

Several versions of the jet unit were designed and built and tested, and eventually friends and acquaintances asked Bill for similar jets, and so a business was founded.

Today, Hamilton jet units are axial flow pumps which suck water in through a grill in the bottom of the boat and discharge it as a propulsive jet straight out at the back. Steering deflectors turn the jet from side to side, a reverse deflector comes down to reverse the direction of the jet when going astern, and the bottom of the boat remains beautifully smooth and free from any appendage. Over the years the engines driving the jet units have become larger: 100 h.p. to 250 h.p. is common, whereas the original boat had a Ford 10 engine, developing little more than 25 h.p., and speeds have risen steadily from the original 17 m.p.h. to speeds in excess of 80 m.p.h. in racing craft.

Today Bill Hamilton's jet units are used to propel a wide variety of craft, from off-shore patrol craft to landing barges, from commercial fishing boats to airport rescue craft, as well as boats for sportsmen and family groups. But all the early practical experience was in shallow-water conditions where Bill Hamilton on his own, and later with a small group of his friends, explored the streams and rivers flowing from the Southern Alps of New Zealand.

As a friend once remarked to me, "It is not for the development of the jet boat that we must thank Bill Hamilton, it is for showing us what to do with them." There is a lot of truth in that, as it took years to develop the technique of navigating the shallow rivers of the plains and the rocky torrents in the mountains. Now it is all relatively easy; the boats are powerful and well made, the New Zealand Jetboat Association has more than a thousand members with all the background skills and experience, and the terrors of wild rivers have given way to a keen interest in the challenge offered by them. The pioneering expeditions of the past are the Sunday family outings of today.

However, there is still a lot of technique to be learned, and it takes several seasons of river boating before one can confidently handle the full range of conditions to be met in different rivers, in different seasons and in different countries. River lore is a wide subject and that, of course, is part of its fascination.

The first two things a new jet-boat driver must learn is the difference between the displacement and the planing condition, and the use of power. When a boat travels slowly it lies deep in the water and is at the mercy of every cross-current and eddy. In contrast, when it is planing, the boat skims over the surface; the draught is negligible and it will be unaffected by cross-currents. What is more, the boat can benefit by the "ground effect" and will rise and flatten its trim when crossing extremely shallow patches. In New Zealand, the beginner soon learns to use plenty of power to get the boat up on to the plane quickly, and then to throttle back for cruising at economical r.p.m.

Learning to read the river takes a little more time: judging just how deep the river is by the look of the ripples as it runs over shallows; deciding whether a wave conceals a rock or is just formed by an irregular bottom many feet down; looking far ahead to get an idea of the pattern of currents and shallows, and, in wild water, sorting out the many hazards is a stimulating business. Bill Hamilton taught us the rudiments of the art of river navigation which he discovered in the first two or three years after building his first jet boat. Since then the art has been refined and polished, but his basic advice still holds true:

Long swells mean deep water; ripples mean shallows. The wave-pattern is often a good indicator of water depth.

Speed over shallows. If very shallow, keep the speed up and turn slightly so that the boat heels to one side; continually position the boat so that the jet intake is in the deepest water and, as you come to each deepening of the stream, decide whether to stop there or to push on, for you cannot slow down on a shallow without grounding.

Beware of sand. Shingle bars are safe – if you ground on one you slide gently to a halt, but if you touch river sand the stop is so sudden that passengers can be thrown out or can suffer cuts and bruises.

Notice the bank. It is a clue to the river bottom: fine shingle beaches mean fine shingle bottom; steep rocky cliffs mean fallen boulders in river; forest country means submerged tree-trunks; wet bank means retreating flood-waters and unexpected shallows, etc.

Subsiding floods are hazardous. In these conditions shallow bars appear where none are expected; the flood has removed old bars and deposited new material, but the river has not had time to carve out a fresh channel appropriate to its reduced flow, and it is particularly difficult for a driver to judge the water correctly.

Beware of still water. Rocks or tree-trunks are usually clearly indicated in moving water by the wave pattern they generate, but in still water they cannot be detected, and the driver must use his river-sense to find the best course.

And in rough water:

Look well ahead. If you are running down a bouldery stretch of fast water, it is more important to have your general course sorted out than to attend too closely to nearby hazards.

Keep the bow up. It can be disastrous when driving upstream to allow the nose to plough under a wave, the boat may swamp or turn end-over-end.

Watch the current. You can skim happily over cross-currents unless the standing waves are large. In that case you must avoid allowing skew water to strike the bow, as it can swing the boat quite violently and you "knife", to use an American term.

But above all, Bill Hamilton's example and encouragement were to lead to experiment with the new form of propulsion, to find out how to navigate previously unthinkable waters, and to develop the skills necessary to travel with safety and certainty over the marvellous waterways which had so quickly become accessible.

In 1959 an American licencee had been appointed to manufacture the Hamilton jet units in the U.S.A. John Buehler, dynamic head of the American company, decided to put four of the new jet boats into an expedition to attempt the first-ever uprun of the Grand Canyon of the Colorado River. He invited Guy Mannering, photographer, and myself as the son of the inventor to take part as drivers, first on a run down the river, to lay off fuel caches, and then on the uprun attempt.

In a river rapid the waves are stationary; there are frequent surges and eddies, and the larger waves may heave and break, but they are standing waves remaining in substantially the same place while the water flows through them. When driving downstream there is little one has to do except keep out of the steepest waves and avoid rocks, and in no time the boat is through a rapid, even if the crew have been doused in the process. Running up a major rapid is a different matter altogether. The boat must have sufficient power not only to beat the current but also to climb the quite steep gradients encountered, and even then it can be a slow process, inching one's way upstream. One small mistake and the boat can be spun round and swept down out of the rapid, perhaps taking water aboard on the way, and you have to pump out the bilges and start all over again.

The Colorado expedition was successful, but in a dozen or more of the major rapids in the Canyon, the standing waves were so large and the water so fast that a complete new technique of driving had to be established. The New Zealand experience counted for little in the new white-water conditions; the same old advice on driving remained true, but we had to get used to the very much larger and swifter water in the major rapids. However, we soon found that the smooth-bottomed jet boats were absolutely ideal for the turbulent water and just couldn't be turned over—or rather, couldn't be turned over sideways. They just might turn end-over-end if we once got the foredeck under water. And that was practically what happened to one of the boats before the end of the nine-day uprun: it was driven to the bottom, bow down, and the crew of two floated out, to be rescued by the following boat.

Since that expedition, further overseas experience, using jet boats with Australian government geologists, up tributaries of the Sepik in New Guinea; with Sir Edmund Hillary on the Sun Kosi River in Nepal; with a private group on the Kafue River in Zambia; on an aid project in the Mekong in Laos and Cambodia; and marathon racing on the Rio Balsas in Mexico consolidated much of the river experience obtained originally in New Zealand and on the Colorado River.

The first really new type of water condition encountered since those early days was with Major Blashford-Snell's Zaïre River Expedition in 1974–5. The Zaïre River has the second largest flow of any river in the world, the Amazon being the largest. The river rises in the rich mineral belt of Katanga and after a thousand miles reaches Kisangani (Stanleyville), already a mighty river with several times the flow of the Mississippi. From here it enters the vast equatorial rain forest of Zaïre and in its next thousand miles it is fed by numerous tributary rivers and streams until it flows at its full volume into Stanley Pool, a huge lake of moving water still a thousand feet above sea level.

From here the river, in a bed of solid rock, plunges down a series of gigantic rapids to reach sea level at the port of Matadi. A typical rapid is a mile or two wide and perhaps a mile long, and the swirls and eddies from it persist for a great distance downstream. We travelled with two eighteen-foot jet boats down these falls for two hundred miles to the big hydro-electric project at Inga, and there refuelled and made the return journey to Kinshasa on the south bank of Stanley Pool. The air-filled rafts of the Zaïre River Expedition arrived from up river and we then shepherded them down the falls to Mafuambo Kibenza, which was as far as the river was navigable for such ponderous craft, before we went on to Inga.

The new and outstanding features of that river were vertical currents. Because of the great depth, the energy developed in the falls was eventually dissipated in vertical eddies and currents as well as in the more normal horizontal ones. The surface evidence of down-flowing water was sudden whirls which would appear in a matter of seconds, grow to perhaps twenty or thirty feet in diameter in a quarter of a minute, and then drift downstream and dwindle. The converse, up-welling water, would appear as a huge boil rising above the surface of the river and spreading out hundreds of feet in diameter.

These features would appear so quickly that it was impossible to avoid them in a jet boat. The boat would drop into a whirlpool, be thrown to one side, and the crew would look with awe at a rapidly rotating core several feet across, with water tumbling down the central hole in a 45-degree spiral. A man would stand no chance in such water, but the boats would climb out of them without any fuss or apparent danger.

The up-welling boils were equally noticeable. A boat would be suddenly lifted, and one would find oneself running down the gentle slope of a small hummock, facing a sharp and growing wave of water formed at the rim of the boil where water, just risen from the deep, was falling back to river level.

This was the first time that vertical currents had really forced themselves on to our notice. We were awed by them, as by the grandeur of scale in that river, and did not expect to find them again in milder conditions.

The jet boats from the Ganges expedition were prepared as load carriers. For a thousand miles we expected flat, calm water, but logistics would be a problem, as we had sixteen men, food and camping gear, an enormous load of film-making equipment, and long hauls up-river between refuelling points. We realised that there would be some rocky rapids in the mountains at the end of the journey, but that was a secondary consideration in the selection of the boats.

These were standard Hamilton Jet 52's, 16 ft long, fibre-glass, with Holden 308 cu. inch V8 engines driving Hamilton model 753 three-stage jet units. The engines had special low compression pistons fitted to suit the 83 octane fuel which is more readily available than premium grades away from the main centres. Each boat had 270 litres of fuel capacity, heat exchanger cooling, a bilge blower to clear possible petrol vapour before starting, and "inboard"-mounted jet units. This last feature leaves less of the jet unit protruding behind the boat and thus reduces the risk of damage from rocks. The bench seat and the steering wheel were raised a few inches as Sir Edmund is a tall man, and this improved the visibility.

Gay yellow and green canopies with ample headroom, designed by Hillary, were supplied by Sears Roebuck from the U.S.A. and these, when fitted, gave the fleet a jolly air as well as providing protection from the sun by day and from rain by night. But not, alas, from the rain on the several occasions we had to travel in it! The open design was excellent for hot weather, but at 30 m.p.h. any warm rain would just drive in and soak us to the skin.

From a driver's point of view, the first section of the expedition was interesting but not remarkable. The great estuary of the Hugli, twelve miles wide, with its large tidal range (often exceeding fifteen feet) and patches of choppy water, the tidal Sundarbans mangrove jungle with its maze of interconnecting waterways and mud of the most slippery and slimy sort, and the Hugli itself, large and docile, presented no problems. But as soon as we ran under the barrage gates at Jangipur and into the mighty flood-swollen Ganga, we realised we were once again in conditions quite different from any New Zealand has to offer. The river was six miles wide, a brown and surprisingly swift current, carrying at that time just thirty times its low-level volume, and already falling.

After twelve miles' travel against this great tide, the river narrowed to a mere mile and a half, and at this point we passed under the Farakka Barrage before nightfall. The next day the river widened again, numerous islands appeared, and we had occasion to recall the advice given by Bill Hamilton long ago: *Observe the bank.* Yes, but the nearest bank was but a suggestion of greenery on a distant horizon of water. *Subsiding floods are hazardous.* Yes, we understood that, but what to do? *Beware of sand.* Crunch—without warning someone would be stopped dead on a sandbar in ankle-deep water. It would take all hands to re-float the boat, and sometimes there were bruises to nurse, too.

For several days the only driving technique which seemed to offer any reduction of the risk of grounding was to run in line astern, and not to be the lead boat! Then, one day, I noticed that Jim Wilson had been running first for rather more than his fair share of the time, was taking a zigzag course for no apparent reason, and was not running aground. The technique he had developed was to *Look well ahead*, but this time in a search for those tell-tale patches of expanding slick water with tiny ripples at the borders which signified up-welling water. They were midget counterparts of the great boils of the Zaïre River, but still up-welling water, and where water up-wells it can't be shallow! Jim had discovered that in many areas he could lead with confidence where the water was so calm that there was no indication at all of shelving sand.

As the expedition approached Hardwar, old Ganga changed her character. No longer was she the broad, brown flood in a meandering course, cutting away banks and villages, building new islands, top-dressing the land with rich silt as she retreated, providing water for irrigation and disposing of all refuse. Now she was a young mountain torrent running on a stony bed between rocky walls. We removed the canopies from the boats, reduced the loads and fitted strong covers aft of the bench seats to reduce the risk of swamping.

A shallow river flowing over an even shingle bed can fall quite steeply, maybe twenty feet to the mile, without presenting the slightest difficulty to boating. A large and deep river, on the other hand, will have swift currents even if its fall is only one foot to the mile and where side-streams have carried rocks and boulders into the main river there can be wild patches of furious water separating quiet and sedate stretches of river.

For a thousand miles from the ocean, Ganga has an even fall of six inches to the mile but even here flood-waters keep the average current at five miles per hour or more. However, from Hardwar on, the grade steepens: five, ten, fifteen, twenty, twenty-five feet to the mile; then above Karnaprayag thirty, forty and finally over fifty feet to the mile. In these upper gorges the monsoon flood had long since passed its peak, but the confining walls kept the river deep and very swift. Many of the rapids were surprisingly steep, but all were just nicely within the capabilities of the lightened boats.

From the driver's point of view the Alaknanda provided some of the most glorious jet-boating imaginable giving plenty of opportunity to practise the careful art of handling big water; but the driving became more and more relentless until the fall at Nandaprayag brought a clear cut end to the boating phase of the expedition.

Appendix Five

Glossary of Indian terms

arati – circular devotional waving of oil lamps or burning camphor

artha – material and social position, prestige, power; one of four aims of life

ashram – retreat; place of meditation and/or teaching, usually centred on a
  particular sage or teacher

bara sahab – big man, big leader

basti – hut, dwelling place

baul – member of a Bengali religious sect of wandering singers

Bhagavadgita – 'Song of God'; a portion of the *Mahabharat* in which Krishna
  reveals himself as the Supreme Being and instructs Arjuna in loving devotion to him

bhagavan – God, Lord

bhajan – devotional song; hymn

cha – tea

chapati – thin unleavened wheat bread, usually round

dal – pulses; spiced lentil soup

darshan – sight or presence (of great man, or of deity); also, true vision or
  knowledge of reality and, hence, system of philosophy

Devlok – the world or realm of the gods

dhanyabad – thanks

dharma – knowledge of the eternal laws of the universe; also moral and
  religious and social duty; one of four aims in life

dharmshala – pilgrims' house

dhoti – length of light cloth wrapped around the waist and drawn up between
  the legs

ek – one

ekais – same

ghat – bathing place on a river bank; wharf

ghee – clarified butter

gopi – cow-girl; love-companion of Krishna in Hindu mythology

hatha-yoga – a stern form of physical and mental discipline believed to lead
  to extraordinary powers

jai – life, victory

kama – sensual enjoyment, sexual and aesthetic; one of four aims of life

karma – the moral law of the universe: the deeds we do, the habits we form,
  influence our future in this life and determine the form and status of our
  rebirth

kosi – river

linga, lingam – penis, symbol of Shiva's creative power

lota—small shapely pot or jar, often copper or brass

lungi—length or sheath of material worn as lower garment, rather like a simple skirt

Mahabharat—ancient Indian epic poem: into the story of a civil war has been woven an immense amount of religious and moral and social teaching

mandir—temple

mantra—Sanskrit chant, spell or prayer

masala dosa—finely spiced vegetables folded inside a crisp pancake made from rice flour

mata—mother

moksha—spiritual freedom, enlightenment, release; highest of the four aims of life

muni—ascetic; one who has renounced worldly life to seek enlightenment

namaste—a greeting

nim—the acidic twigs of this tree fray at the end when chewed, and are used for cleaning teeth

pakora—fragments of vegetable deep-fried in spicy batter

pandit—learned man, scholar, teacher

pani—water

prasad—offering to a god; boon, blessing

prayag—junction (of rivers)

puja—worship, devotional ceremony

pujari—priest

puri—flat cakes of wheat dough deep fried

Ramayan—the second great Indian epic: it tells how Ram, incarnation of Vishnu, searches for and releases his abducted wife, Sita, then returns from exile to his kingdom

rasgulla—Bengali sweet

rishi—sage

roti—bread

sadhu—saint, hermit, holy man

samsara—the universe of moving forms, infinite in space, and endlessly circling in time; for living forms, the cycles of death and rebirth, endless unless moksha (release) is realised

Saraswati—goddess of learning

satyagraha—literally 'holding to truth'; used by Gandhi to refer to his non-violent method of opposing the South African Government and then British rule in India

sepoy—soldier

Shiva—destroyer and re-creator; one of the great Gods of Hinduism; a name for the Supreme Being

siddha—possessor of extraordinary powers (siddhi—achievements, powers)

sitar—seven-stringed instrument, played with the fingers

tilak—spot-mark on forehead, placed on participants during religious and other ceremonies

Veda—the earliest Indian scriptures, a collection of hymns and chants; term extended to refer also to the *Upanishad*, mystical teachings

Vishnu—sustainer of the universe; the other great God of Hinduism; a name for the Supreme Being walla—fellow, person

yatra—pilgrimage

yoga—ancient Indian discipline of body and mind, believed to bring extraordinary control and powers, and, more importantly, to lead to enlightenment

yogi—advanced practitioner of yoga

Index

Adventure World of Sir Edmund Hillary, 41–42
Aickman, Dr Colin, 139, 227, 230
Air India, 28, 39, 48
Akash Parbat, 212, 235, 241
Alaknanda River, 17, 18, 24, 149, 150, 163 190, 192, 207
Allahabad, 17, 121–126, 240
Arjuna, 208, 236
Arun River, 13, 34, 156, 165
Aryans, 101
Asoka, 101, 242
Assistant River Surveyor – see Choudhury
Attewell, Waka, 45, 66, 73, 75, 131, 138, 139, 146, 185, 211–237
Awnings, 28, 151, 210

Babul trees, 109
Badrinath, 17, 18, 24, 123, 186, 199, 201, 207, 208, 210, 221, 225, 228, 236, 240, 241
Balakun, 203
Banadevi, 58–59, 245
Bangladesh, 17, 54, 87
Bankipore Club, 98, 99
Bareilly, 226, 227, 230, 231, 241
Base Camp, 206, 208–211, 241
Battacherjee, Mr 47
Bawa, Major, 206, 207, 209, 220–222, 225, 228–229
Bay of Bengal, 18
BB – see Bhatia, Bridhiv
Behrampur, 80, 82, 84, 85, 128, 239
Belakuchi Realignment, 189, 190, 225, 240
Benares – see Varanasi
BG – see Dewari, B. G.
Bharat Petroleum Co, 32, 79, 166, 179
Bhagirathi River, 16, 25
Bhagirathi – Hugli River, 81, 86, 87, 163
Bhatia, Bridhiv (BB), 39, 47, 58, 65, 66, 72, 78, 111, 123, 134, 135, 137, 162, 185, 190, 195, 205, 226, 246
Bhotias, 203, 206, 210
Bihar, 90, 94, 239
Bijnor, 140, 240
Bindumati, 242, 257, 259
Birds, 52, 93, 130
Birehi, 150, 187, 225, 240
Bithur, 128
Blisters, 189
Bore tide, 67
Brahman, 244
Buddhism, 101
Buffaloes, 131
Buxar, 83, 102, 239

Calcutta, 32, 47, 50, 61, 63, 65, 69–71, 77, 239
Calcutta Port Trust, 32, 66
Camping, 91

Carpet-making, 117
Cawnpore – see Kanpur
Chait Singh, 106, 116
Chait Singh Palace, 105, 106, 111
Chamoli, 187, 225, 240
Chandrashekar, Mr 126
Choudhury, Mr K. T. Das, 64, 71, 82, 89
Chunar, 116
Chute, The (rapid), 25, 172–176, 240
Colgong, 90, 239
Colorado expedition, 264
Country boats, 90, 92
Crabs, 64
Crocodile, 61
Crowds, 78–80
Cycle-boat, 87
Czech expedition, 151, 177, 187
Czech Hat Rapid, 177, 178, 240

Daily Himachal Times, 200, 213, 232
Damodar River, 64, 70
Darshan, 18, 89, 119
Dasashwamedh *ghat,* 113, 245
Deer's Leap Rapid, 172, 173, 240
Delhi, 31, 47, 70, 130, 137, 139, 239, 240, 246
Deoprayag, 17, 24, 163, 240
Dept of Forests, 47, 50, 53, 55
Dept of Tourism, 28, 40, 67, 138
Devlok, 200, 232
Dewari, B. G. 45, 53, 102, 185
Dharma, 242
Dhows, 90, 92
Dhulian, 87
Dillon, Mike, 44–45, 56, 58, 73, 75, 92, 112, 158, 185, 187, 211–237
Dingle, Graeme, 36, 48, 55, 75, 94, 99, 110, 132, 133, 135, 136, 139, 149, 178, 191, 211–237
Discord Rapid, 164
Doab, 130
Dutt, Raj, 117
Dutts of Bijnor, 140
Dysentery, 64, 95

Everest, 18, 38, 39, 66, 67–68, 78, 80, 88, 95, 103, 205, 246, 255

Farakka, 26, 86, 87, 88, 89, 239, 266
Farrukhabad, 132, 240
Fatehgarh, 132, 240
Fatephur, 127
Film, 30–46
Finance, 27–32
Flow-rates of rivers, 87, 153, 268
Forest Dept, 47, 50, 53, 55

Gandhi, Mahatma, 98
Ganga, 13–18, 23–27, 50, 87, 101, 107, 138, 140, 188, 242–259

Ganga Canal (upper), 143–145
Ganga Sagar, 17, 19–22, 32, 49, 50, 239
Ganga water, 20, 110
Ganges—see Ganga
Gangotri, 17, 39, 128
Garhmuktesar, 137, 138, 139
Garhwal, 17
Gazeteer of India, 14, 65, 70, 122
Ghangaria, 194, 198, 240
Ghurkas, 199
Gill, Mike, 13, 35, 41, 56, 72, 74, 81, 86, 94, 95, 96, 124, 126, 131, 135, 138, 181, 184, 185, 211–237
Gomukh, 17, 128
Governor of West Bengal, 66, 68, 74–75, 239
Govindghat, 192, 198, 240
Govt of India, 28
Gradient of river, 154, 181, 267–268
Greenfield, George, 31
Groundings, 52, 81, 96, 102
Gurudwara, 194
Guru Govind Singh, 197

Haldia, 32, 48, 62, 63, 239
Hamilton, Bill, 261
Hamilton, C. W. F. & Co, 28, 29, 97
Hamilton, Jon, 13, 21, 34, 48, 56, 57, 67, 81, 97, 99, 132, 137, 146, 153, 157, 161, 170, 177, 181, 261
Hamilton, Joyce, 160, 162, 166, 173
Hamilton, Mike, 21, 34, 48, 96, 99, 145, 157, 171, 180
Hardwar, 17, 26, 31, 141–148, 240, 254, 267
Har-ki-pairi *ghat*, 145–147
Helicopter, 218, 220–225, 231
Helong, 240
Hem Kund, 186, 196–198, 254
Herobhanga, 52
High Camp, 211–237, 241
Hillary, Peter, 35, 52, 54, 56, 60, 65, 68, 74, 84–85, 97, 98, 125, 135, 137, 146, 177, 193, 201–205, 211–237
Hillary, Sir Edmund, 60, 67, 75–76, 79–80, 84, 88–89, 97, 100, 103, 106, 110, 113, 133, 147, 151, 152, 164, 167, 211–237
Himachal Times, 200, 213, 232
Hinduism, 15, 59, 77, 101, 120–121, 242–259
Hindustan Oil Co, 32
Howrah Bridge, 73
Huan Tsang, 122, 147
Hugli River, 17, 50, 63–64, 81, 239
Hungry Boy, 210, 220

Imperial Gazeteer of India, 14, 65, 70, 122
Indian Air Force, 220–232, 241
Indian Army, 31, 78, 151, 191, 224, 225
Indian Customs, 31
Indian Everest Expedition, 38, 39
Indian Mountaineering Federation, 28, 36, 38
Indian Mutiny, 128
Indian Oil Co, 31, 32, 72, 99, 117, 123, 127, 134, 250, 256
Indian War of Independence (First), 128
Indo-NZ Ganges Expedition, 28, 38
Indus Valley Civilisation, 101

Jahngir Island, 93, 239
James and Mary Sands, 64

Jamuna River, 17, 121
Jangipur, 86, 87
Jeena & Co, 138, 149, 150
Jet-boats, 13, 28–30, 120, 261–268
Jones, Murray, 23–27, 35, 60, 68, 90, 98–99, 111, 125, 137, 139, 158, 171, 172, 176, 177, 192, 201–205, 211–237, 243
Joshimath, 190–192, 225, 231, 240, 241

Kaipo Wall, 41
Kakar Bhali, 172
Kaliasaur Rapid, 167
Kamikaze Kids, 137
Kanauj, 131
Kanpur, 128–129
Kapil muni, 16
Karnaprayag, 179–180, 225, 240
Kipling, Rudyard, 71
Kohli, Captain Mohan, 28, 68, 139, 147, 172, 176, 181, 185
Krishna, 208, 246
Kumb Mela, 122, 125

Lokpal, 97
Lowe, George, 201
Lungi, 68, 78, 110

Mahabharat, 101, 208, 209
Maharajah of Benares, 105, 115, 240
Mahmudpur, 134, 135, 240
Mana, 203, 208, 209, 212, 223, 225
Mandakini River, 149, 168
Man of War Jetty, 65, 67
Mike's Hover, 180
Mingma Tsering Sherpa, 13, 39, 94, 100, 102, 131, 134, 137, 151, 165, 205, 211–237
Minocha, Commander, 21, 50
Mirzapur, 116–121, 240, 245
Mitra, Mr, 32, 51
Mogadon, 204, 213, 234
Moghuls, 70, 101, 102, 116, 130
Mokameh, 94
Monsoon, 27, 116
Moonlight, Rapid, 158–159, 240
Mukut Parbat, 205
Murshidabad, 85–86, 239

Nabadwip, 78–80, 239
Naik, Mr, 31
Naini Tal, 232
Namkhana, 51, 239
Nandaprayag, 180–184, 186, 225, 240, 259
Nar Parbat, 204, 205, 208, 233–234, 240, 241
Narayan, J. P., 98–99
Narayan Raja, 188, 221
Narayan Parbat, 36, 192, 203–205, 208, 240
Narwa Barrage, 136, 240
Nehru, Jawaharlal, 14, 27
Nehru, Mrs Rajen, 126
Newby, Eric, 22
New Delhi—see Delhi
New Zealand High Commission, 118, 221
Nilkanta, 201, 203, 211, 212

Padma River, 87
Pai, Miss Vatsala, 28, 31, 138
Pandavas, 207, 208

Pandit Raj Bali Mishra, 118–120
Pataliputra, 101, 242
Patna, 95–99, 239
Paul, Commander, 63, 64, 81, 85, 86, 89
Pearl, Max, 37, 102, 118, 124, 136, 137, 160, 165
Pemma Sherpa, 40, 92, 100, 211–237
Pindar River, 180
Pipalkoti, 188, 225, 240
Plassey, Battle of, 82–83
Police Training Centre, 78
Porpoises, 80
Porters, 206, 209, 210
Prayag, 17, 121, 122, 240
Puja, 19–20, 113–114, 147–148, 163, 245, 256
Purna, Chandra Das, 66

Rahman, Mr M. A., 23
Raja Narayan, 188, 221
Ramakrishna, 77, 107, 248, 249, 257, 258
Ranikhet, 225, 226, 232
Rapids, 155–157, 262–268
Rats, 206, 209, 236
Rawal of Badrinath, 208
Recce Report (Wilson-Jones), 23–27, 149, 150, 158, 162, 166, 172, 176, 182, 183, 190, 192
Rishikesh, 17, 24, 39, 148–150, 240, 267
Rudraprayag, 24, 149 , 166, 168–171, 240

Sangam, 125
Saraswati River, 122, 123, 208
Sarin, Harish, 23, 28, 31, 38–39, 62, 63, 80, 81, 83, 86, 91, 94, 95, 97, 100, 109, 128, 139, 186, 230, 231
Satopanth Glacier, 203, 208, 240
Sears, 31, 57, 266
Shankaracharya, 101, 191, 208
Shipton, Eric, 18, 205
Shiva, 16, 201, 246
Sikhism, 197
Singh, Joginder, 39, 139, 172, 227

Siwalik Hills, 142
Snake-charmers, 111
Soron, 133, 240
Srinagar, 165, 166, 240
Sultanganj, 93, 239
Sundarbans, 32, 50–62, 239, 247
Sun Kosi River, 13, 33, 95, 247
Swamping, 161
Swamp Two Rapid, 182

Tenzing Norgay, 67–68, 80, 103, 255
Thugs, 117
Tigers, 32, 54–58
Tilak, 20
Tongues, 155
Trees, 109

Vaidya, Prem, 19, 45, 81, 85, 115, 120, 133, 135, 176, 185, 186
Vaishno-Devi, 195, 246, 248
Valley of Flowers, 186, 194, 196, 240
Varanasi, 17, 104–115, 239, 245, 256
Vasodara Falls, 208
Veda, 122
Vindyachel Devi, 120–121, 245
Vishnu, 207, 208, 246
Vishnuprayag, 25, 192
Viyasi Rapid, 161, 240

Wilson, Ann, 33
Wilson, Jim, 13, 21, 23–26, 30, 33–34, 48, 56–62, 67, 75, 94, 95, 100, 102, 103, 106, 107, 113–115, 118–119, 123, 133, 139, 142, 146, 149, 157, 164, 167, 171, 177, 178, 190, 191, 211–237, 242, 267
Wives, 37

Yoga, 111, 118–120

Zaïre River Expedition, 264, 265, 268

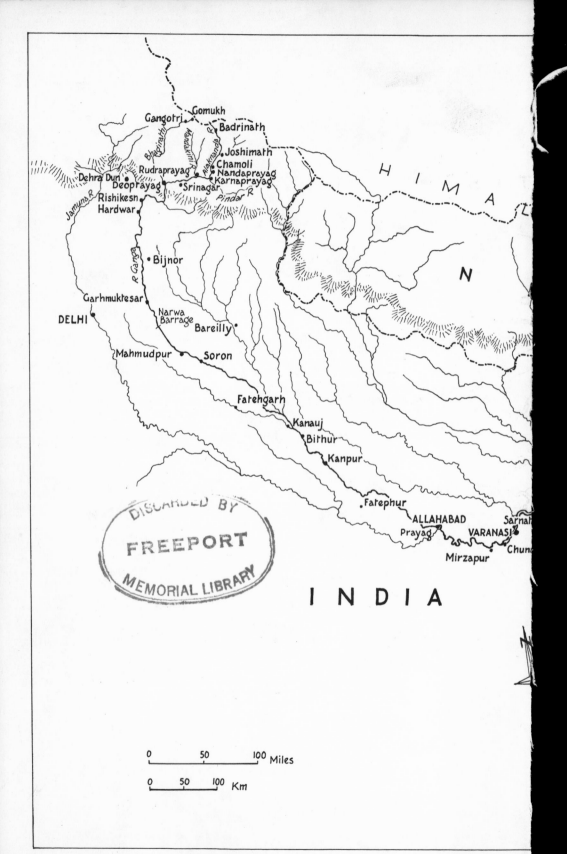

Gomukh
Gangotri
Badrinath
Joshimath
Chamoli
Rudraprayag
Nandaprayag
Dehra Dun
Karnaprayag
Deoprayag
Srinagar
Rishikesn
Pindar R
Hardwar
Jamuna R
R Ganga
Bijnor
Garhmuktesar
Narwa
Barrage
DELHI
Bareilly
Mahmudpur
Soron
Fatehgarh
Kanauj
Bithur
Kanpur
Fatephur
ALLAHABAD
Sarnah
Prayag
VARANASI
Mirzapur
Chun

HIMAL

N

INDIA

0   50   100 Miles

0   50   100 Km